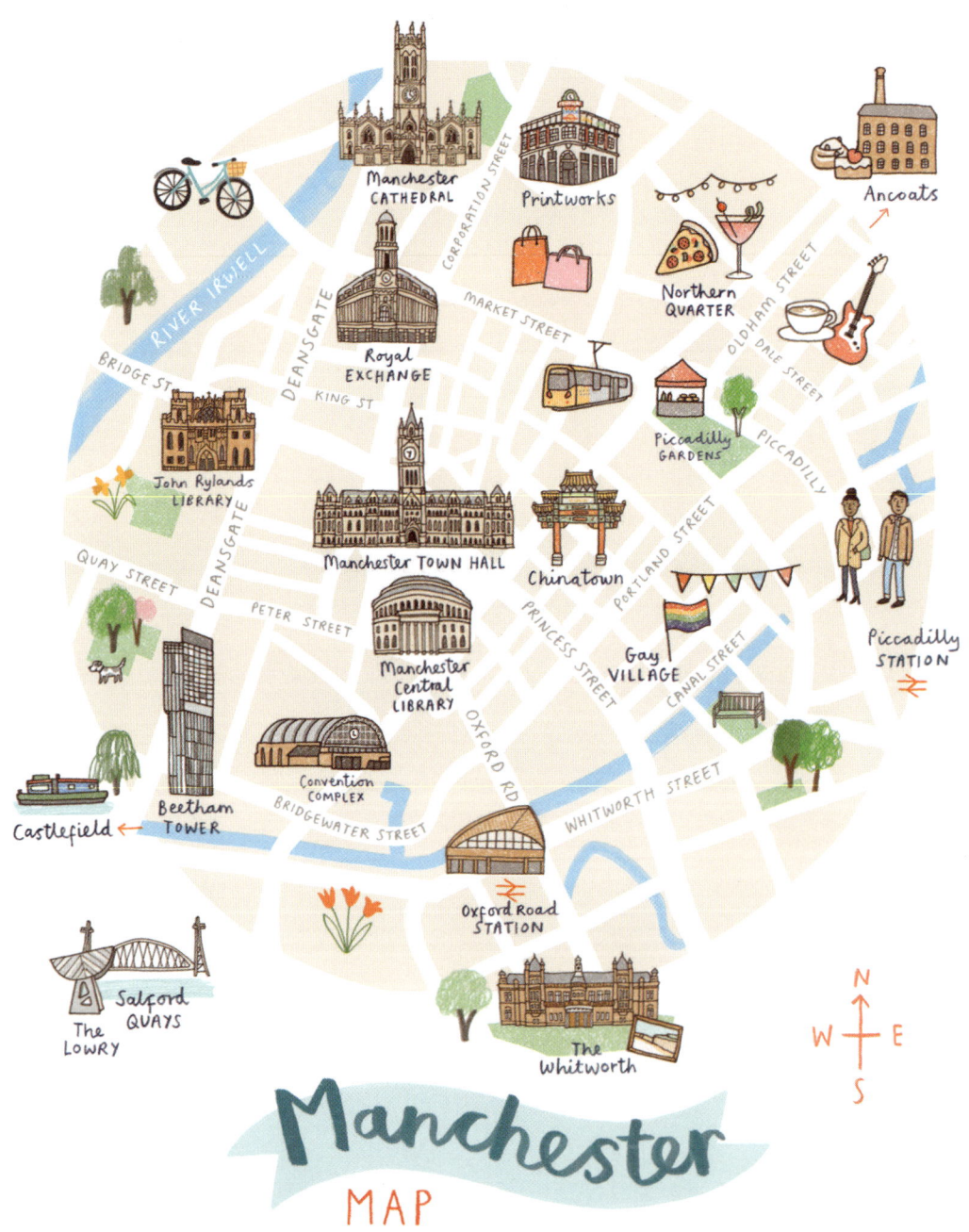

Manchester
CATHEDRAL

Printworks

Ancoats

Northern
QUARTER

RIVER IRWELL

BRIDGE ST

DEANSGATE

CORPORATION STREET

MARKET STREET

OLDHAM STREET

DALE STREET

PICCADILLY

Royal
EXCHANGE

KING ST

John Rylands
LIBRARY

DEANSGATE

Piccadilly
GARDENS

QUAY STREET

PETER STREET

Manchester TOWN HALL

Chinatown

PORTLAND STREET

Piccadilly
STATION

Manchester
Central
LIBRARY

Gay
VILLAGE

CANAL STREET

PRINCESS STREET

OXFORD RD

Beetham
TOWER

Convention
COMPLEX

BRIDGEWATER STREET

WHITWORTH STREET

Castlefield ←

Oxford Road
STATION

The
LOWRY

Salford
QUAYS

The
Whitworth

N
W   E
S

Manchester

MAP

HERBERT PRESS
Bloomsbury Publishing Plc
50 Bedford Square, London, WC1B 3DP, UK
Bloomsbury Publishing Ireland Limited,
29 Earlsfort Terrace, Dublin 2, D02 AY28, Ireland

BLOOMSBURY, HERBERT PRESS and the Herbert Press logo are trademarks of
Bloomsbury Publishing Plc

First published in Great Britain in 2025

A catalogue record for this book is available from the British Library
Library of Congress Cataloguing-in-Publication data has been applied for

ISBN: HB: 978-1-9068-6097-4; eBook: 978-1-9068-6098-1

2 4 6 8 10 9 7 5 3 1

Printed and bound in China by RR Donnelley Printing Solutions Ltd

To find out more about our authors and books visit www.bloomsbury.com and sign
up for our newsletters

For product safety related questions contact productsafety@bloomsbury.com

THE
MANCHESTER
ART BOOK

THE CITY THROUGH THE EYES OF ITS ARTISTS®

EDITED BY EMMA BENNETT

HERBERT PRESS

LONDON • OXFORD • NEW YORK • NEW DELHI • SYDNEY

Acknowledgements

The Manchester Art Book has been made possible with the enthusiasm and talent of the contributing artists and to them I am eternally grateful.

In the lively city of Manchester an illustrious panel of local art and city experts helped select images for publication. I am indebted to them for their creative input.
They are:

- Malcolm Taylor, RBA PS

- Ian Whadcock, Senior Lecturer, Manchester Metropolitan University

- Alex Reuben, Director, The Contemporary Six Art Gallery

- Hayley Flynn, Director of Skyliner

- Jo Tunmer, Lead Panellist, *The City Through The Eyes of Its Artists*® book series

- Len Grant, Artist

Thank you to Bloomsbury for supporting *The City Through The Eyes of Its Artists*® book series. To my family thanks for ongoing support, especially Craig, William, Molly, Len, Val and my Mom, Toni. Clare Barry, thank you for our supportive book chats over tea/coffee, long may they continue. Brenda Purkiss, who loves Manchester, thank you for all your neighbourly help and for forcing me to take swimming breaks in all weathers.

To my fellow MA students Mish Kelly, Kerry Mosley and Sarah McBarnet thank you for your friendship and support whilst I juggle work and studies.

Jo Tunmer, my art and travel buddy, thank you for everything, your friendship and generosity means the world. Luke Tunmer, thanks for indirectly supporting the book series!

Thank you finally to the talented comedy writers from Manchester and its surrounds, who have given me so much joy over the years. To my heroine the late Victoria Wood, born in nearby Prestwich, thank you for the laughs that will always live on, you are much missed.

CONTENTS

FOREWORD

Welcome to the award winning city known throughout the world for its art…
and football. Footballers love art too. I once took a footballer from Manchester United
to see an exhibition called "Poet Slash Artist" which was curated by Hans Ulricht Obrist
of Serpentine Art Gallery and myself. Manchester loves art and art loves Manchester.
The former Director of The Whitworth Art Gallery, Maria Balshaw, is now Director
of the Tate and subsequently one of the most powerful people in the arts in Britain.
Manchester's love of art is central to the nation's love of art.

You came to the right place. You opened the right book.

Manchester International Festival brings leading artists from around the world to
the city and its unquenchable thirst for art. In June 2023 Factory International opened
in Manchester: it is a global destination for arts, music and culture. Manchester loves
artists and artists love Manchester. Immerse yourself in our art. Lose yourself in the
galleries. This city itself is an art gallery. Find work in public spaces. Open your eyes
and open your heart to experiences you may never forget, experiences that might
change you forever. Welcome.

Lemn Sissay OBE
Trustee of The Foundling Museum
Visiting Fellow of Jesus College Cambridge
Hon. Chair in Creative Writing at The University of Manchester

PREFACE

Even if you've never visited Manchester, this city will probably already be a part of your subconscious, the things that we gain from it, possibly a part of your everyday life. This vibrant city has a long list of firsts; the first ever inner-city railway, the UK's first working canal, the world's first steam-driven mill and largest cotton producer. It was The University of Manchester which split the atom for the first time. In this city Suffragette Emmeline Pankhurst was born, with Manchester the birthplace of the campaign for votes for women.

If history isn't your thing, then you may know Manchester as home to two of the biggest professional football teams in the world. Go to the most remote, far away places on earth and you will find someone wearing a football shirt emblazoned with the name 'Manchester'.

If history or football don't connect with you, you may know Manchester as a city that helped define and shape the British music scene. If you've heard of Brit-Pop, then you have heard of Manchester, a city responsible for musical genres recognised globally.

If you haven't realised by now that Manchester is probably a subconscious part of you, then turn your thoughts to TV. *Coronation Street*, the world's longest-running TV soap opera is filmed in the city. If you love comedy, you will be familiar with *The Royle Family* or *Cold Feet*, or the myriad stand-up comedians that Manchester and its surrounds has produced.

So if you feel like you know Manchester but have never visited, pack your bags and see the city and all it has to offer for yourself. If you are a local, you will know the place Manchester holds in the world and the love held for it. Local or visitor, take a stroll through this fantastic city, with *The Manchester Art Book* in your hand and stand for a while in the footsteps of an artist.

Emma Bennett

Creator and Editor of *The City Through The Eyes of Its Artists*® book series

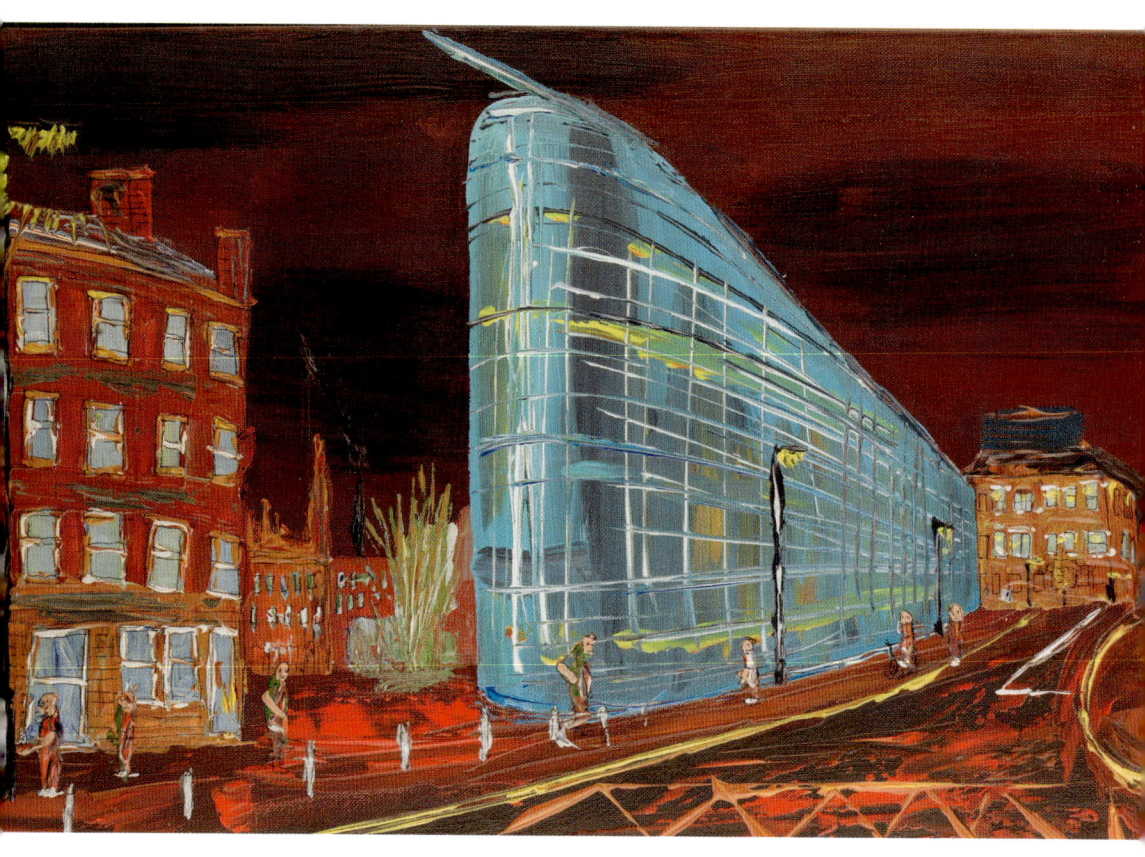

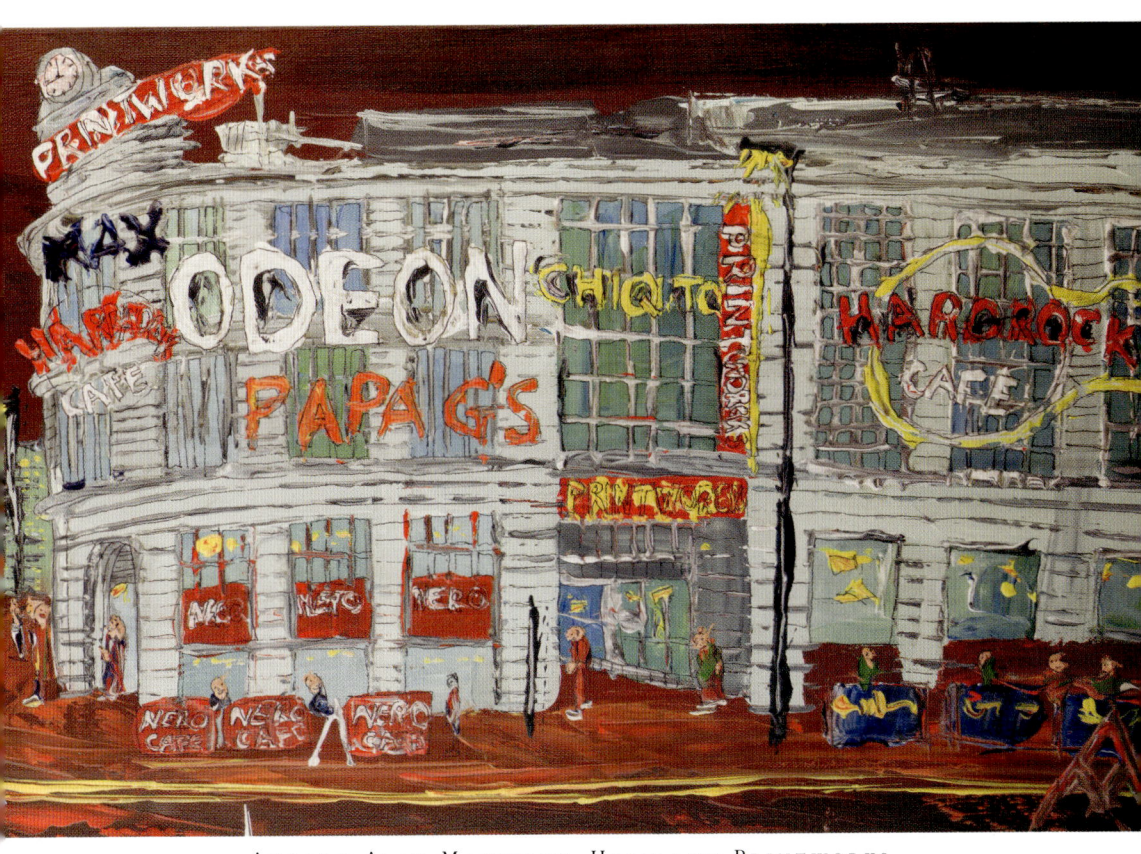

ANDREW ALAN MATTHEWS, URBIS AND PRINTWORKS

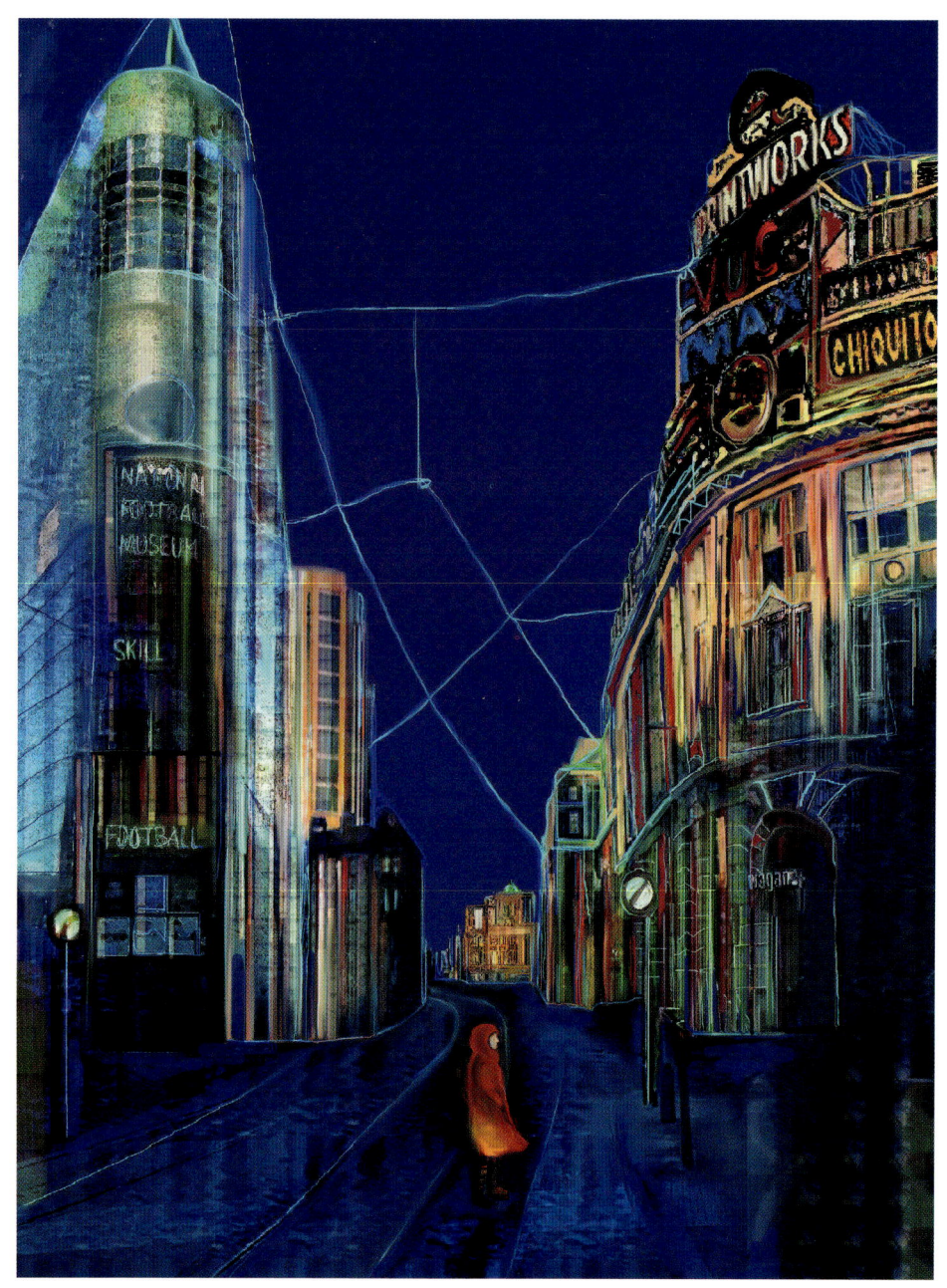

CLAIRE RILEY, VICTORIA

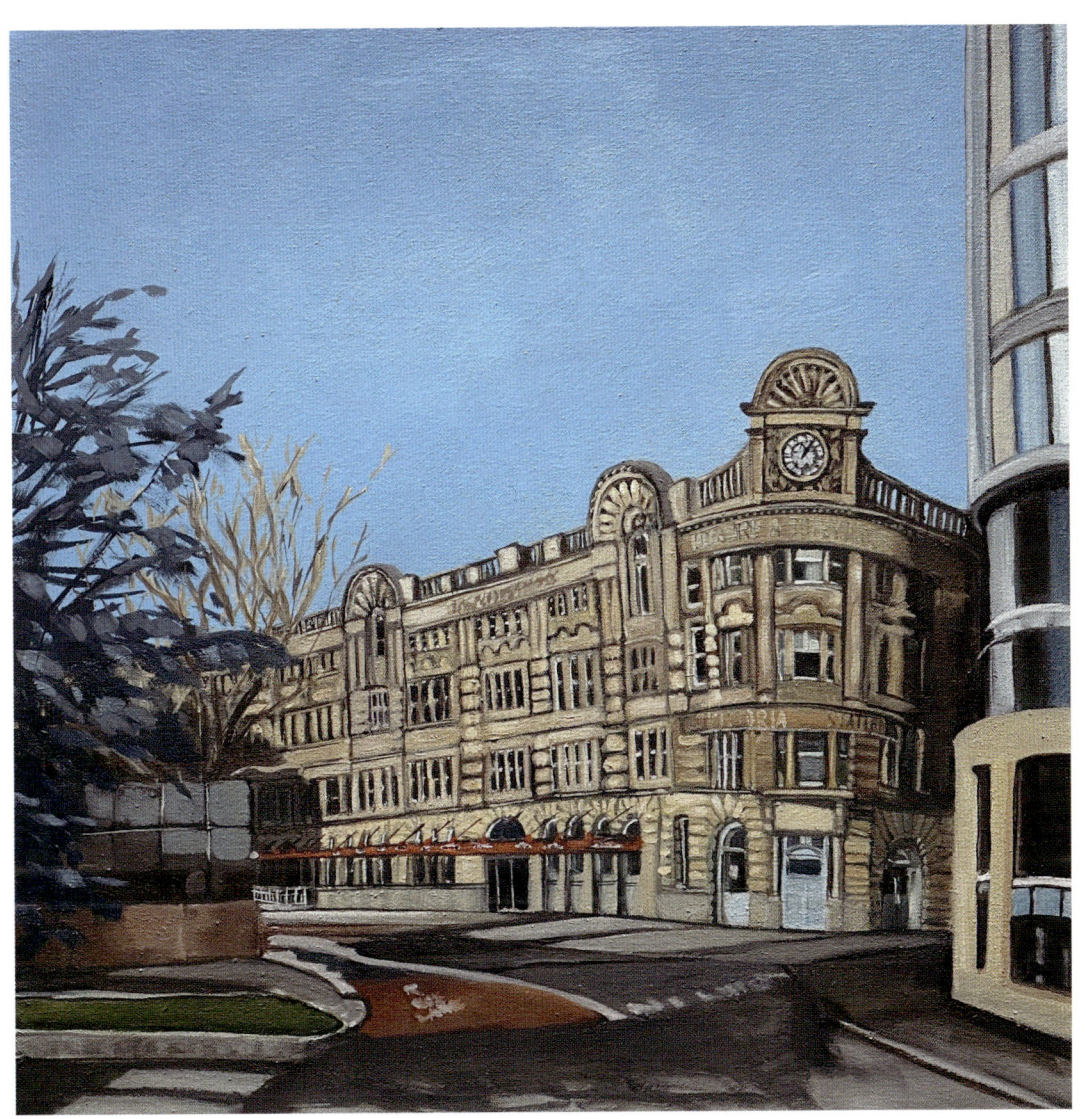

SOPHIE NIXON, VICTORIA STATION

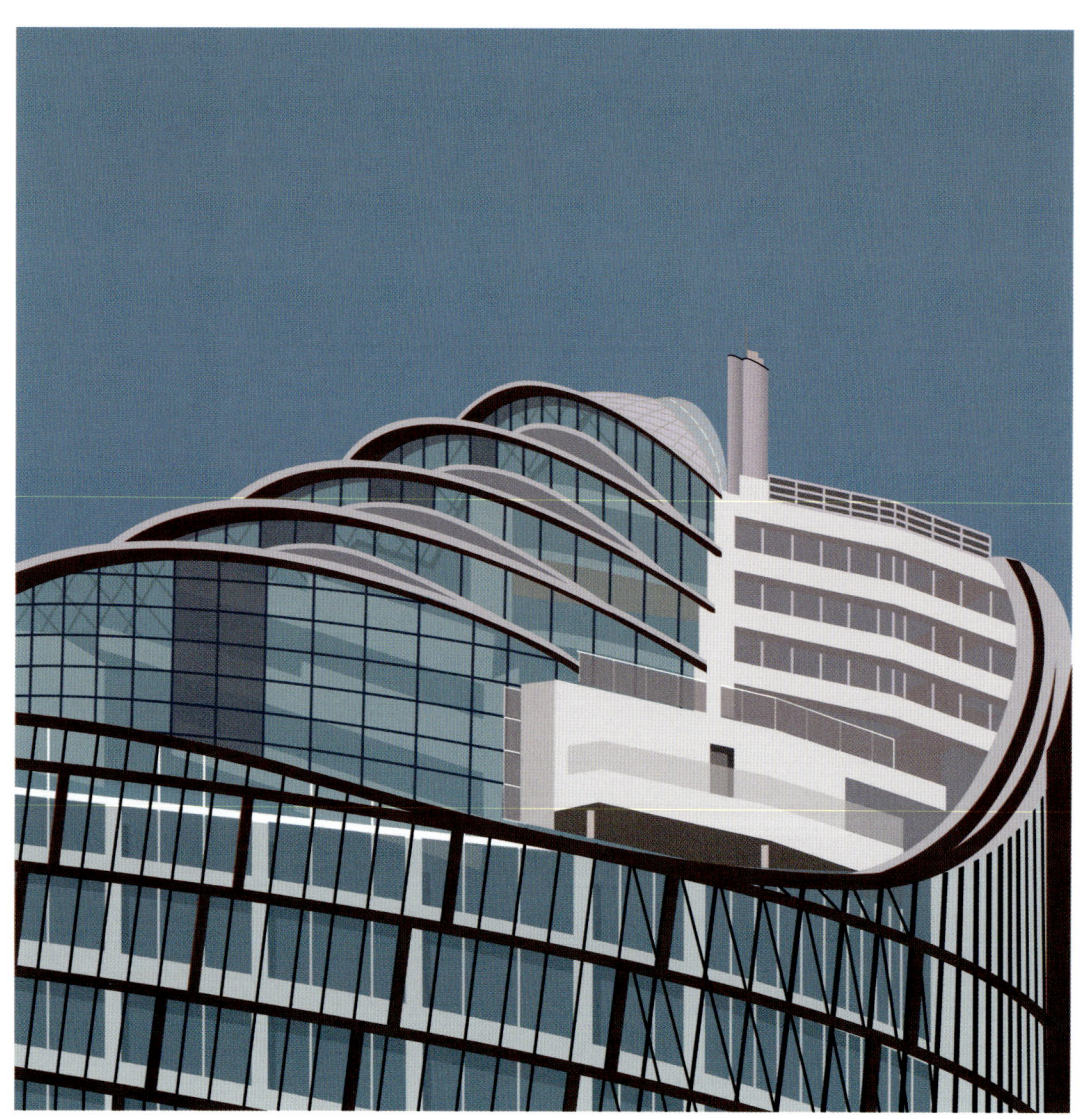

EAMONN MURPHY, ONE ANGEL SQUARE

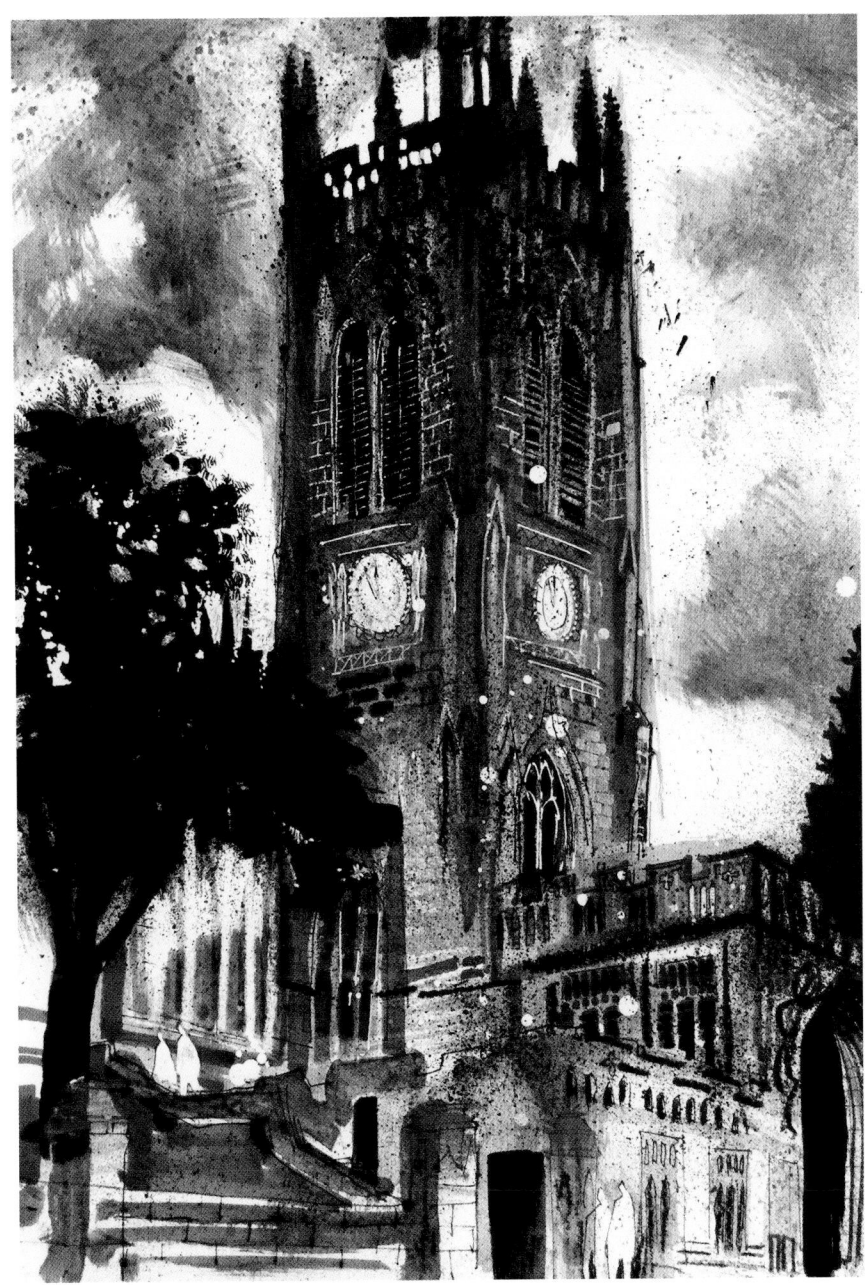

David Lowther, Manchester Cathedral

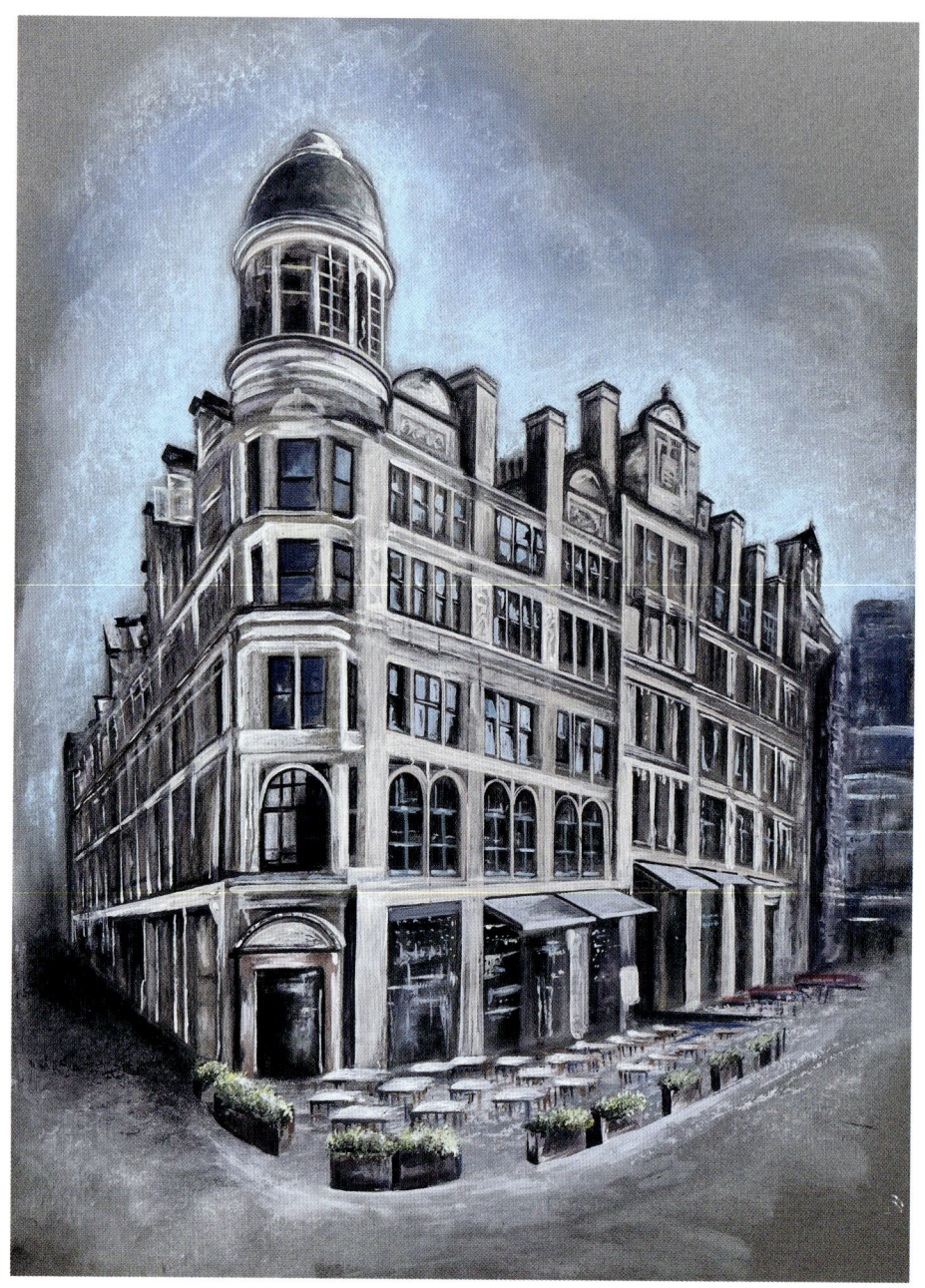

LISA HASELDEN, THE CORN EXCHANGE

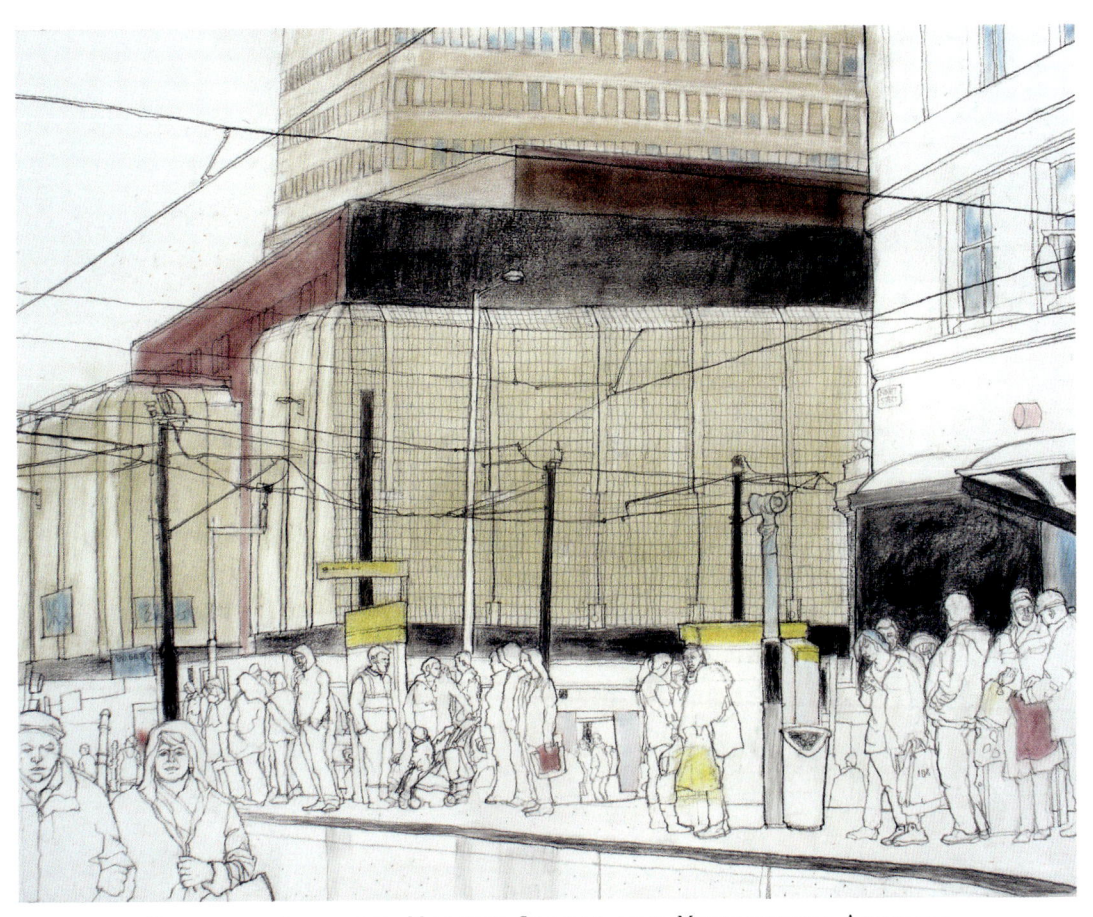

CAROLINE JOHNSON, MARKET STREET AND MANCHESTER ARNDALE

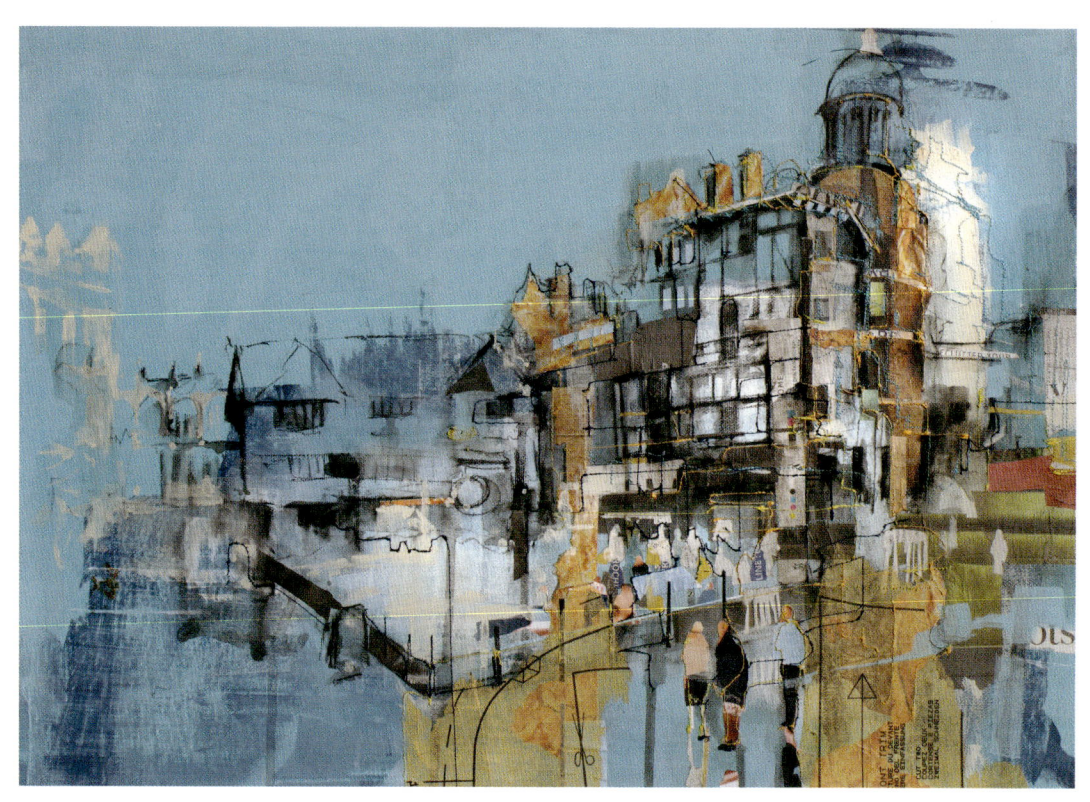

ROB WILSON, SHAMBLES SQUARE

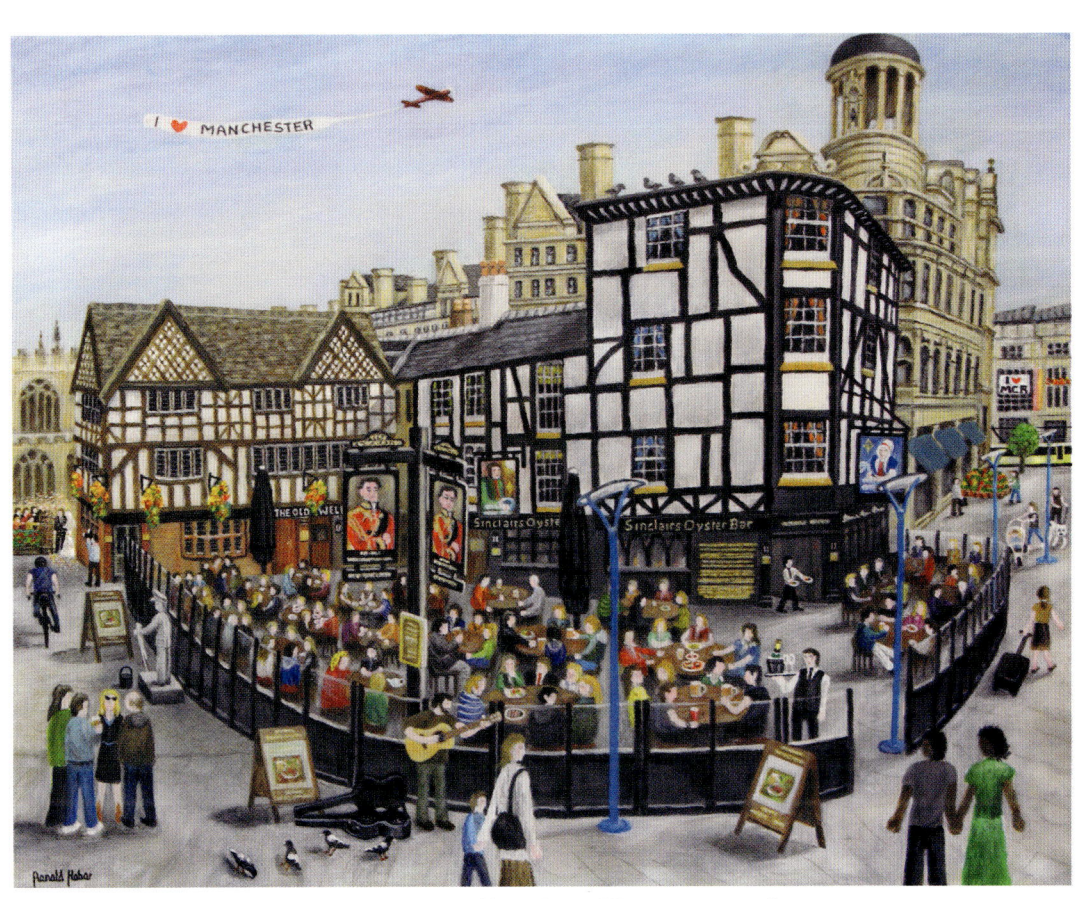

RONALD HABER, THE OLD WELLINGTON INN

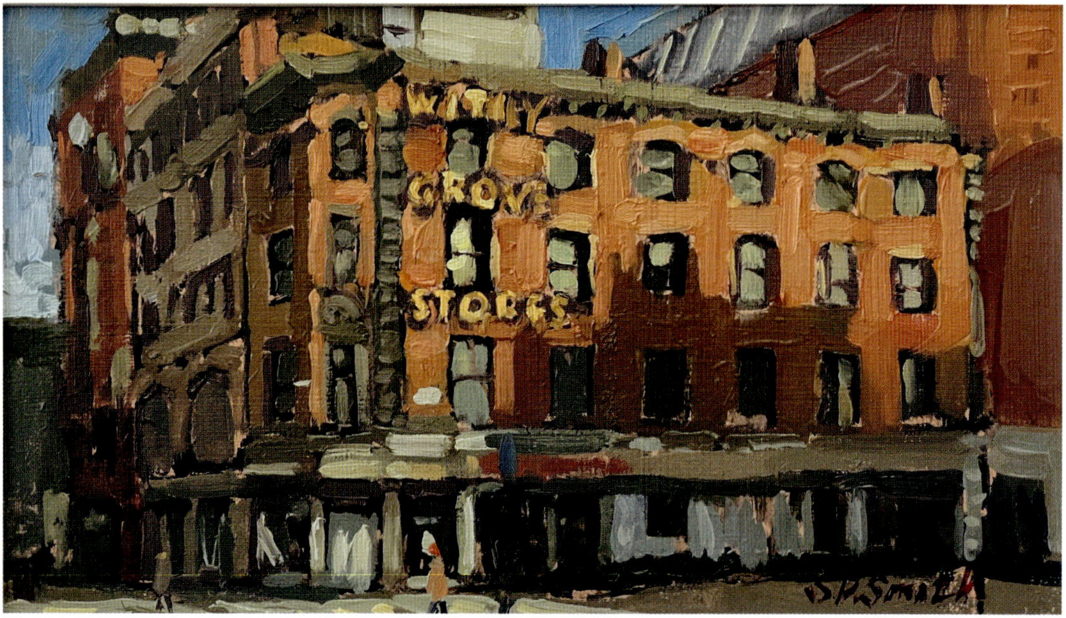

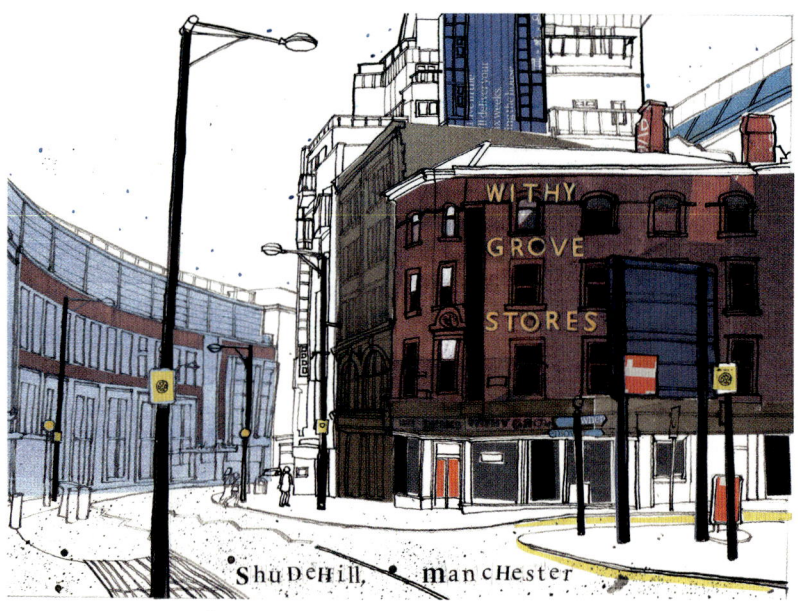

STEVEN P SMITH, WITHY GROVE STORES

CAROLINE JOHNSON, SHUDEHILL

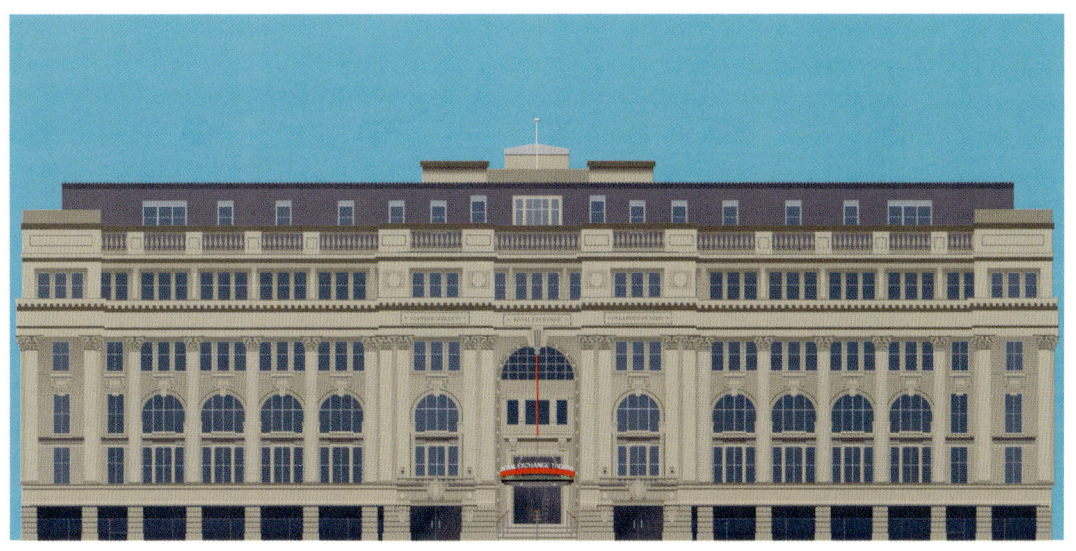

EAMONN MURPHY, ROYAL EXCHANGE

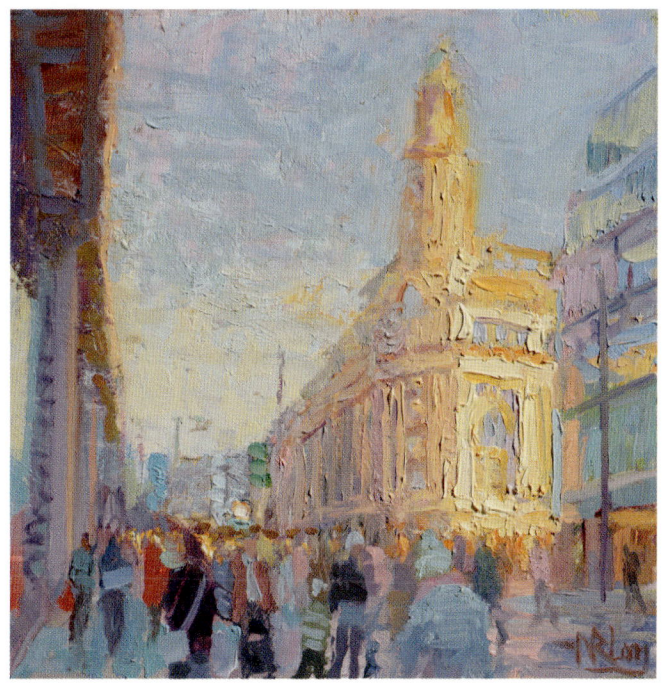

NORMAN LONG, ROYAL EXCHANGE THEATRE

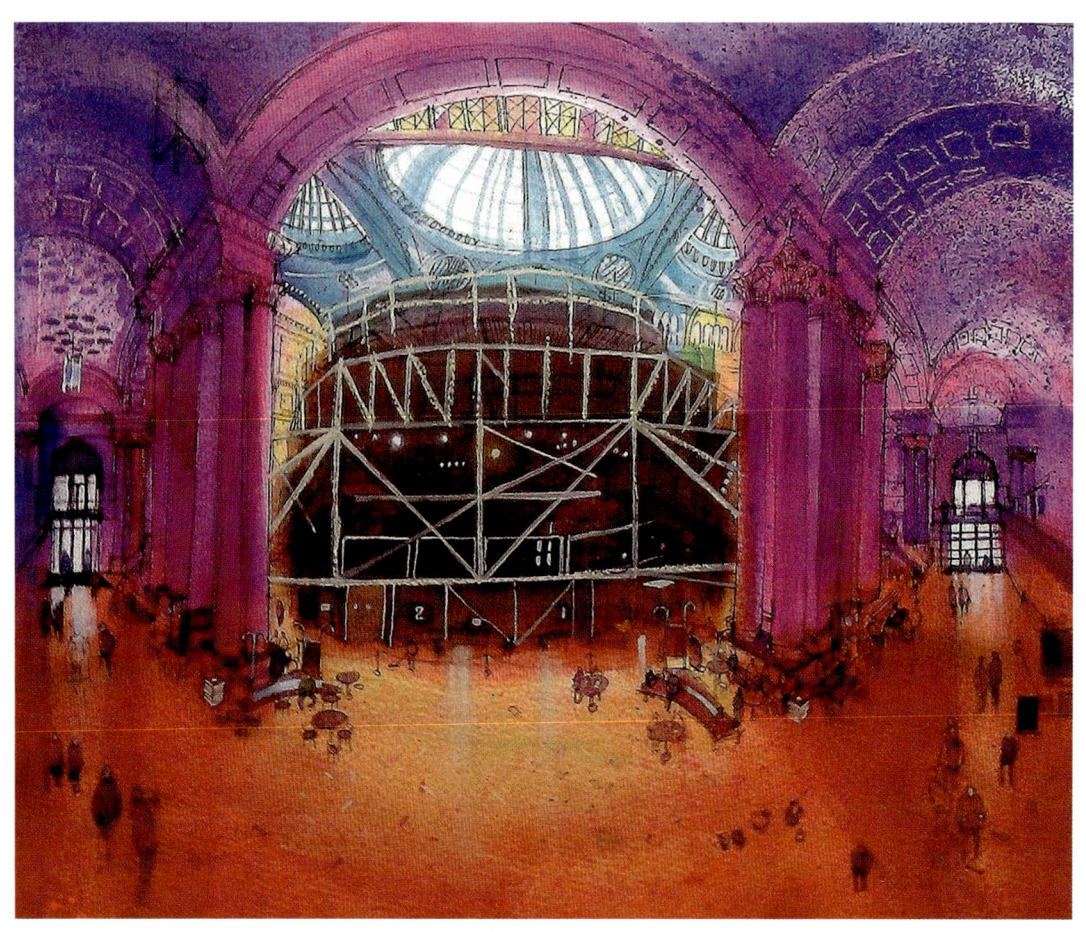

DAVID LOWTHER, ROYAL EXCHANGE THEATRE

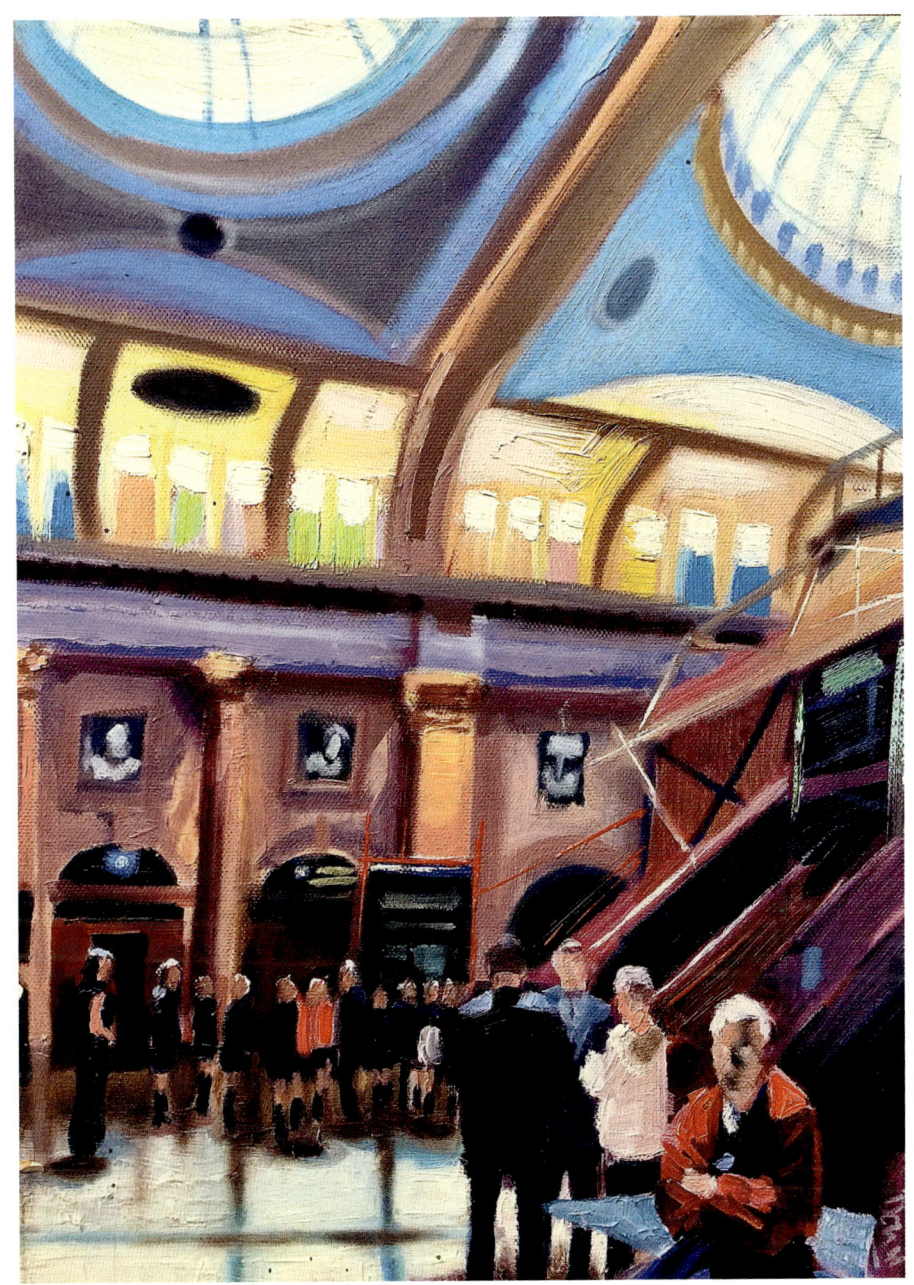

DAVID LOWTHER, ROYAL EXCHANGE THEATRE

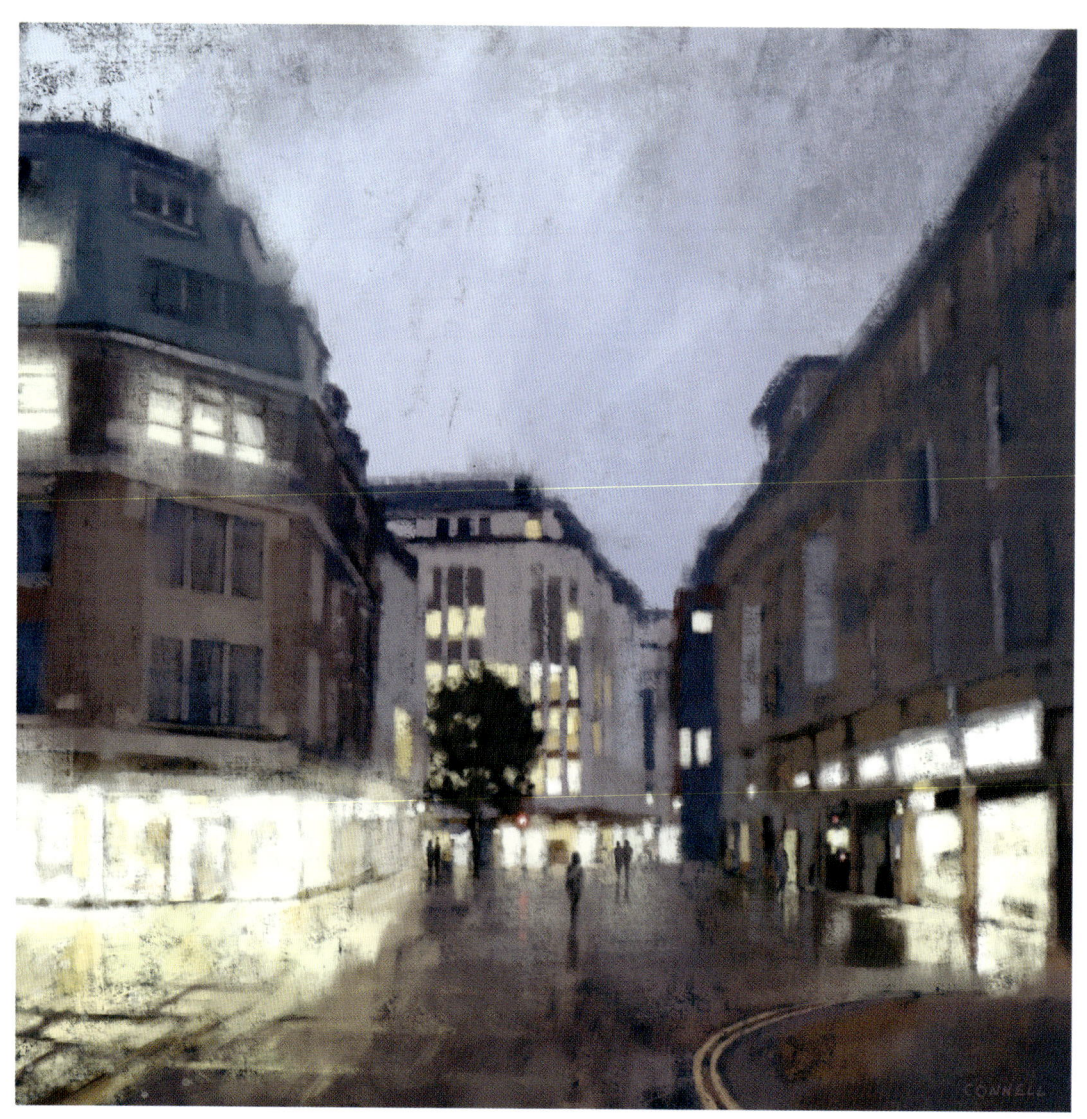

SARAH CONNELL, ST ANN'S SQUARE

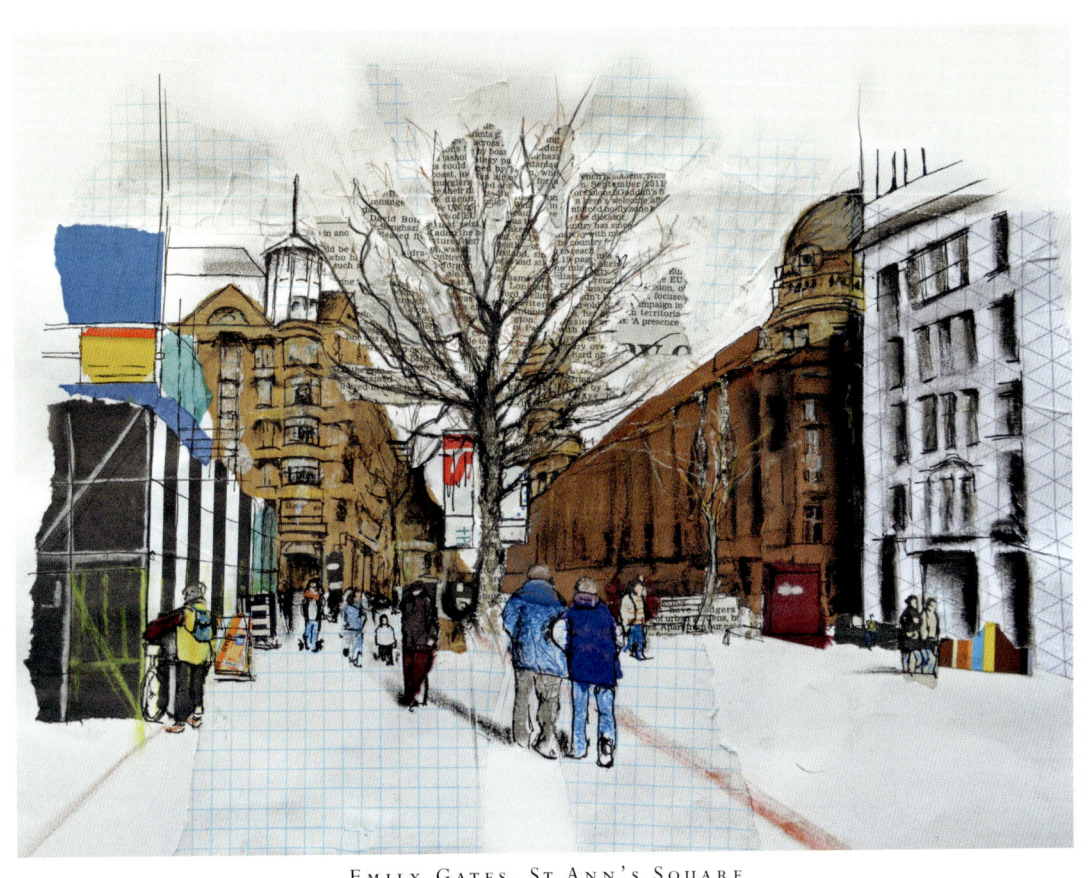

EMILY GATES, ST ANN'S SQUARE

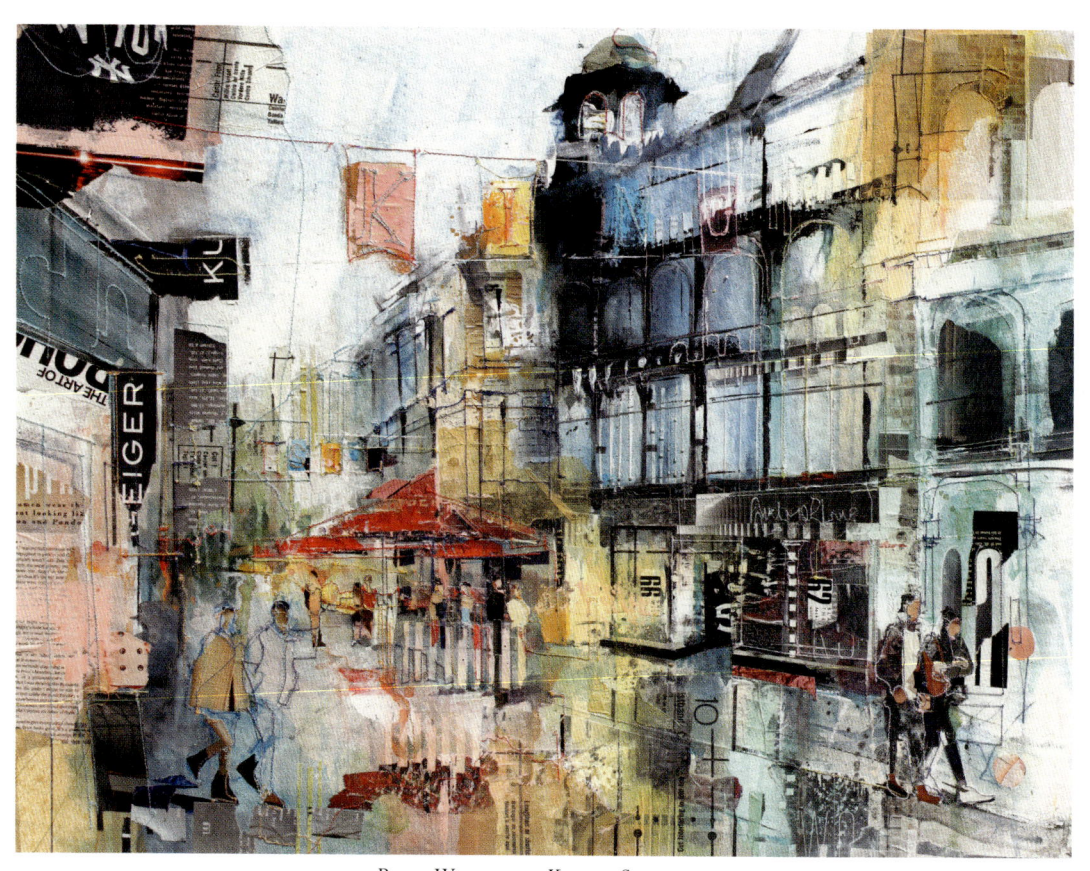

ROB WILSON, KING STREET

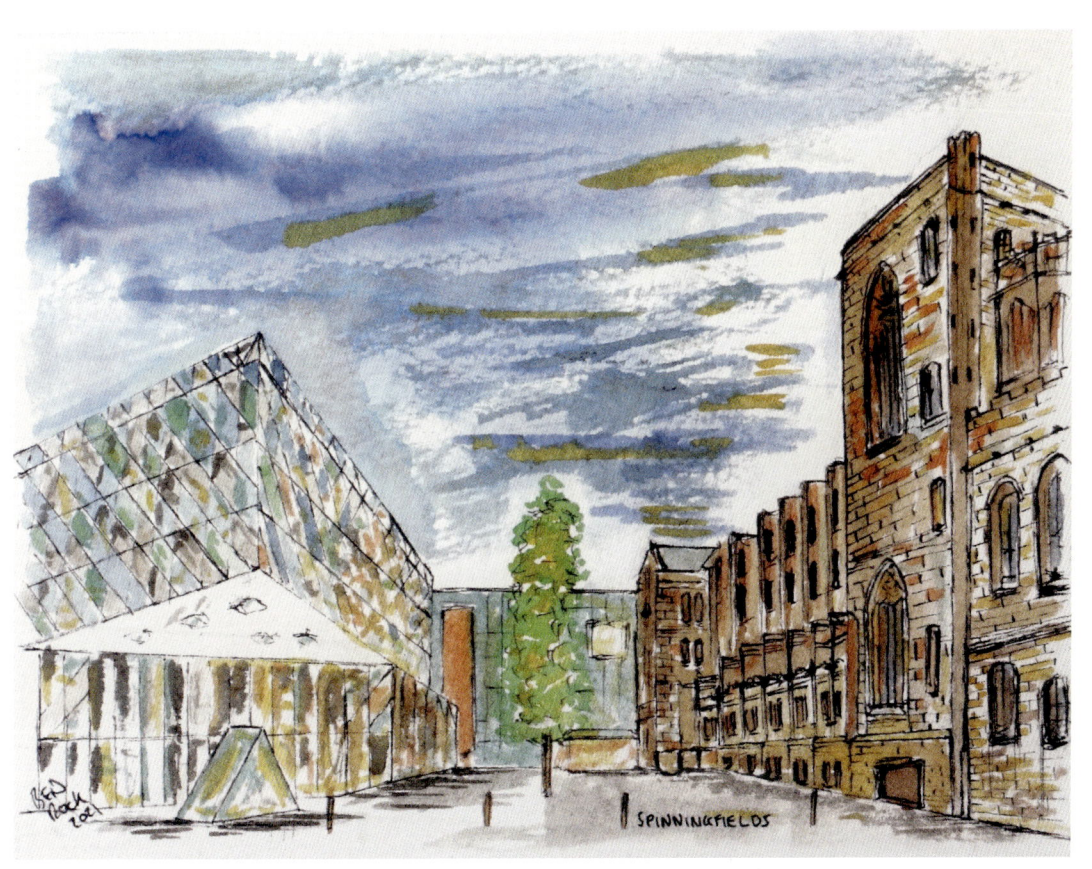

SPINNINGFIELDS

BEN ROCK, JOHN RYLANDS LIBRARY

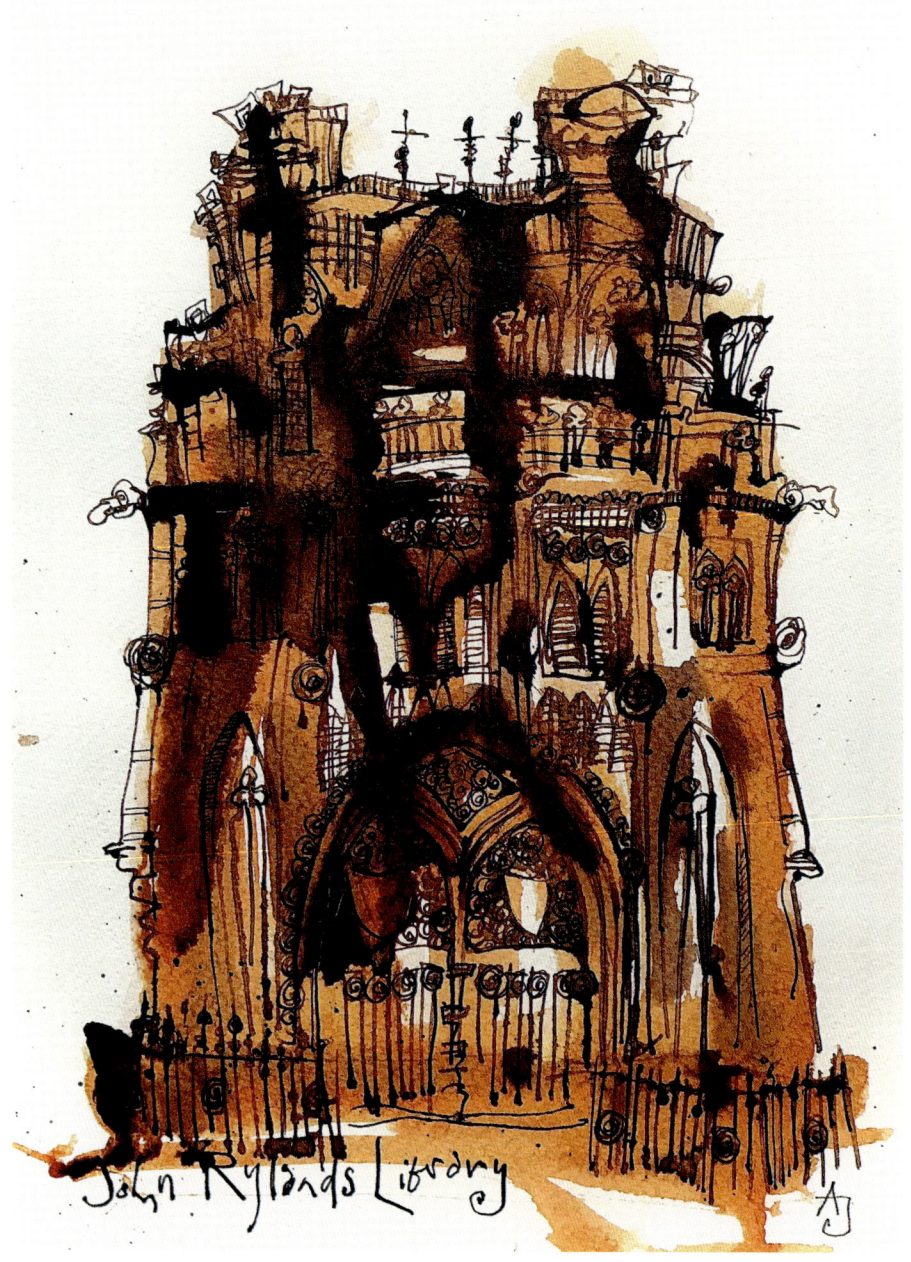

ANDREA JOSEPH, JOHN RYLANDS LIBRARY

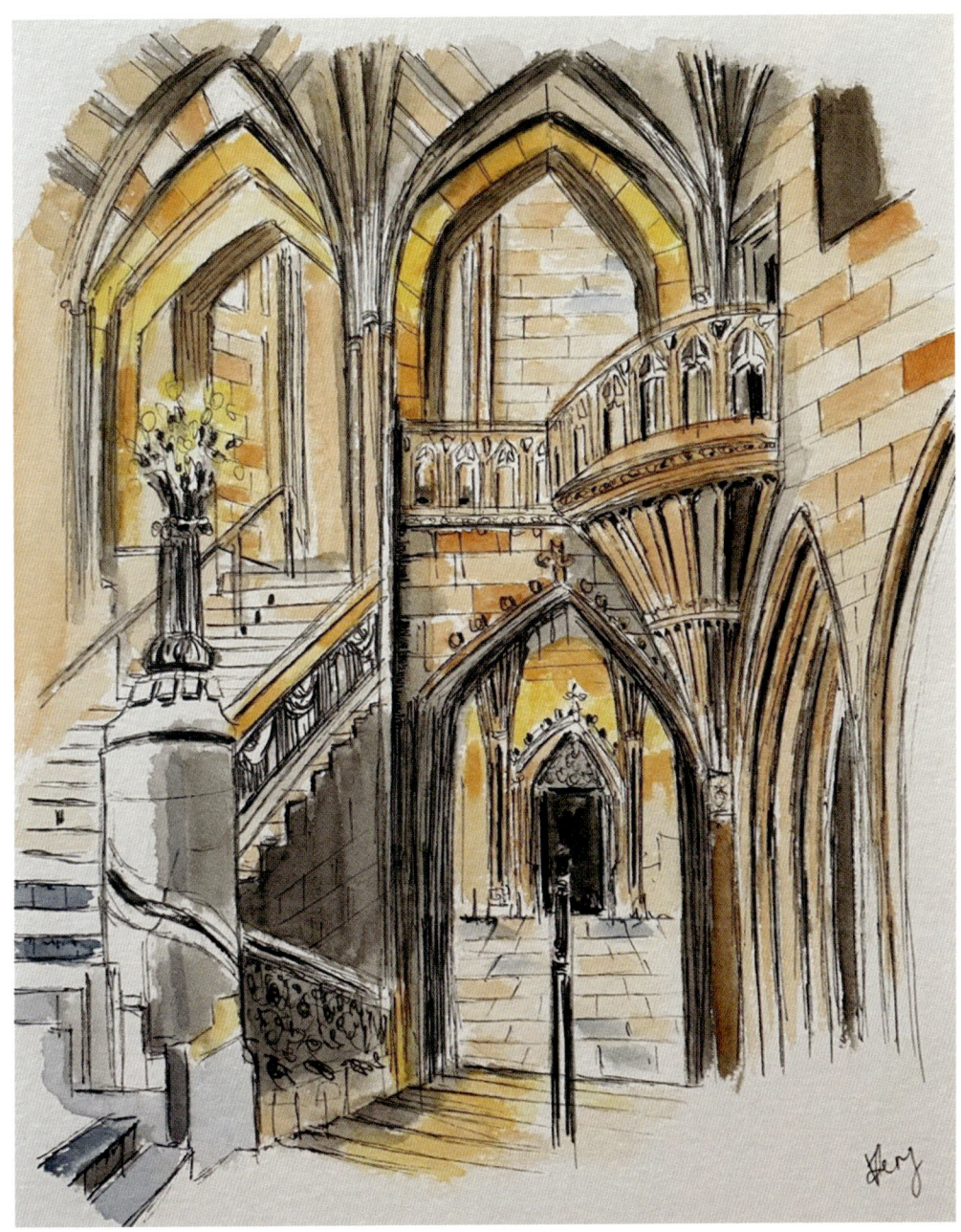

VICTORIA WOOD, JOHN RYLANDS LIBRARY

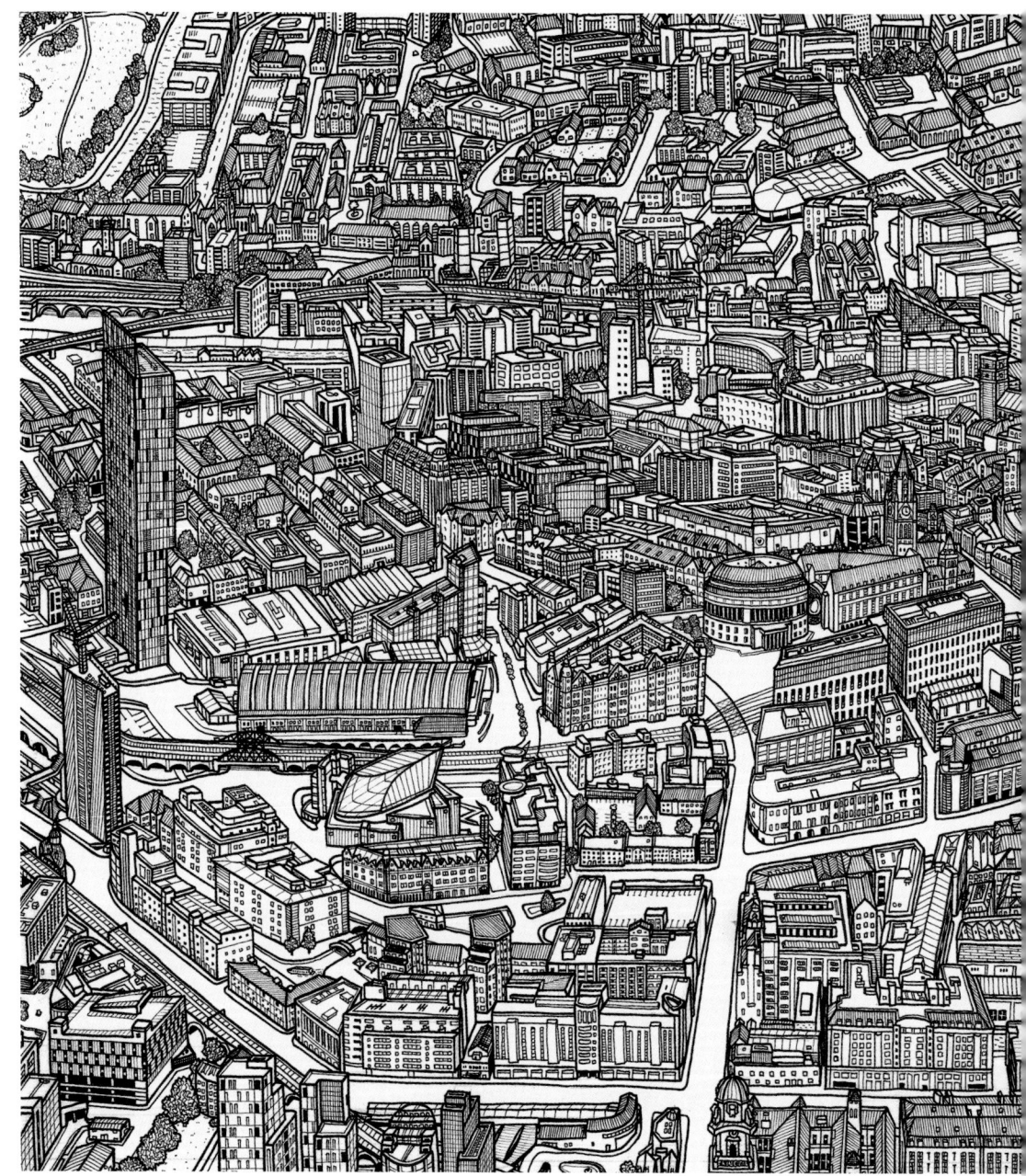

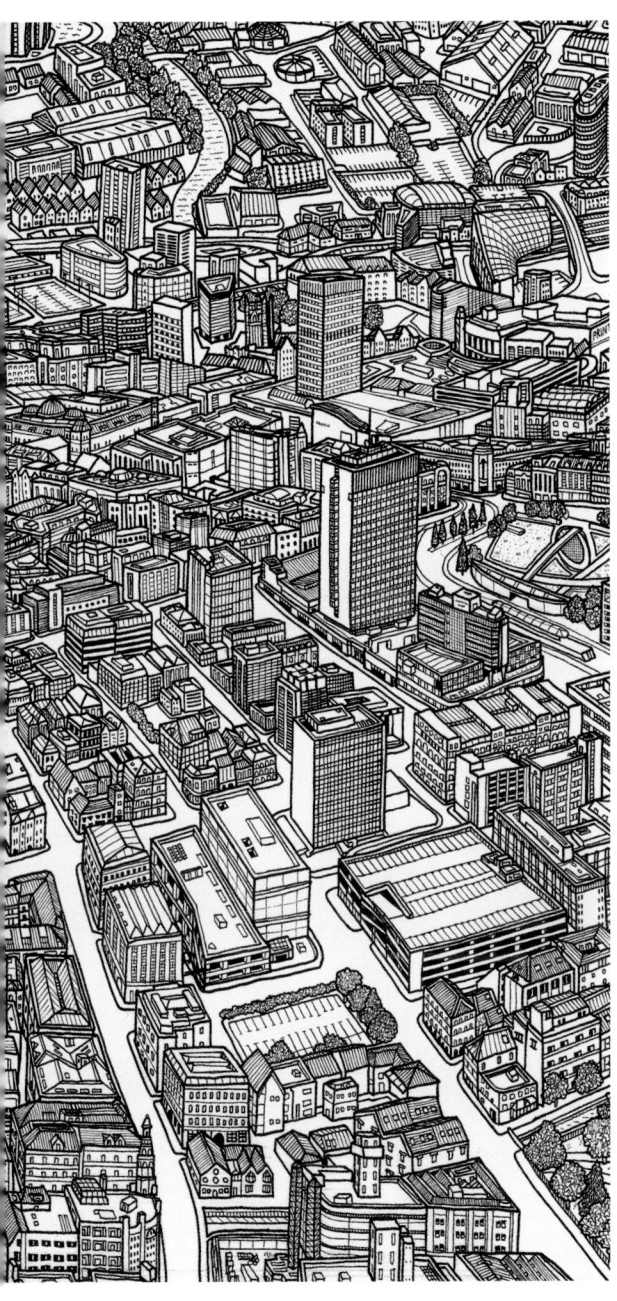

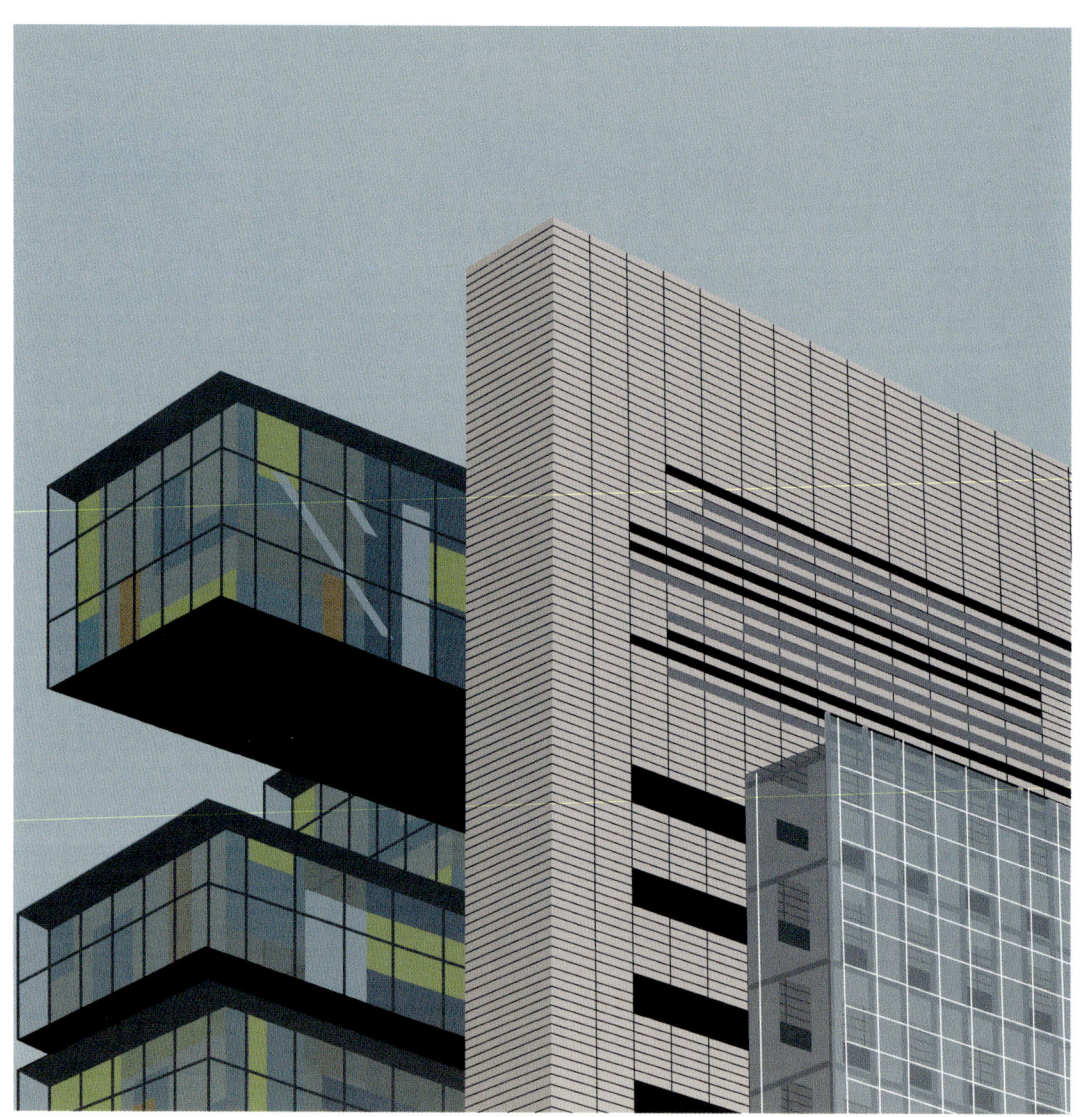

EAMONN MURPHY, CIVIL JUSTICE CENTRE

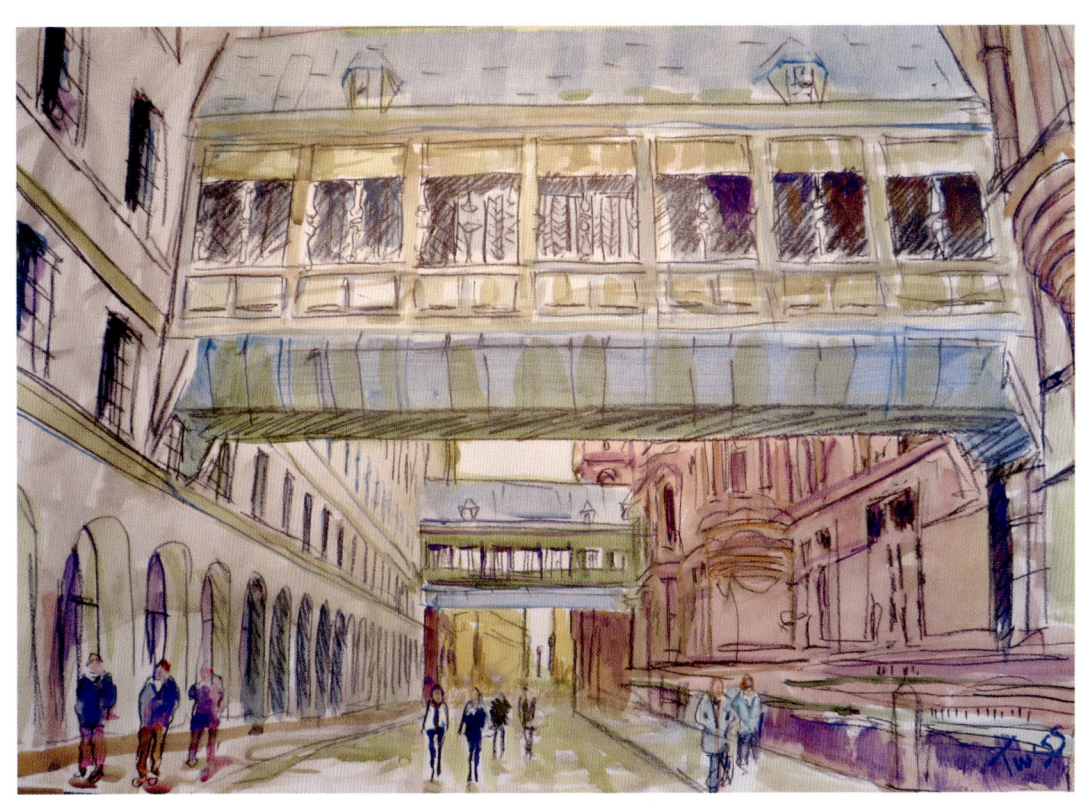

JUSTIN TWIGG, LLOYD STREET

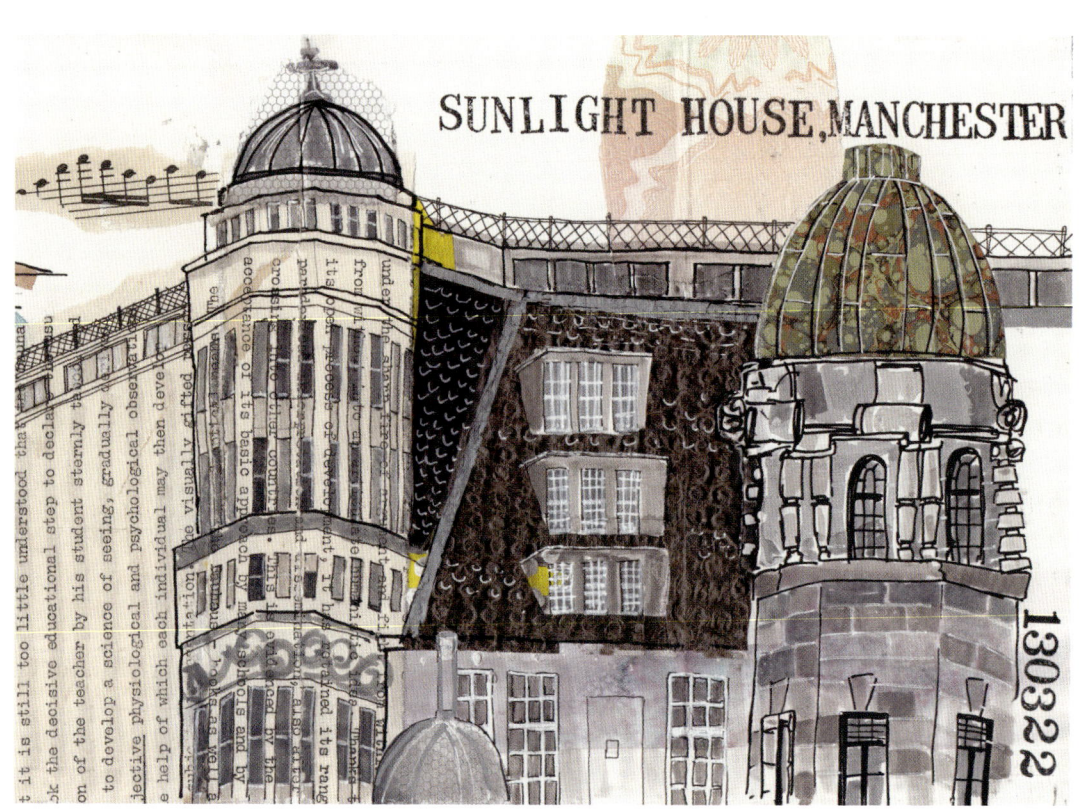

SARAH FRANKLIN, SUNLIGHT HOUSE

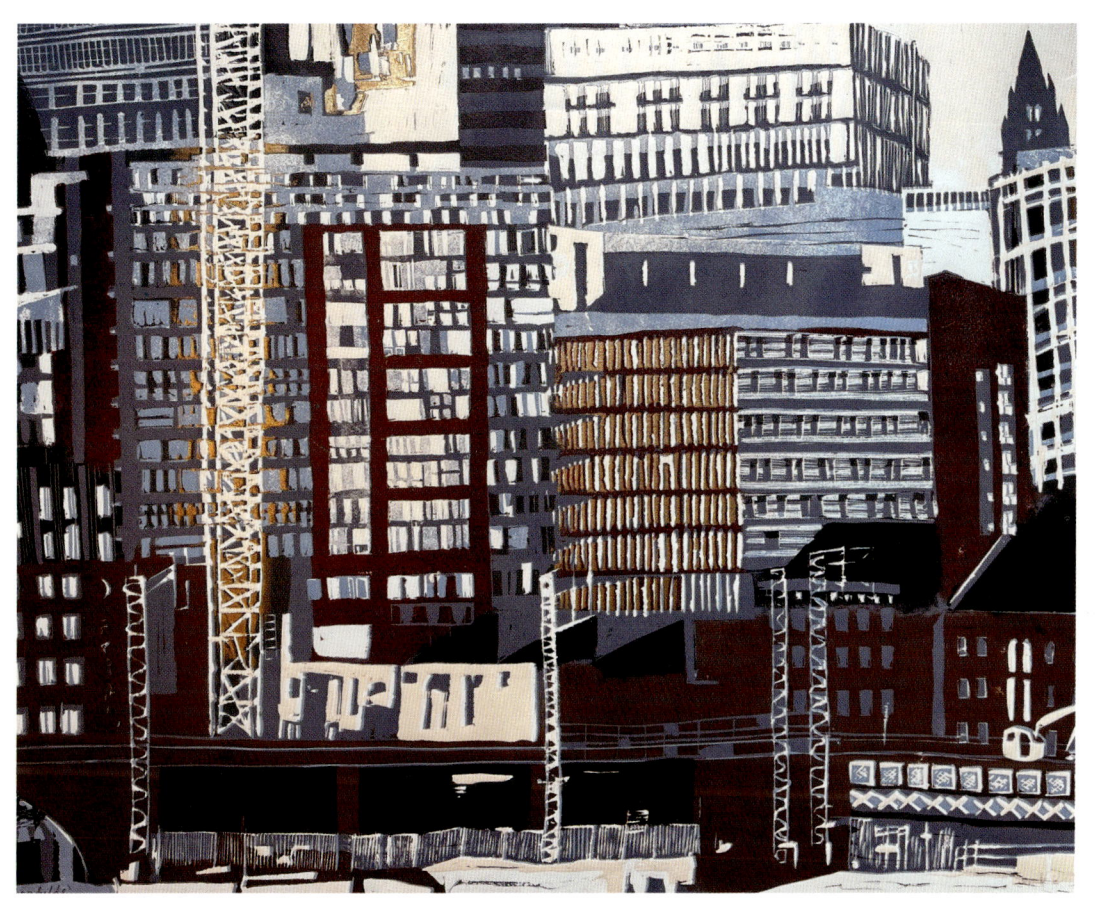

Jayne Pellington, Spinningfields

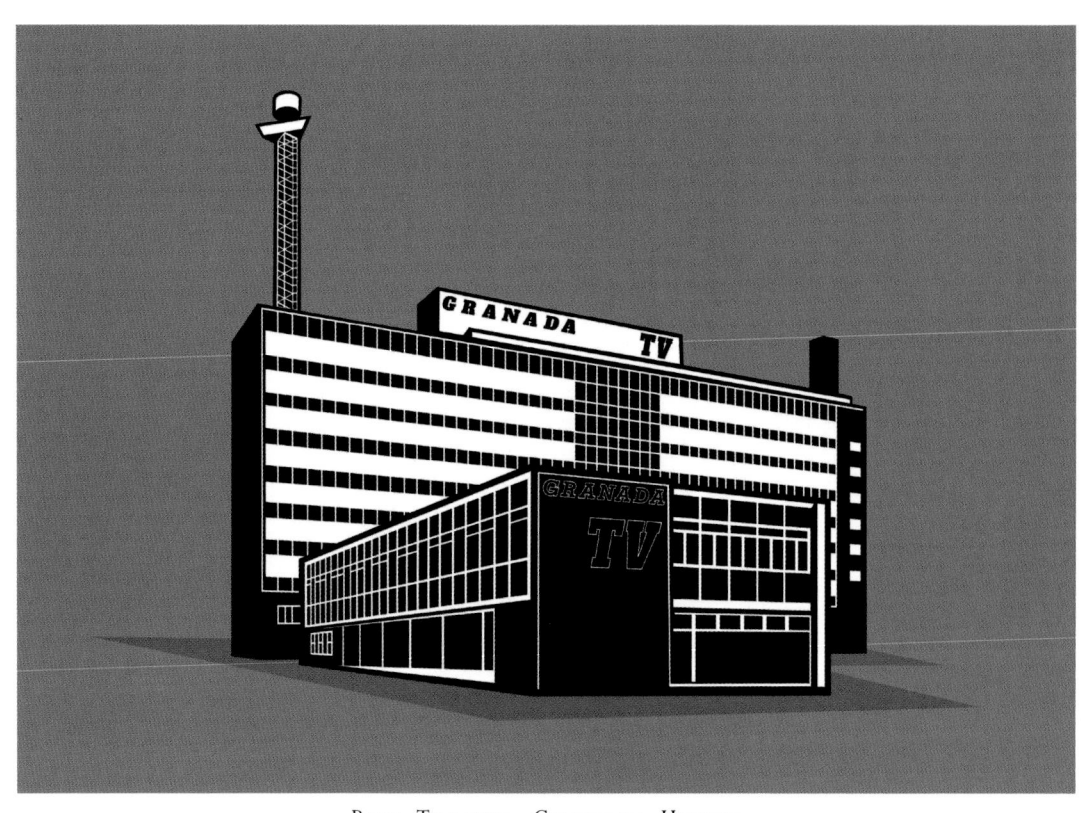

PHIL TURNER, GRANADA HOUSE

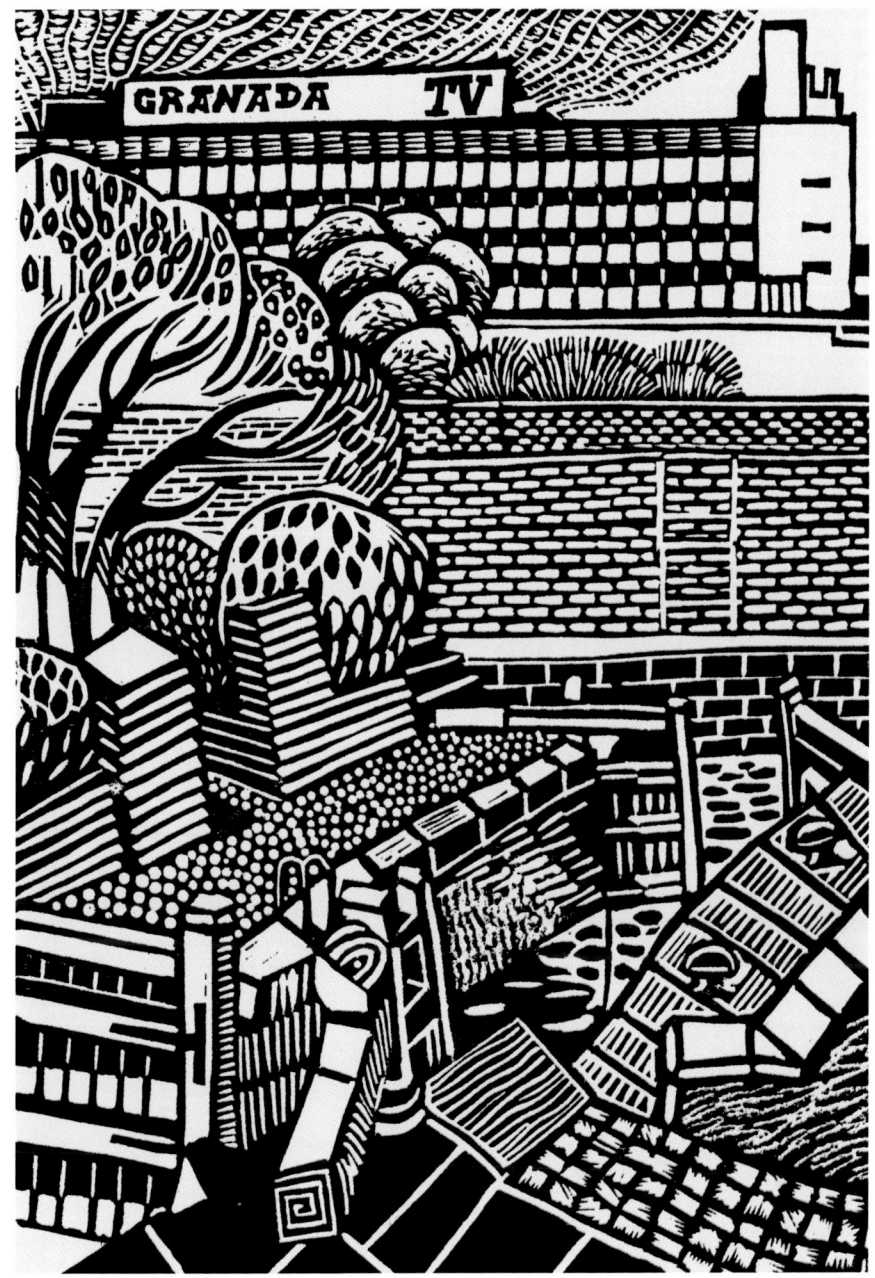

ERIC GASKELL, ENTRY LOCK – MANCHESTER AND SALFORD JUNCTION

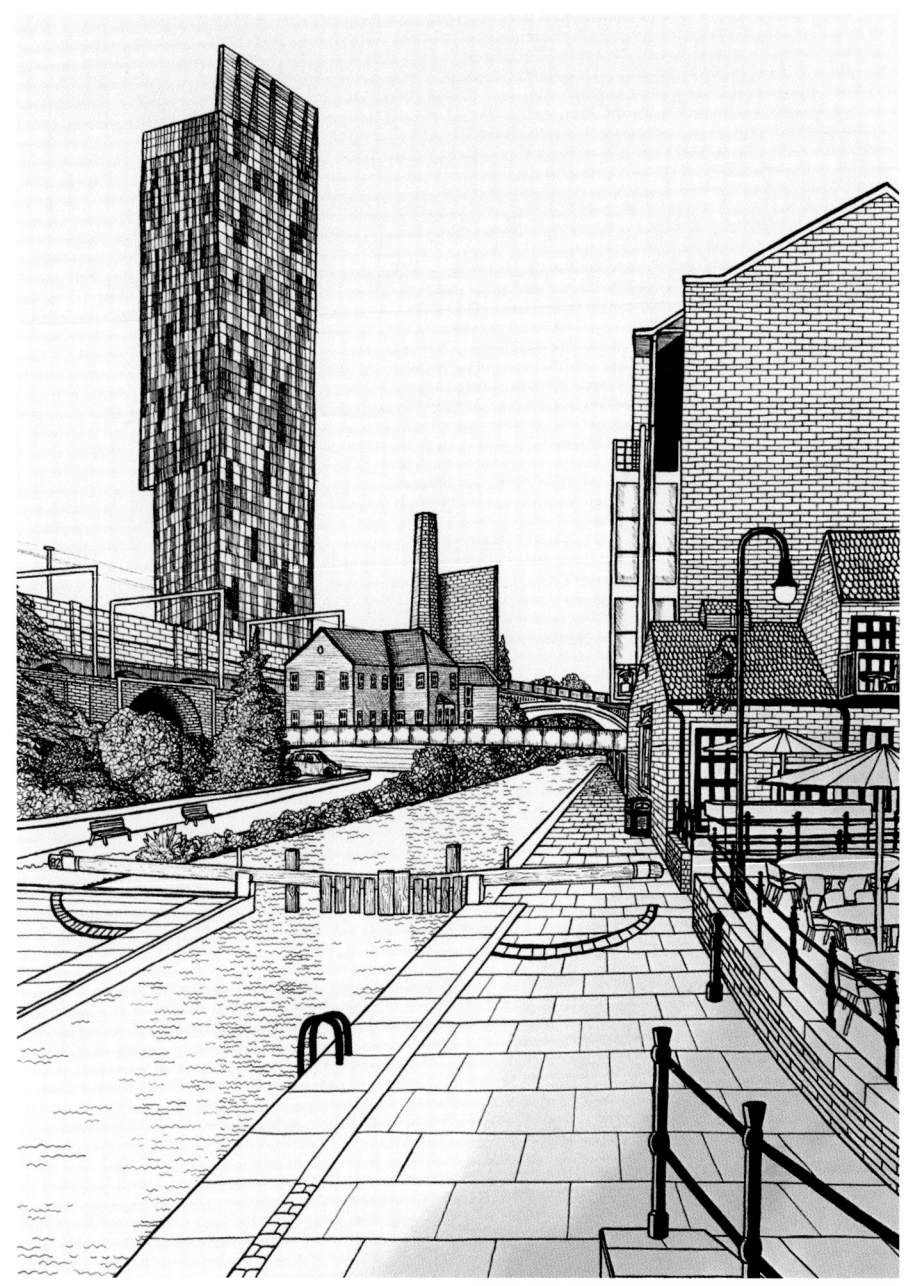

JIM KITE, CASTLEFIELD LOCKS

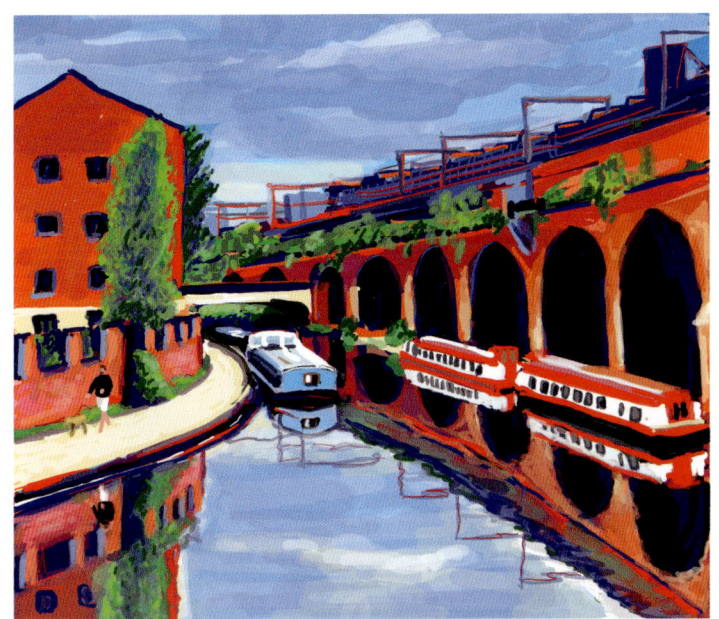

KATIE PATEL, CASTLEFIELD URBAN HERITAGE PARK

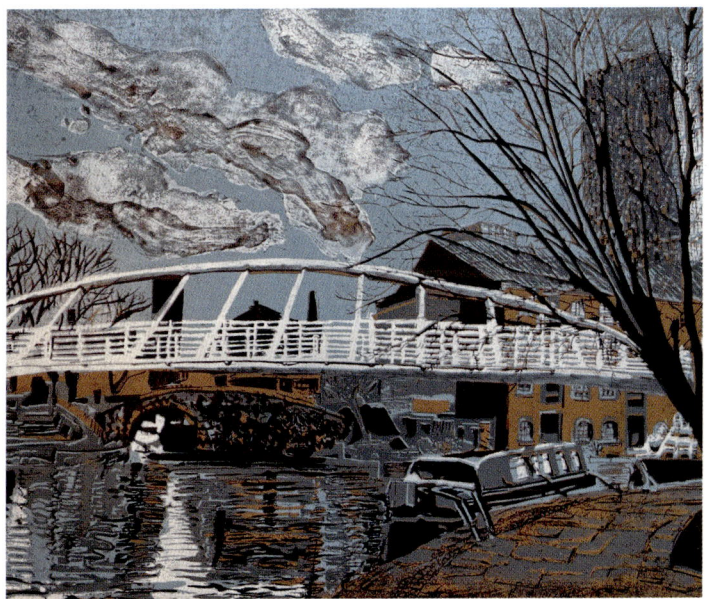

JAYNE PELLINGTON, CASTLEFIELD

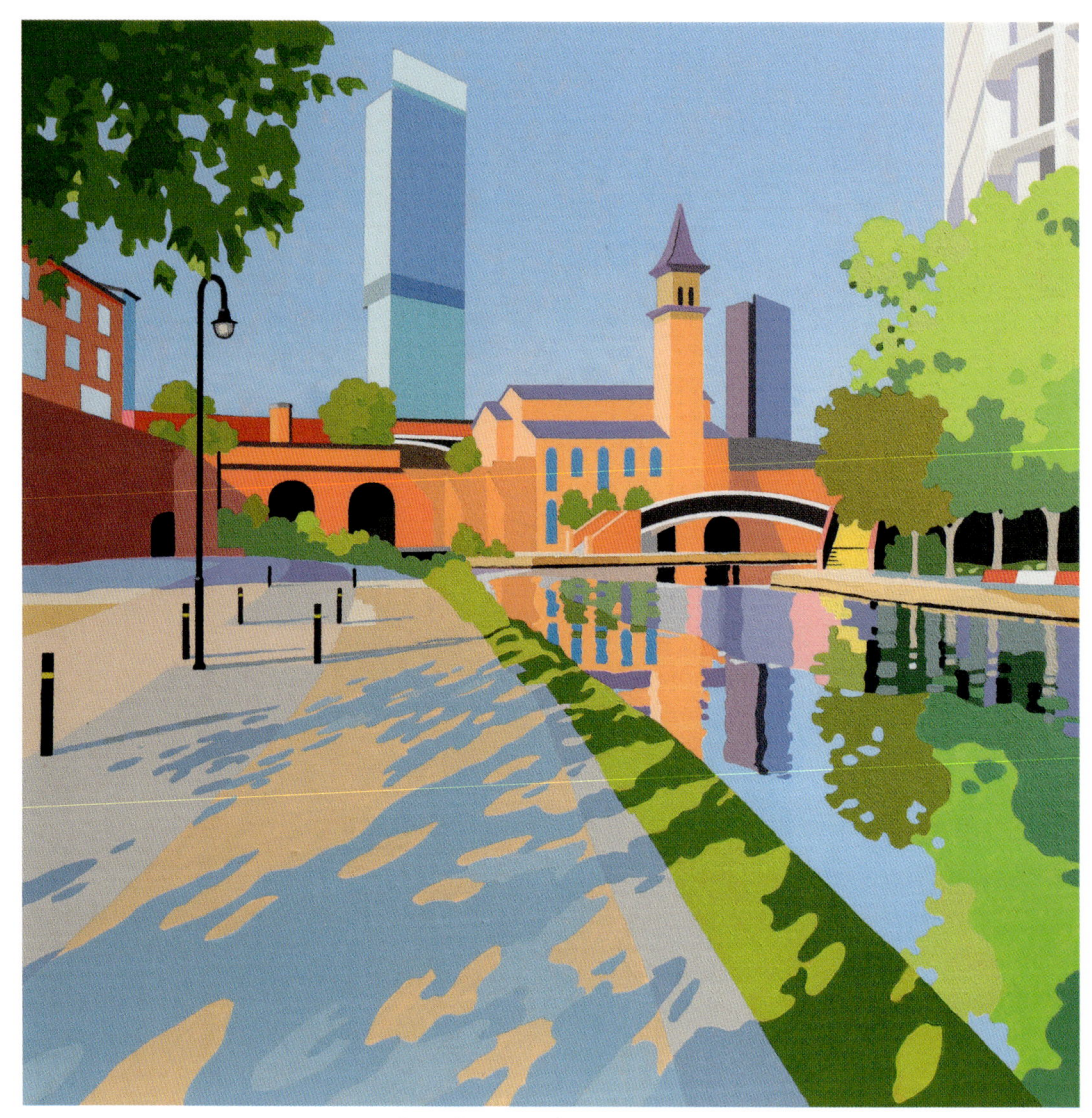

SUE SCOTT, CASTLEFIELD

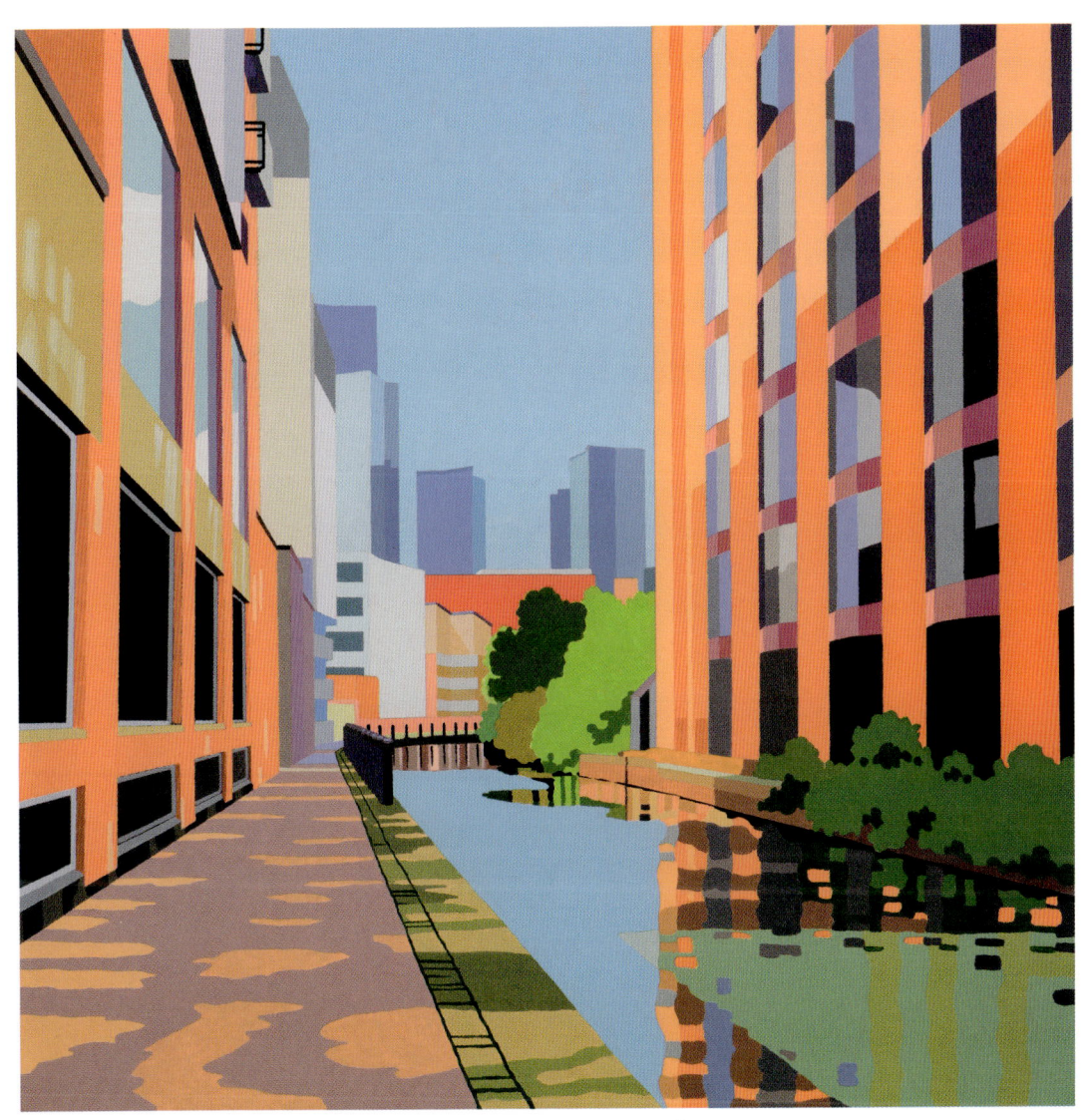

SUE SCOTT, MANCHESTER CANAL

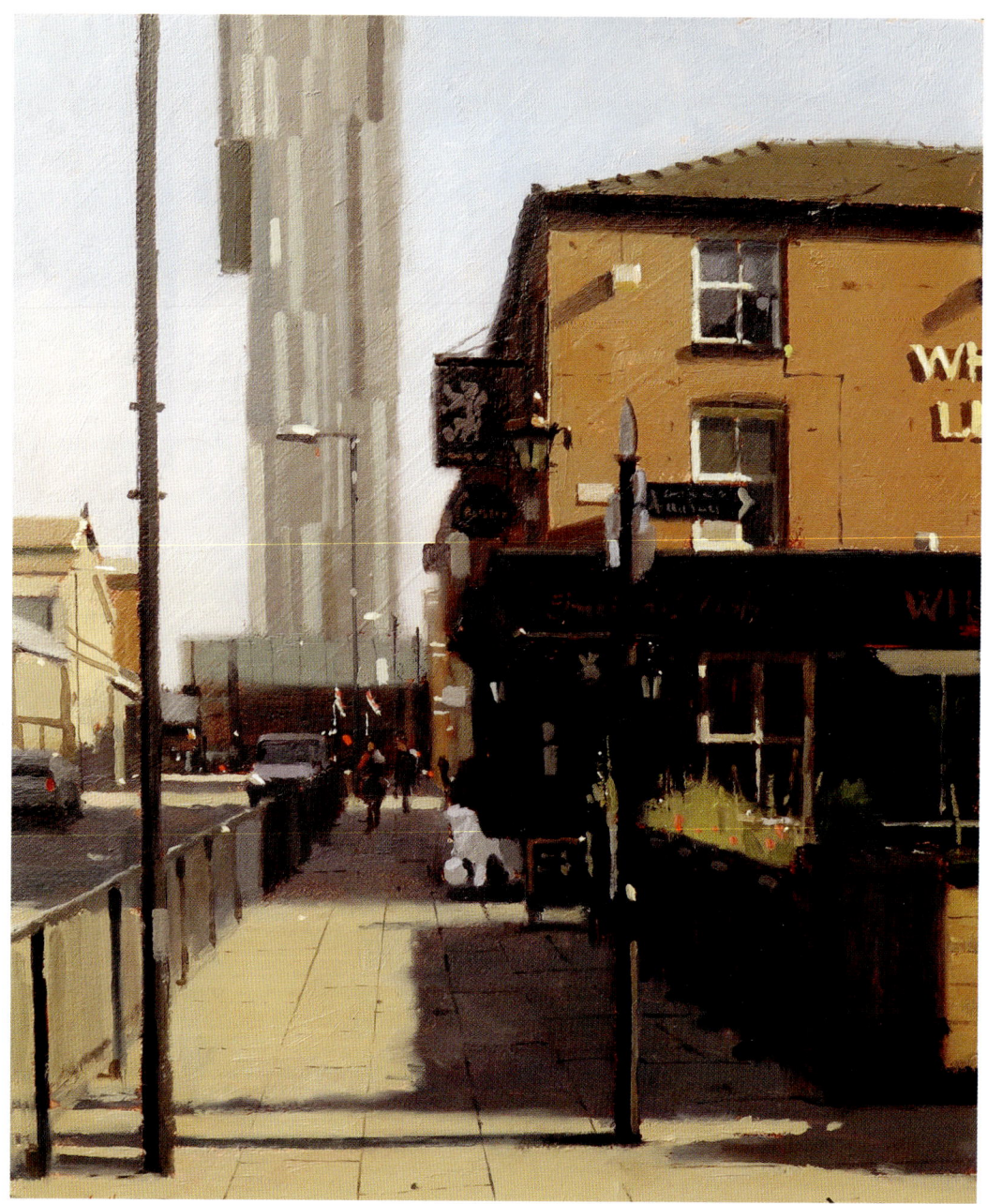

MICHAEL JOHN ASHCROFT, THE WHITE LION

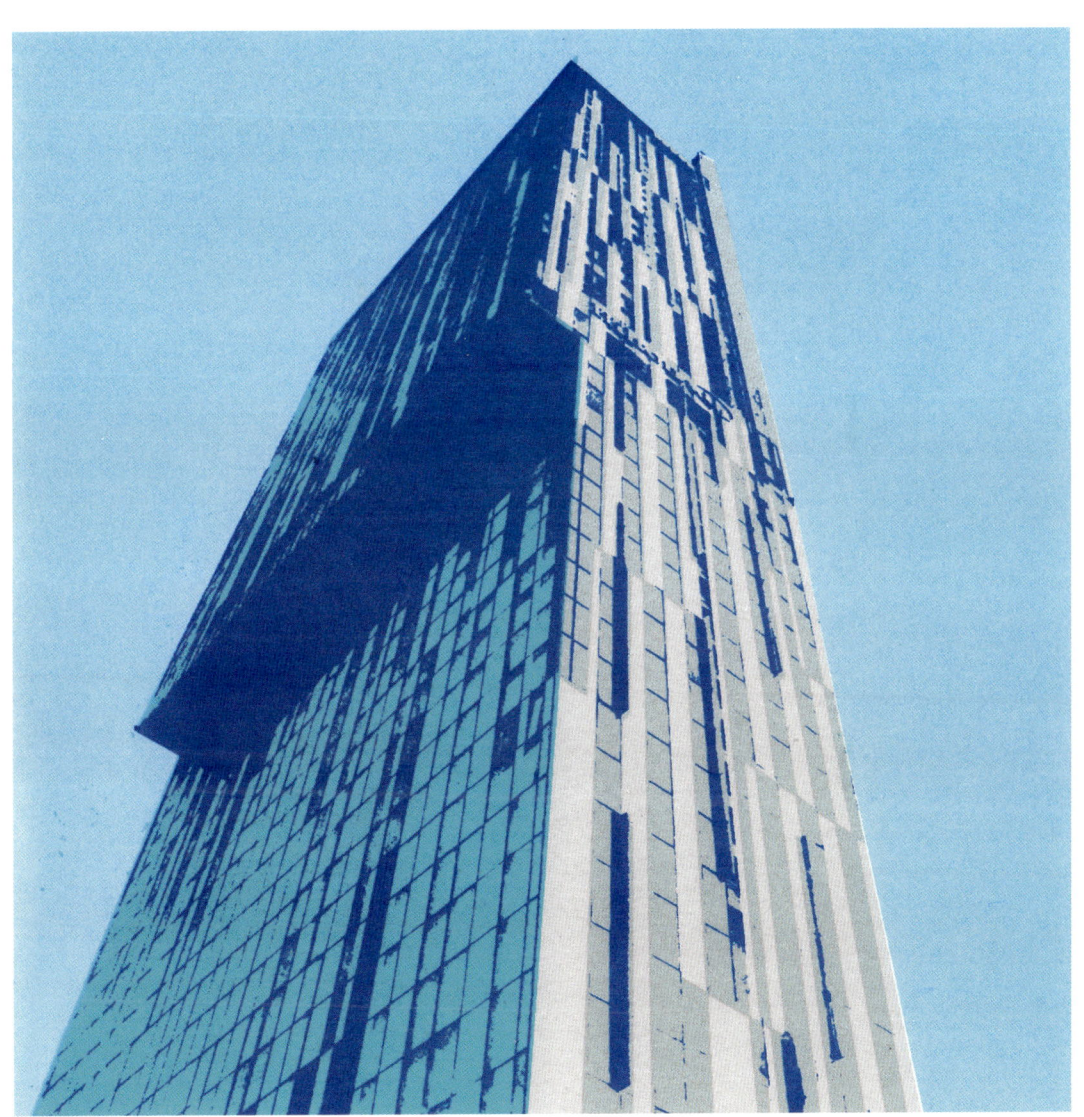

MICHAEL HITCHENS, BEETHAM TOWER

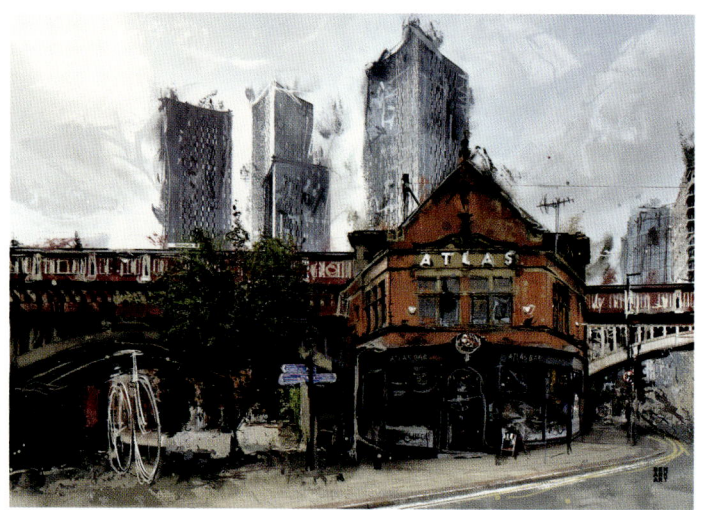

BEN ARK, ATLAS BAR

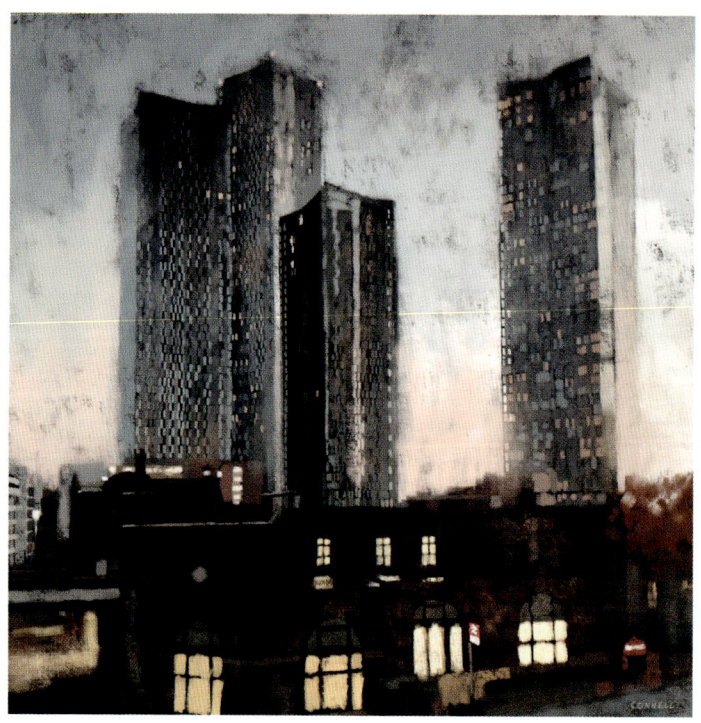

SARAH CONNELL, DEANSGATE TOWERS

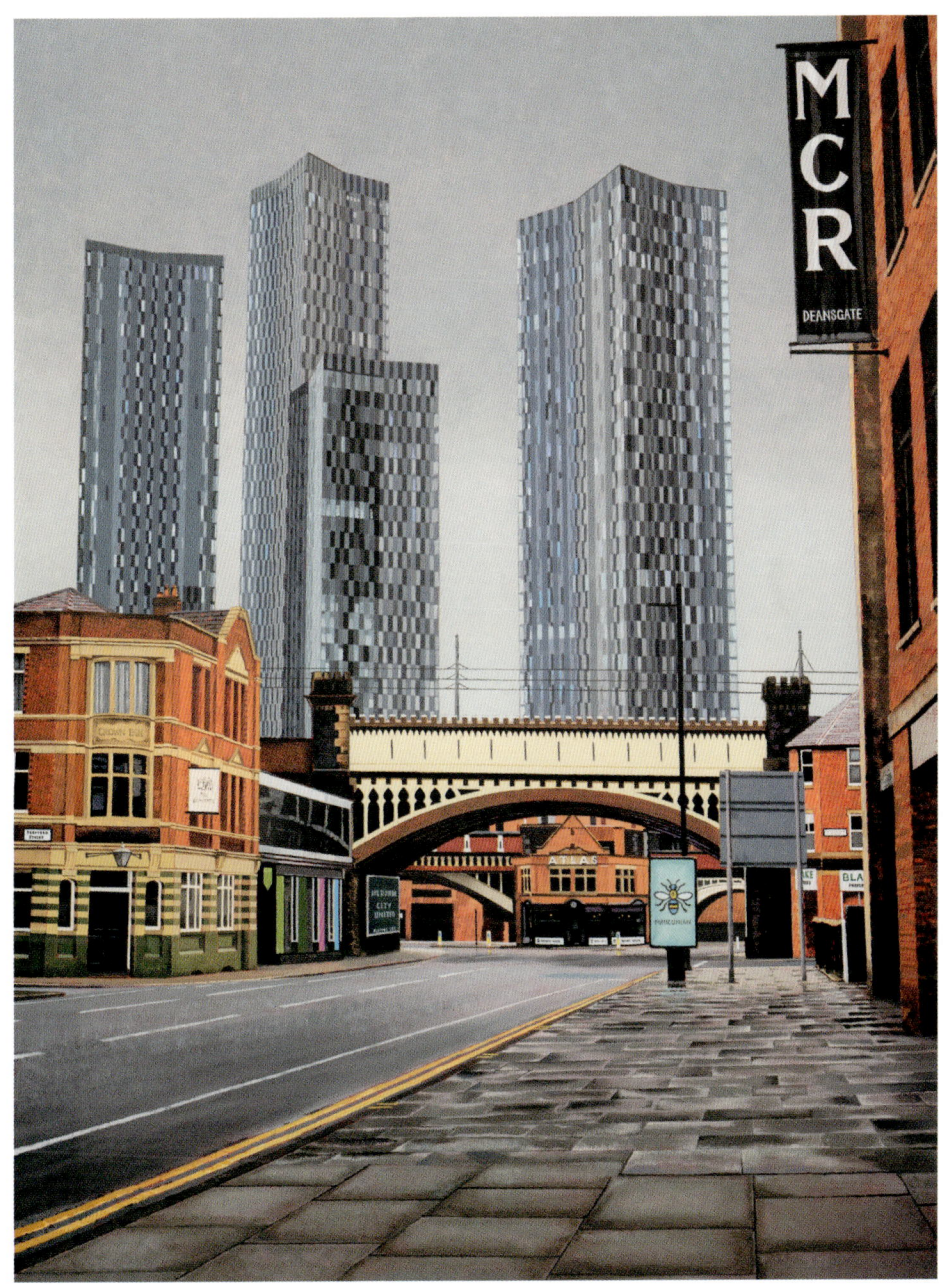

SUE SCOTT, DEANSGATE

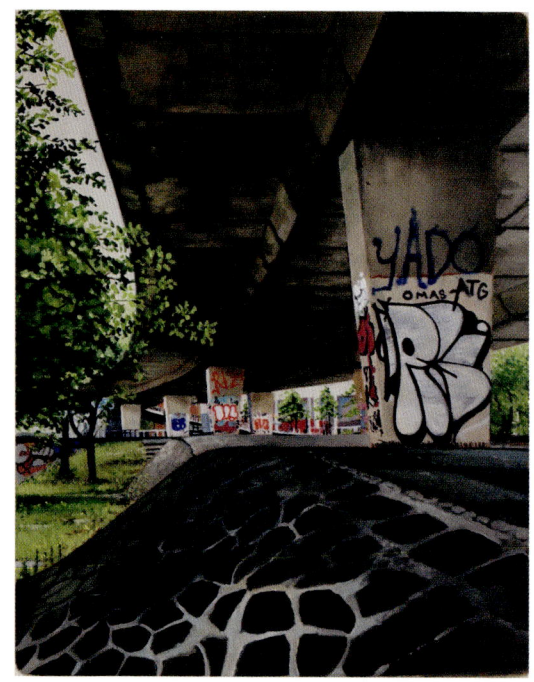

JEN ORPIN, MEDLOCK ROUNDABOUT (CONCRETE CRAZY)

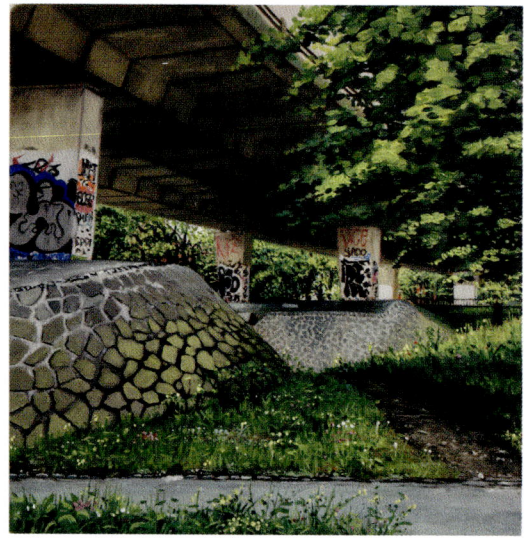

JEN ORPIN, MEDLOCK ROUNDABOUT (PARADICE)

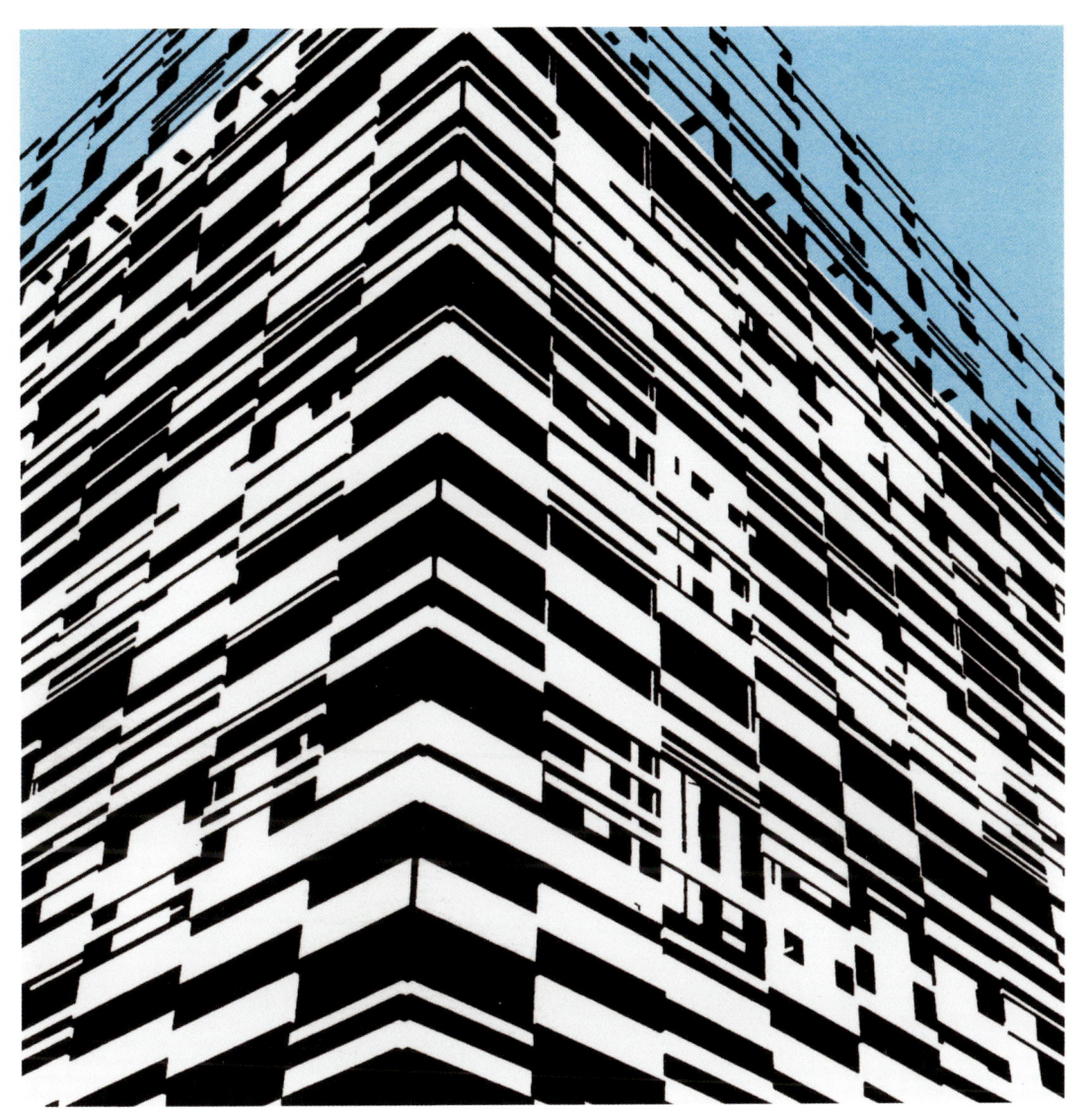

MICHAEL HITCHENS, BROOKS BUILDING

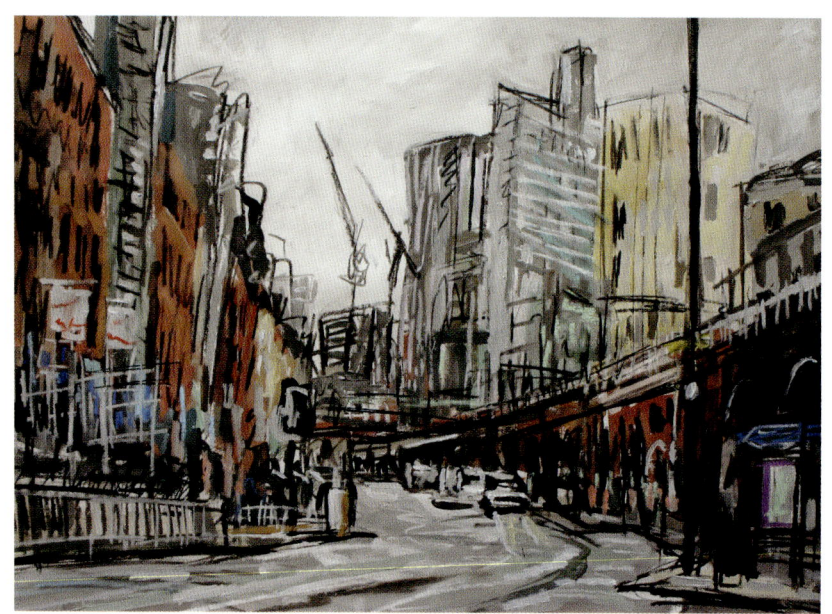

MATTHEW THOMPSON, VIEW FROM CITY ROAD INN

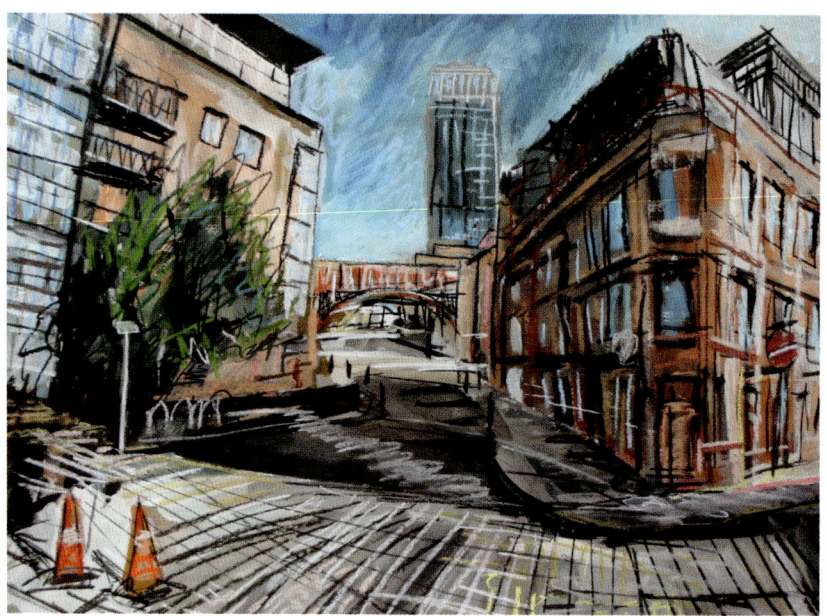

MATTHEW THOMPSON, TOWARDS DEANSGATE STATION

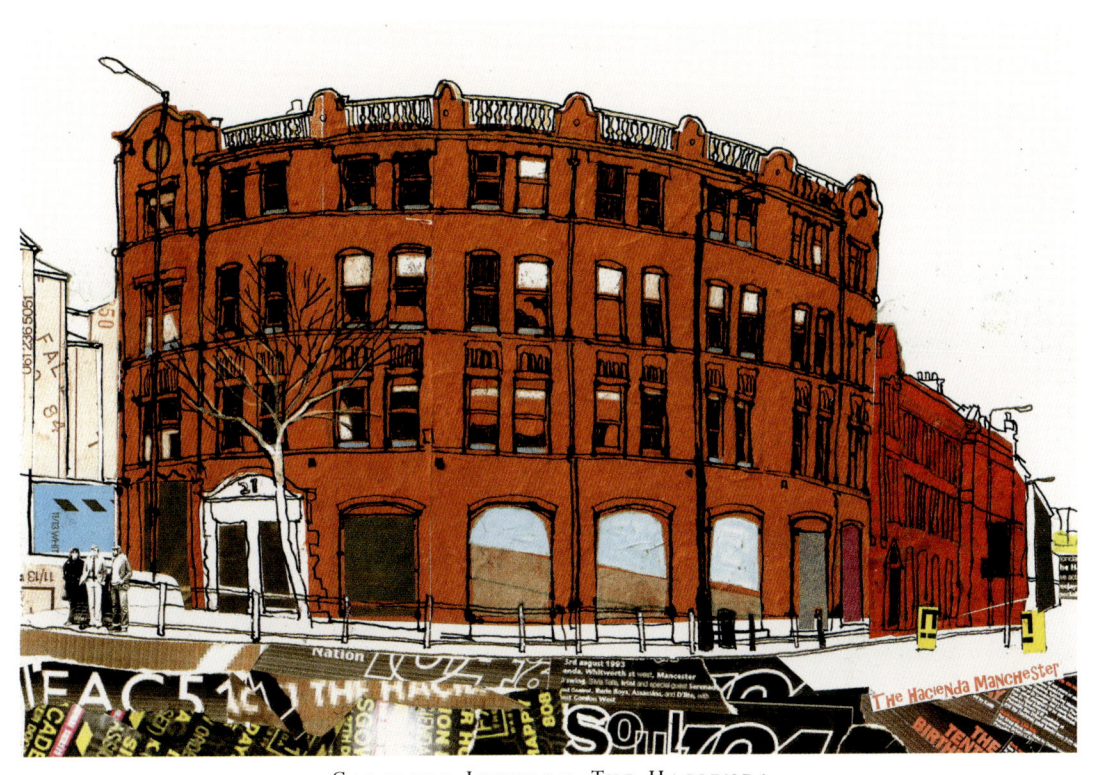

CAROLINE JOHNSON, THE HACIENDA

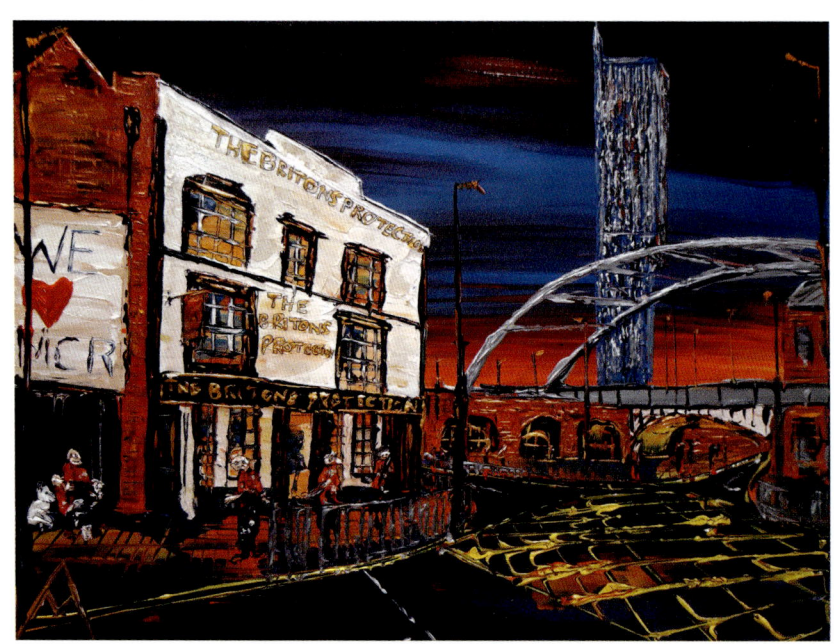

ANDREW ALAN MATTHEWS, BRITONS PROTECTION

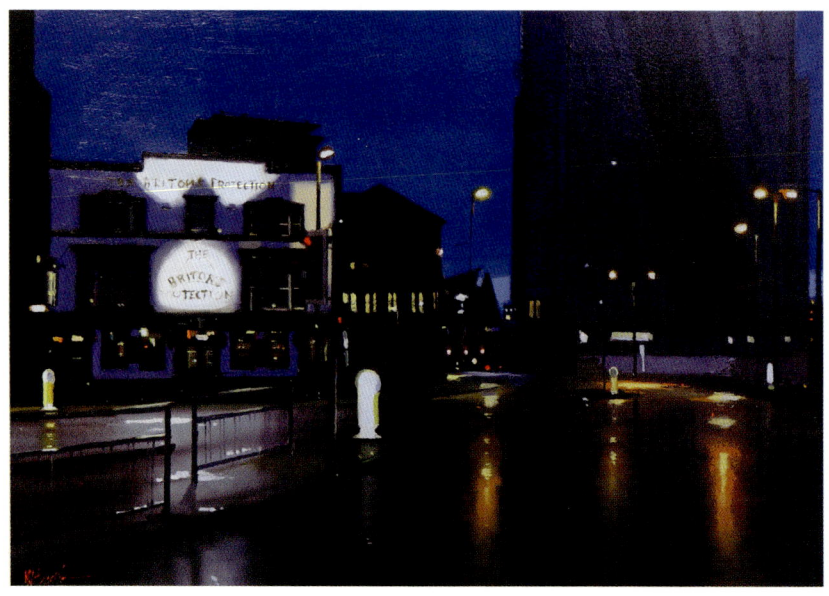

MICHAEL JOHN ASHCROFT, THE BRITONS PROTECTION

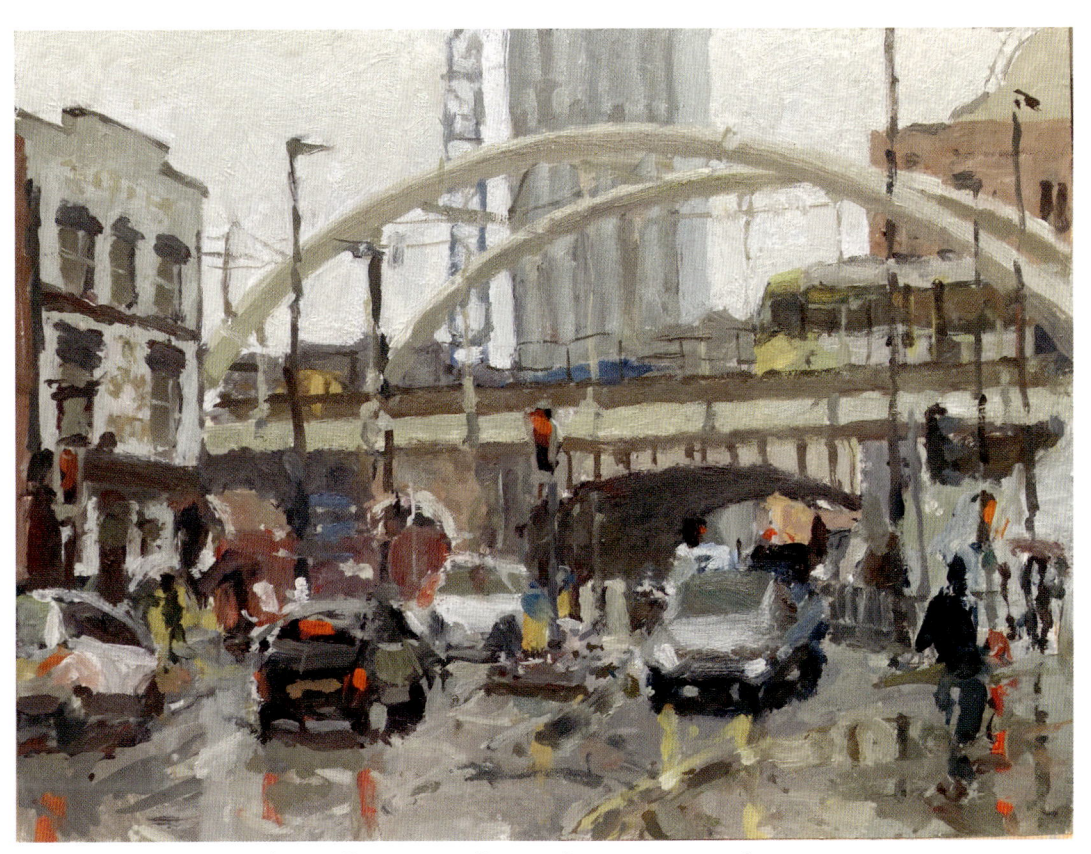

ADAM RALSTON, GREAT BRIDGEWATER STREET

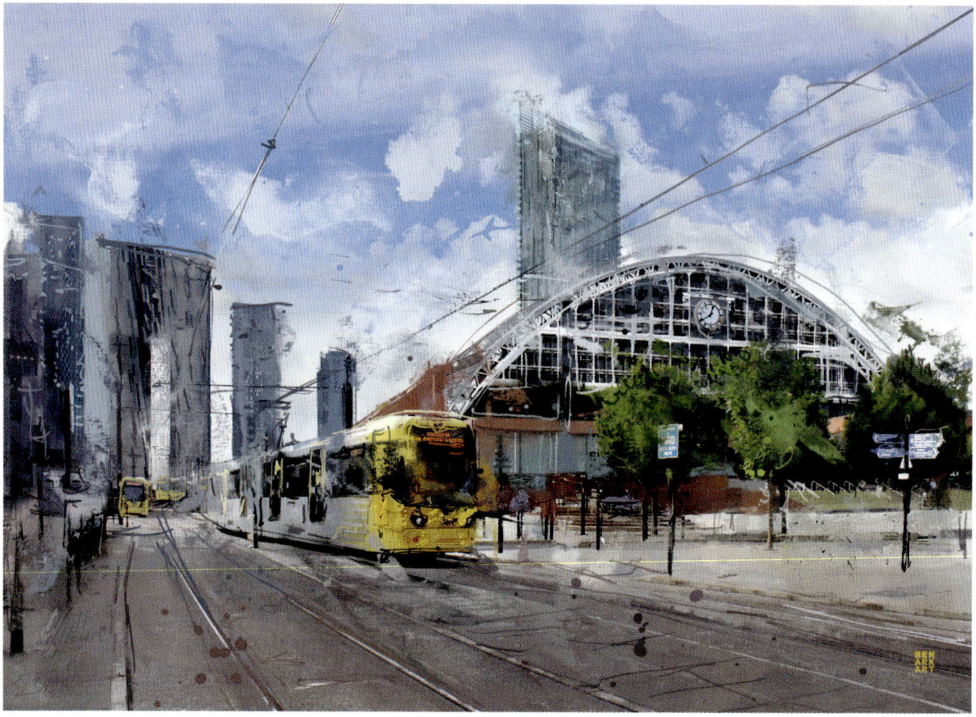

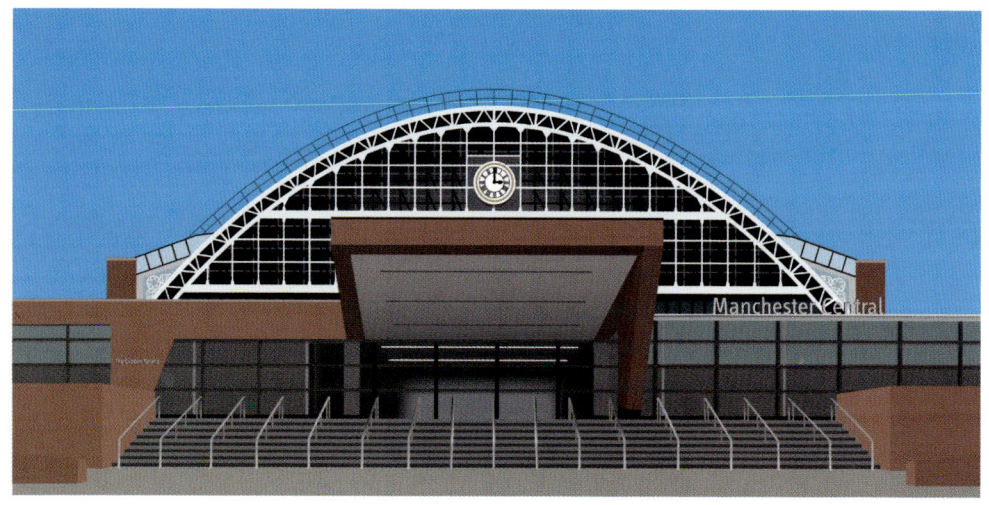

BEN ARK, MANCHESTER CENTRAL

EAMONN MURPHY, MANCHESTER CENTRAL

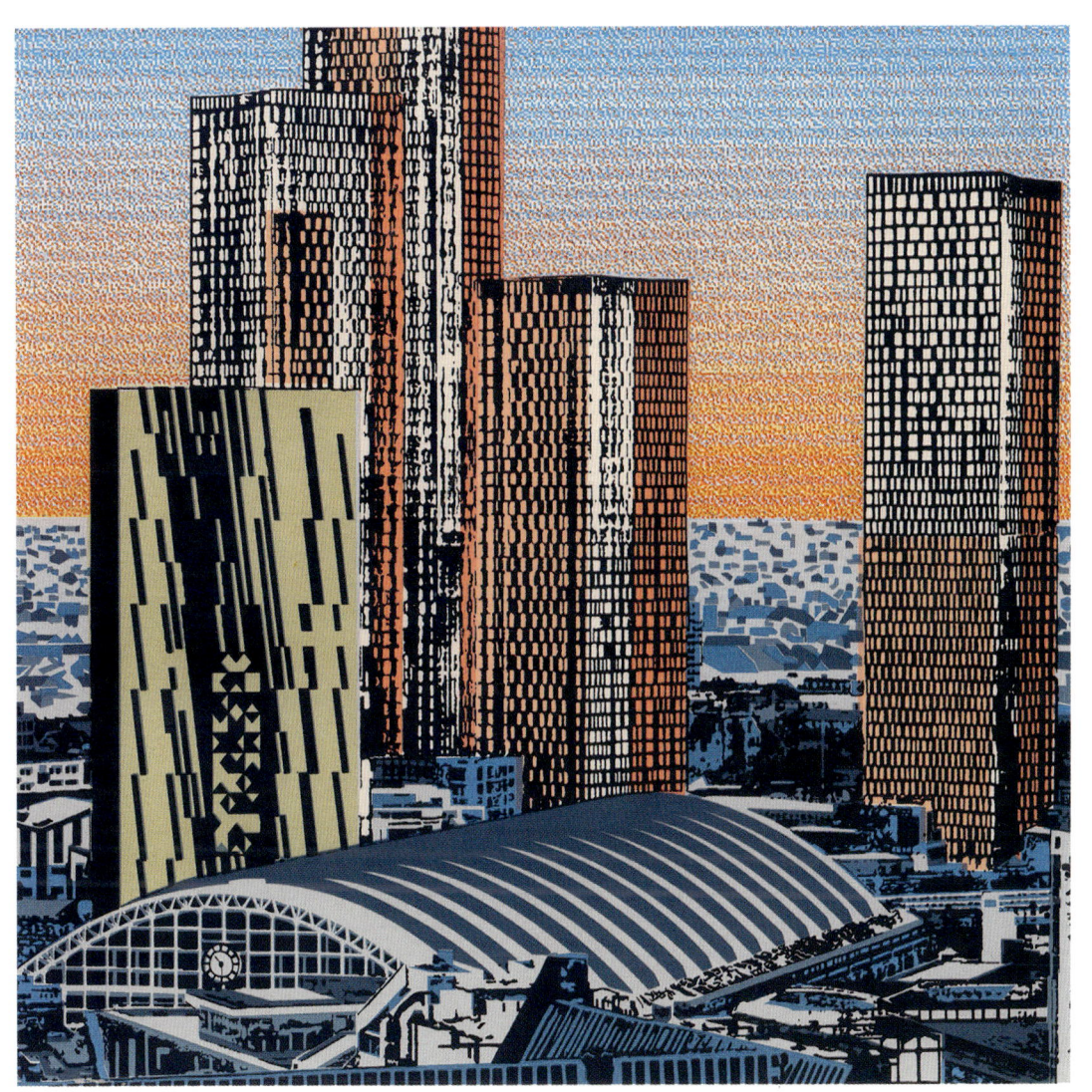

Michael Hitchens, Manchester

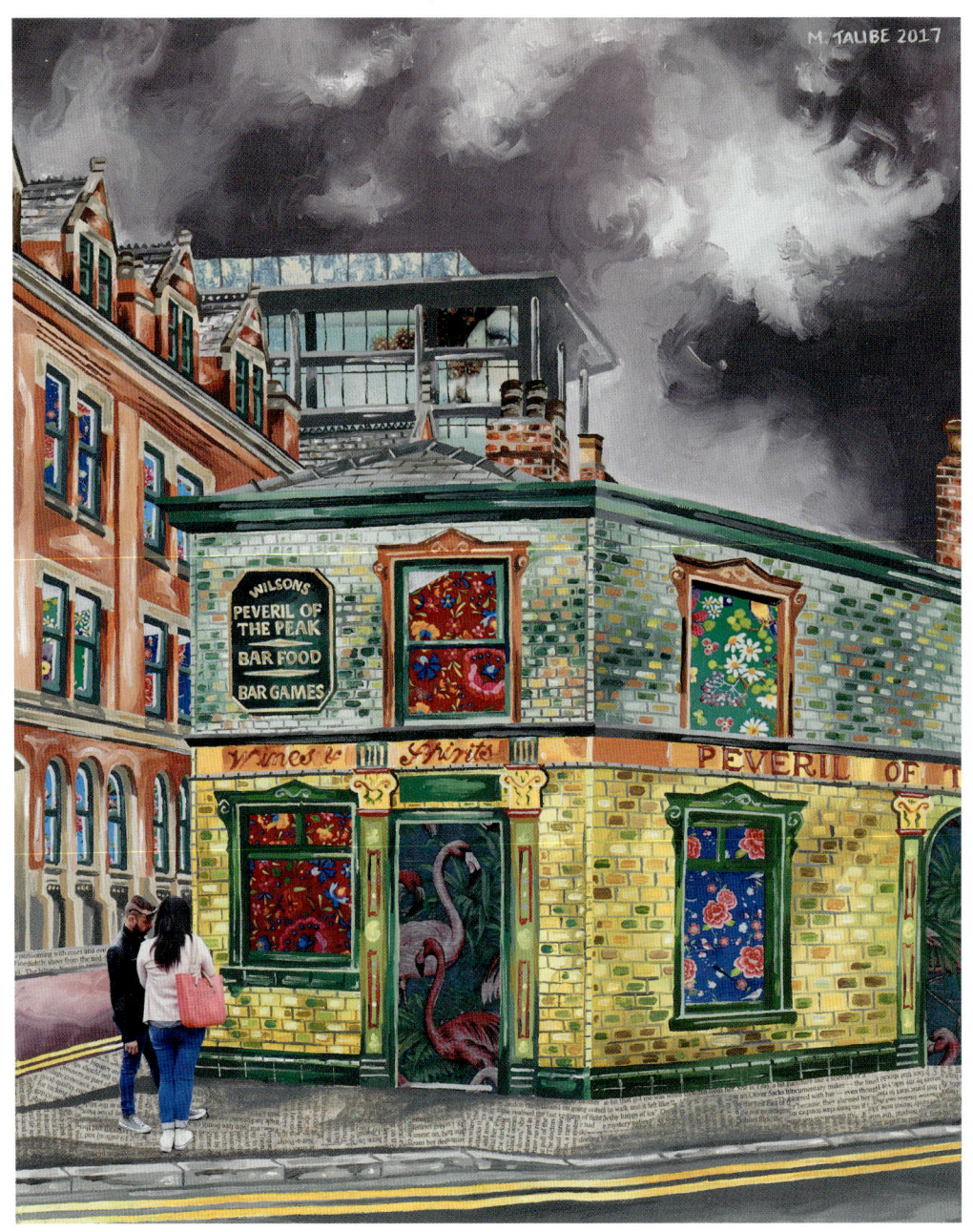

MICHELLE TAUBE, PEVERIL OF THE PEAK

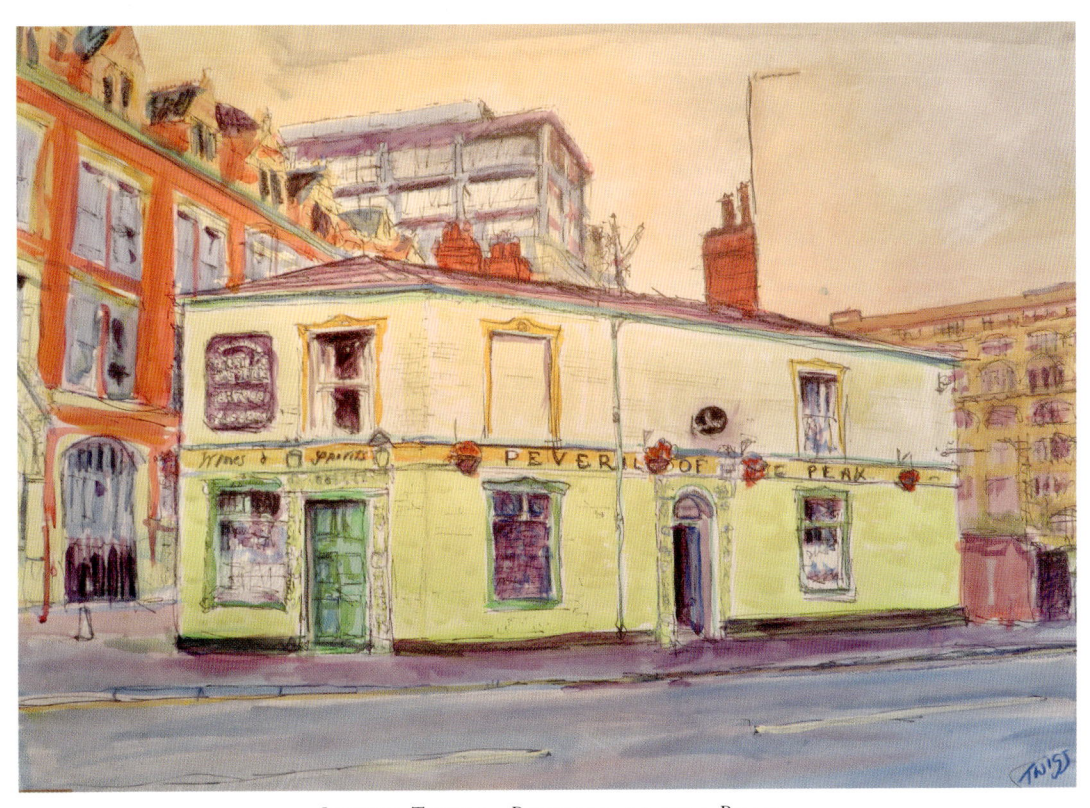

JUSTIN TWIGG, PEVERIL OF THE PEAK

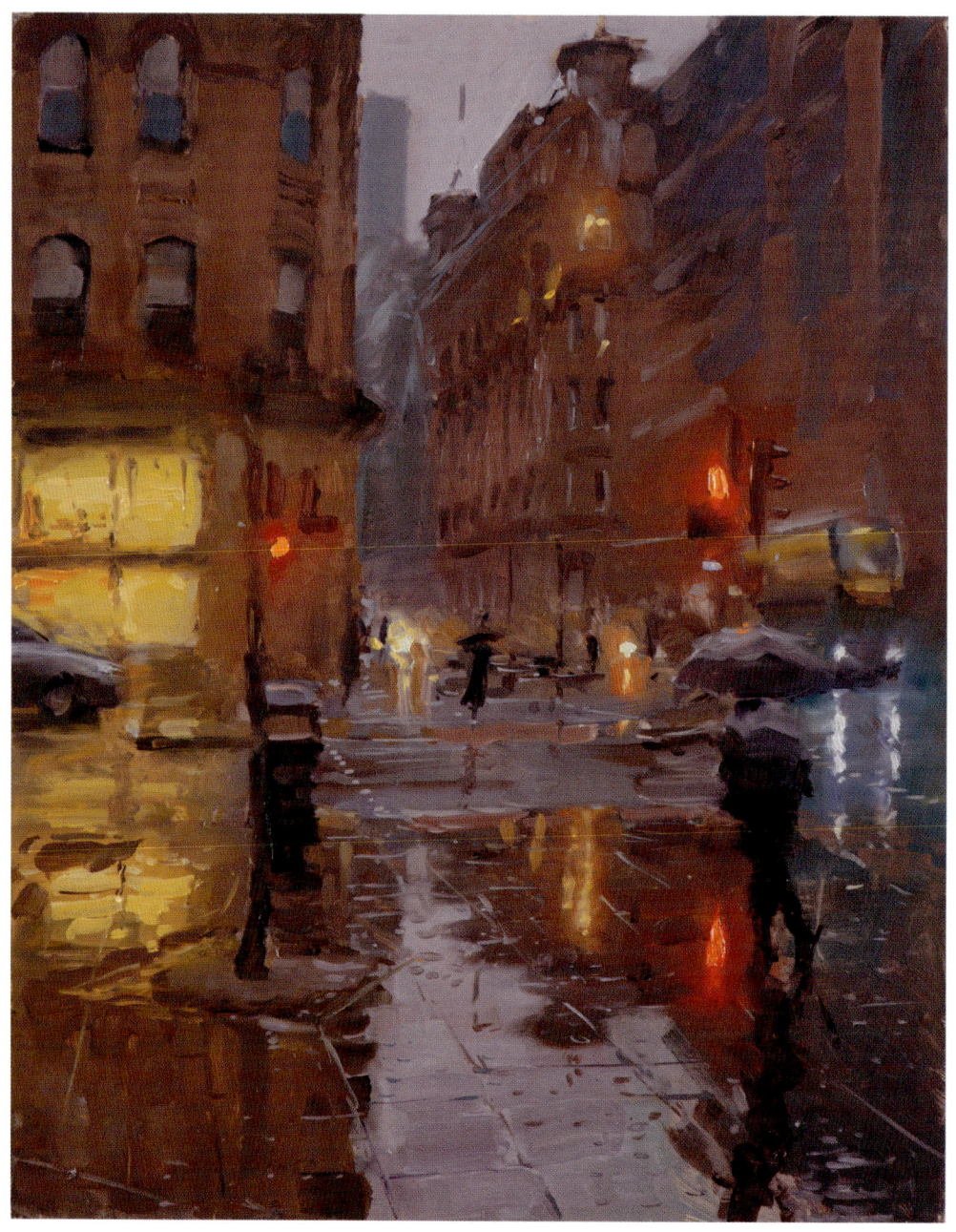

Rob Pointon, Portland Street crossing Oxford Road

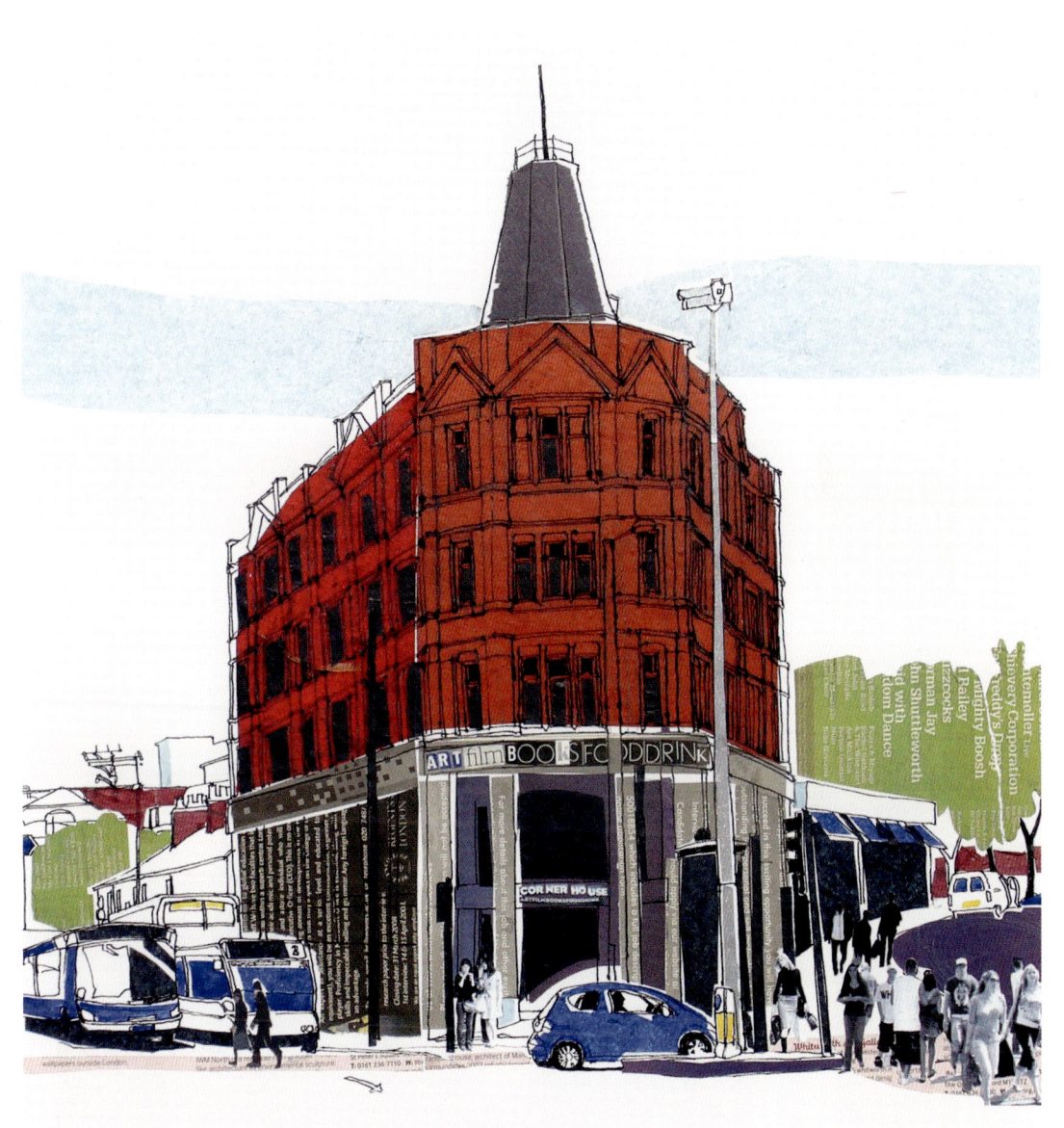

CAROLINE JOHNSON, THE CORNERHOUSE

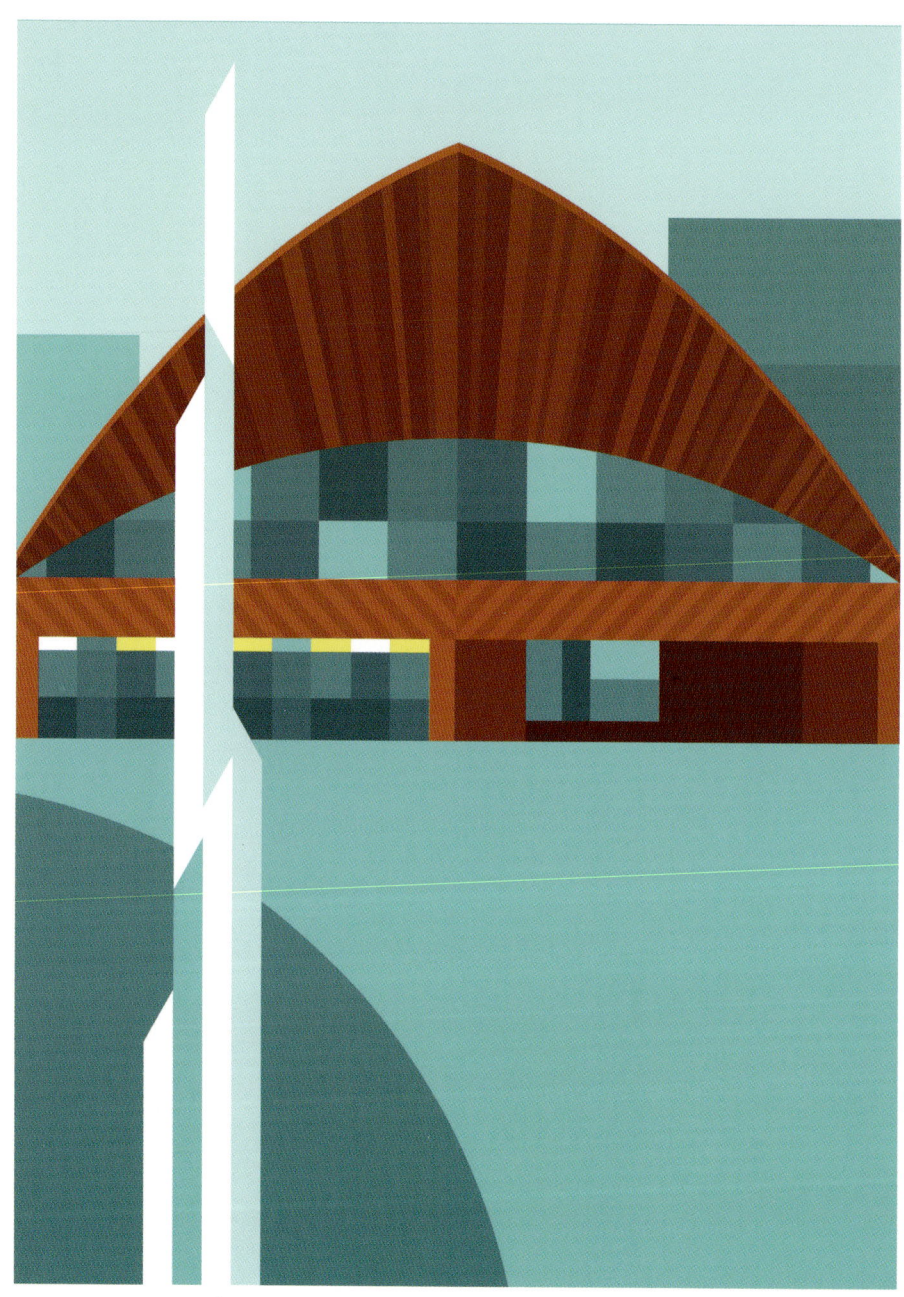

STANLEY CHOW, OXFORD ROAD STATION

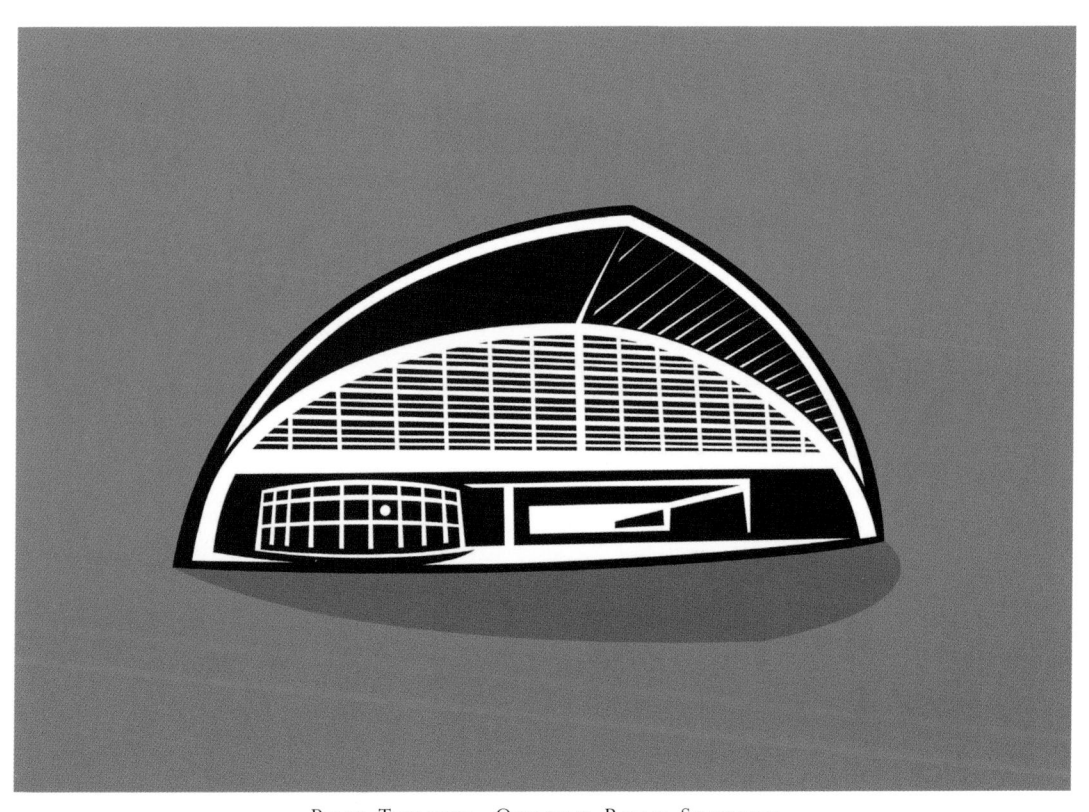

PHIL TURNER, OXFORD ROAD STATION

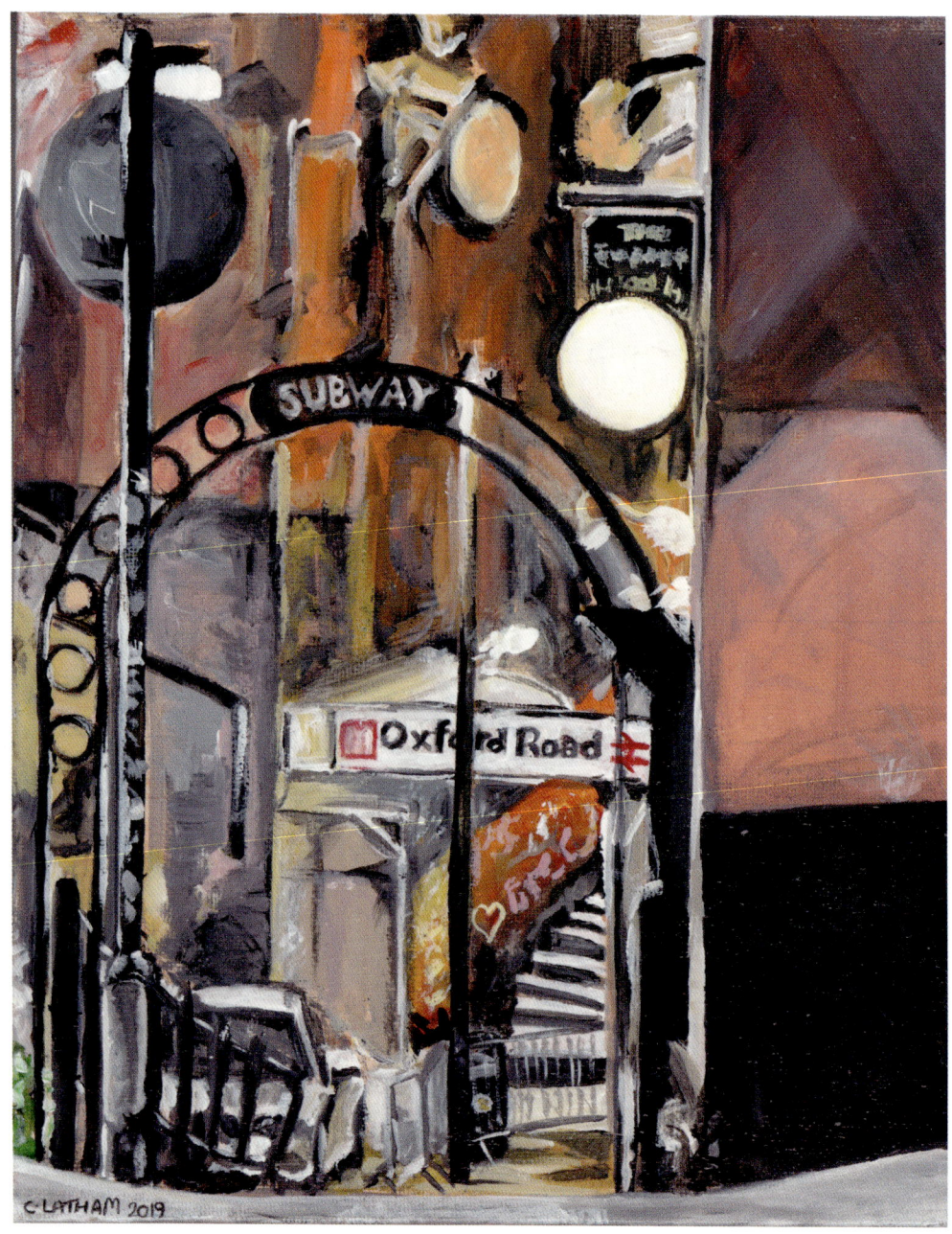

Caz Latham, Oxford Road

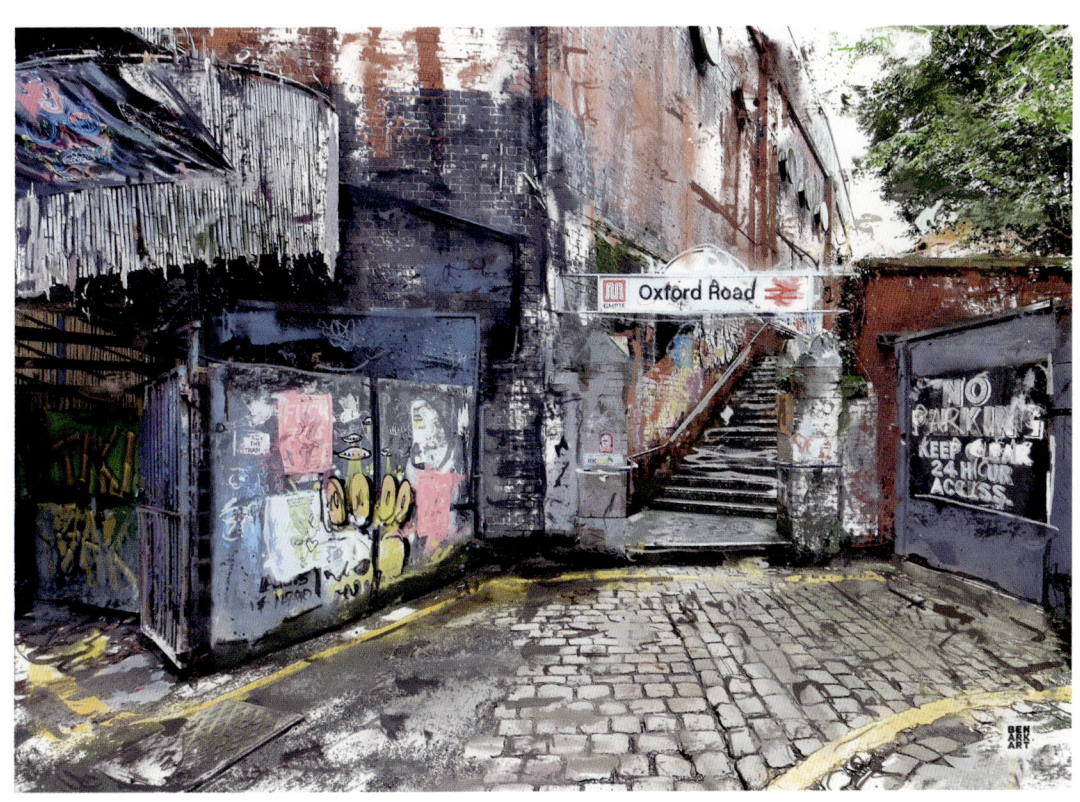

BEN ARK, OXFORD ROAD STEPS

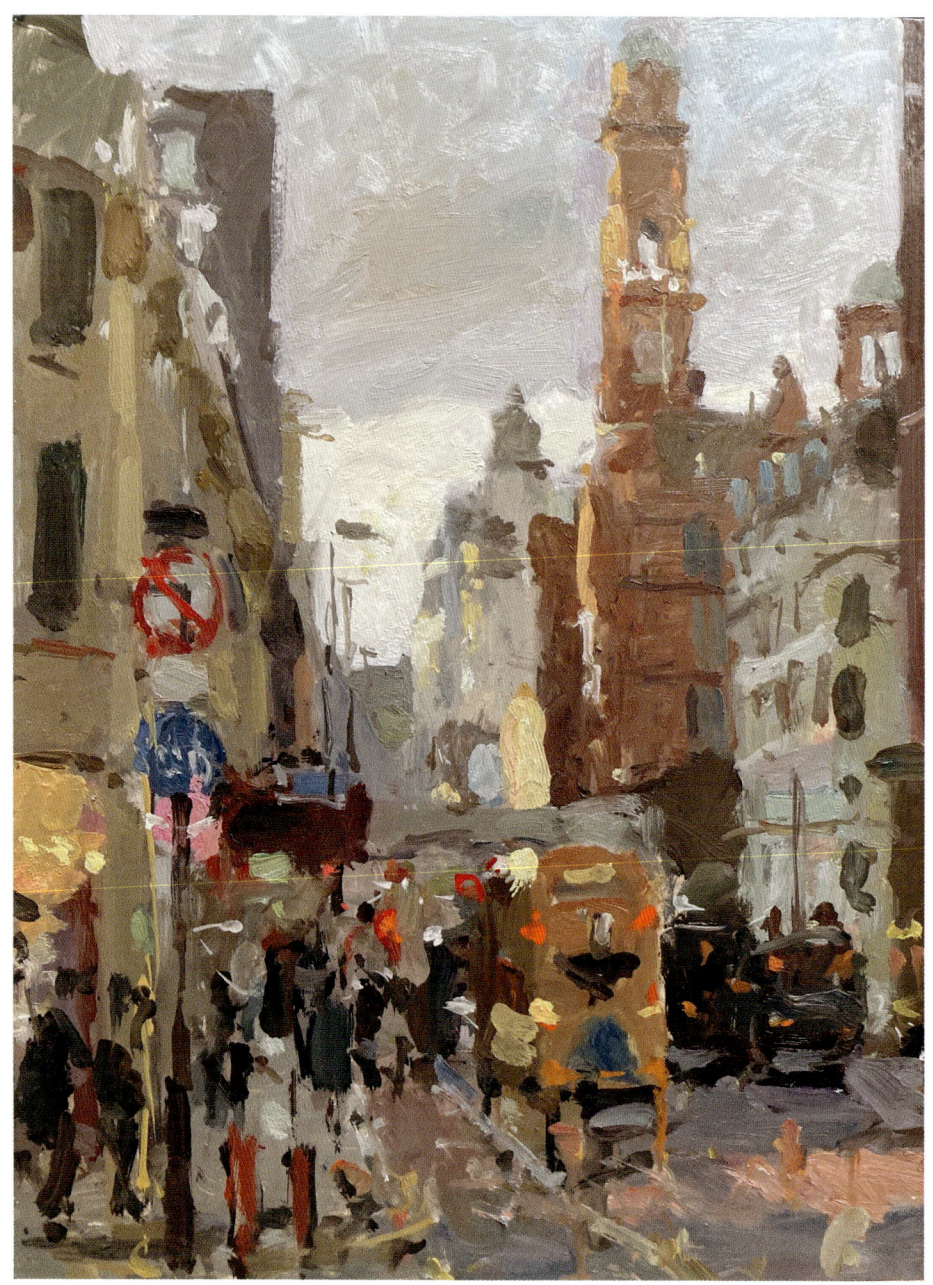

Adam Ralston, Last Light, Oxford Road

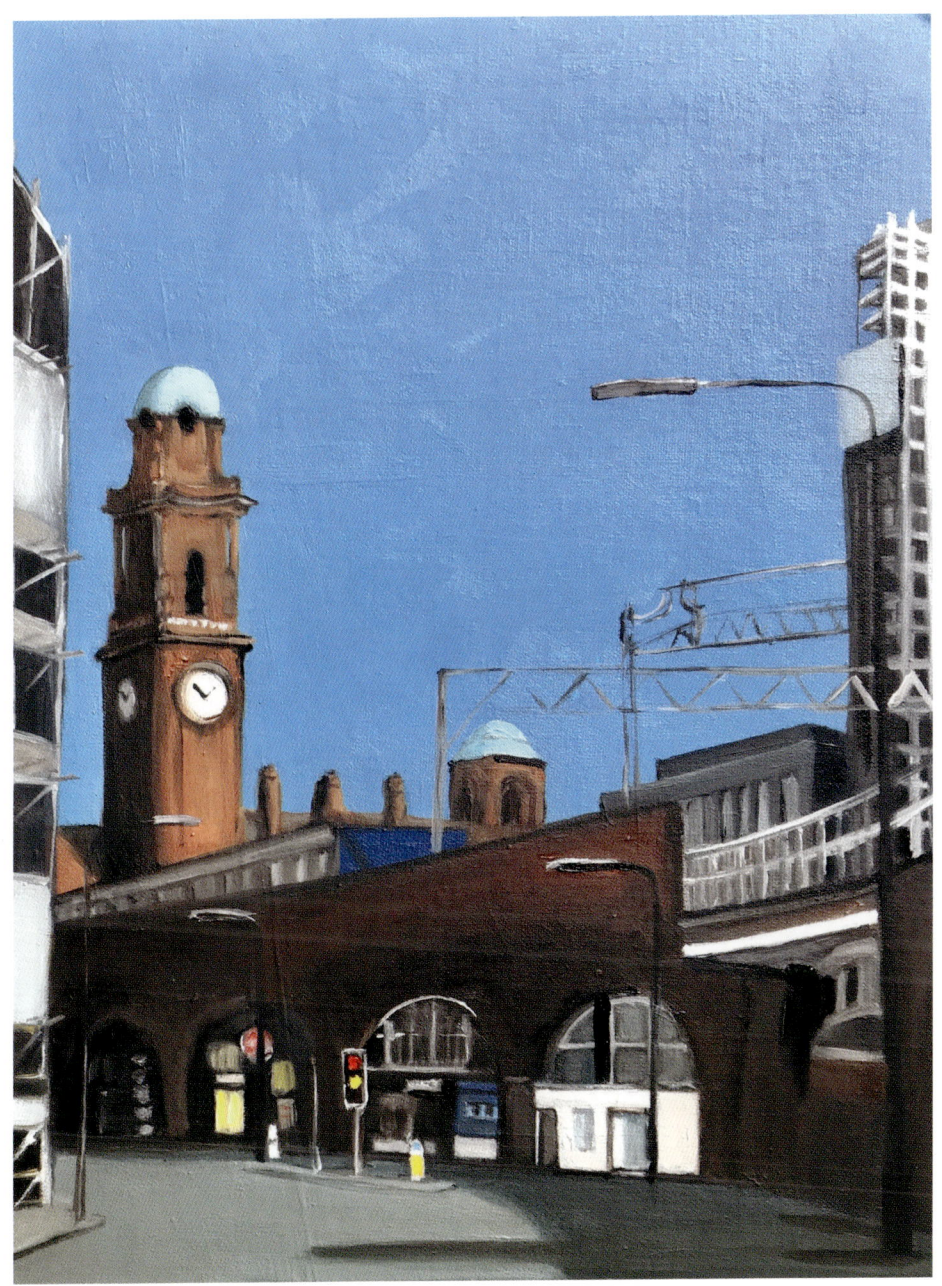

SOPHIE NIXON, REFUGE FROM WHITWORTH

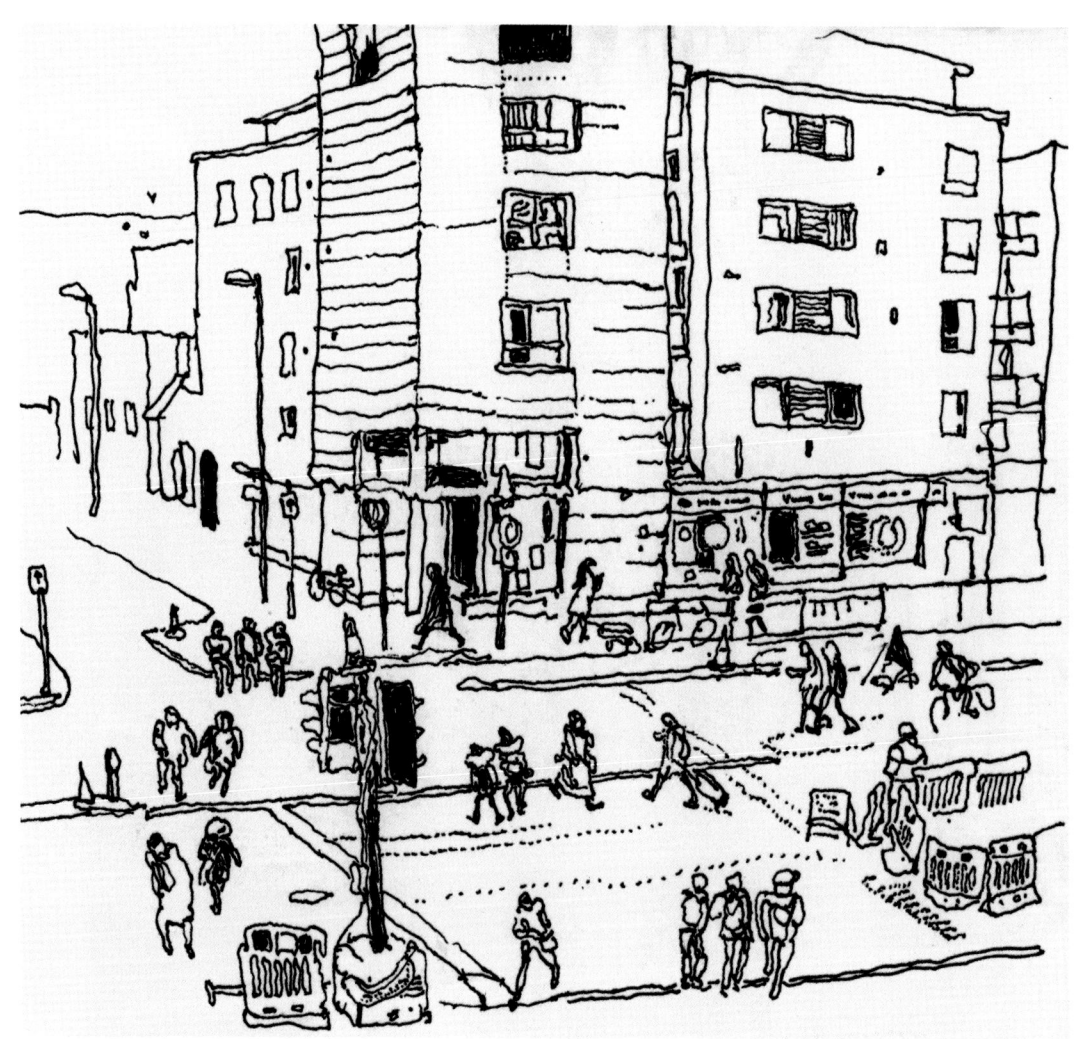

JOHN HEWITT, OXFORD ROAD WITH STUDENTS CROSSING

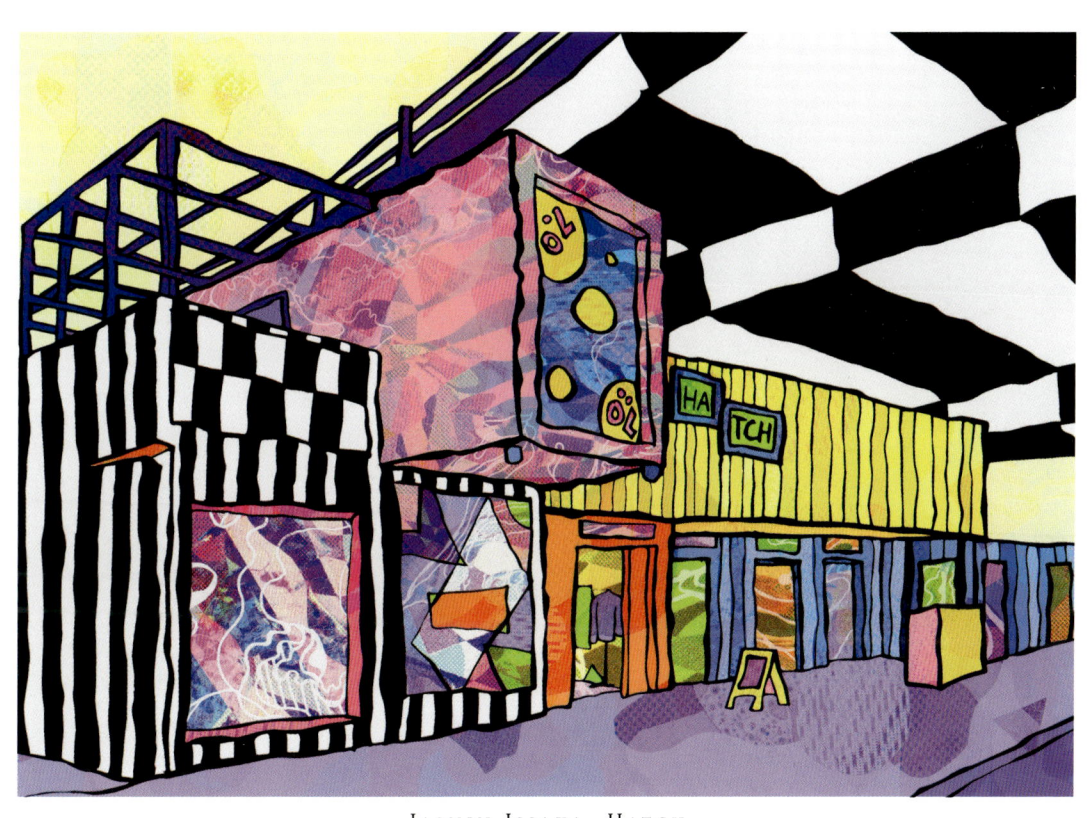

JASMIN ISSAKA, HATCH

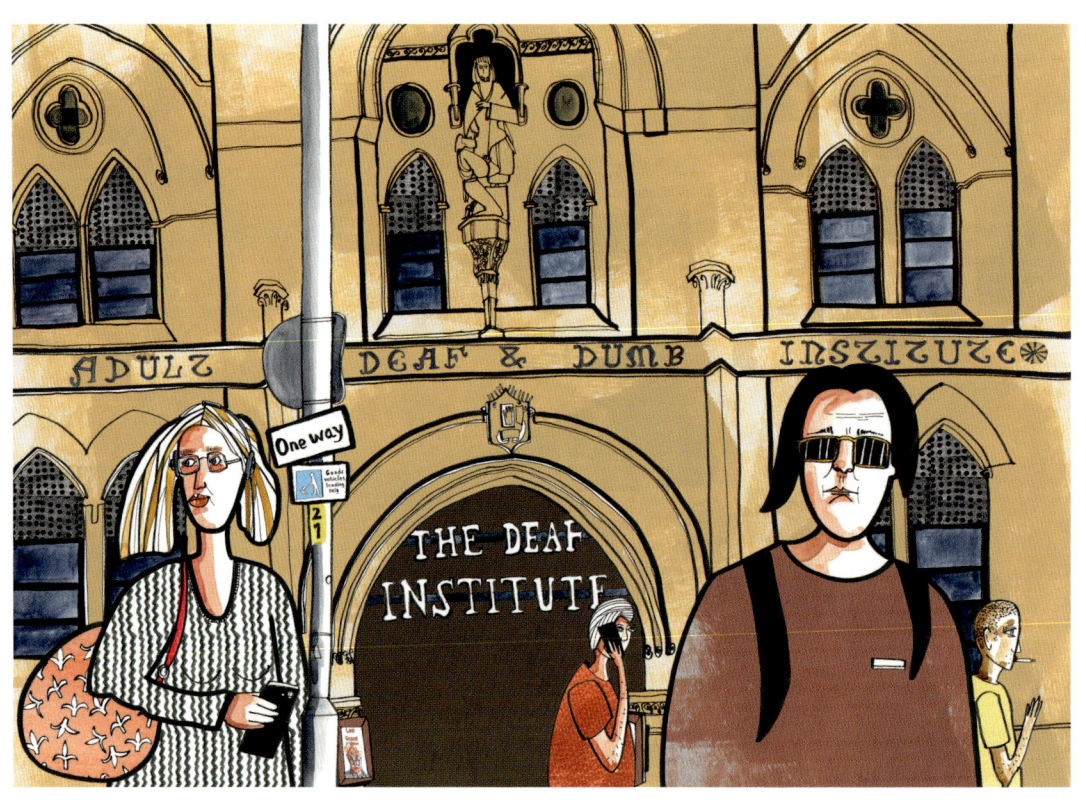

Len Grant, The Deaf Institute, All Saints

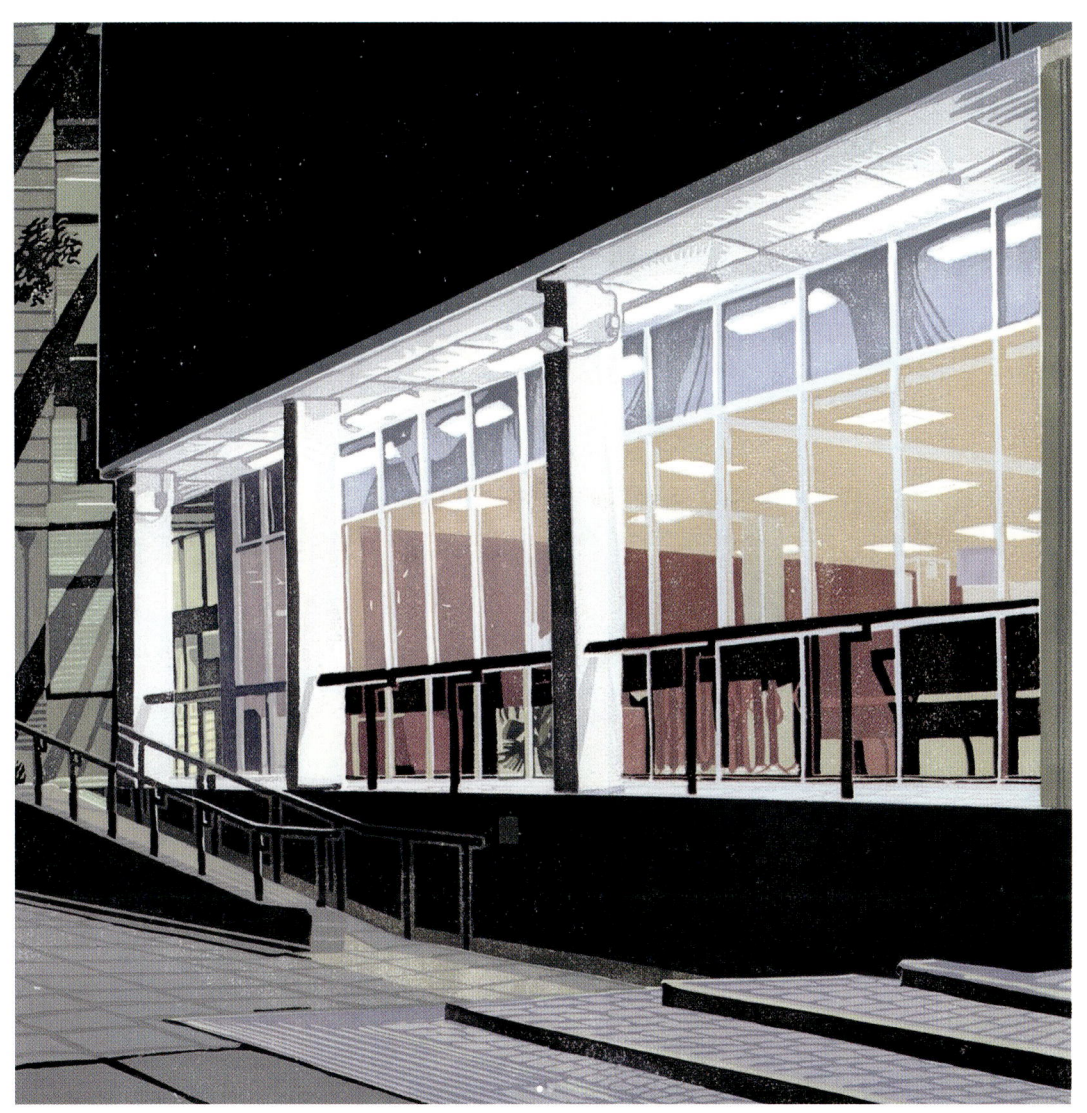

DANIEL HOWDEN, STOPFORD BUILDING

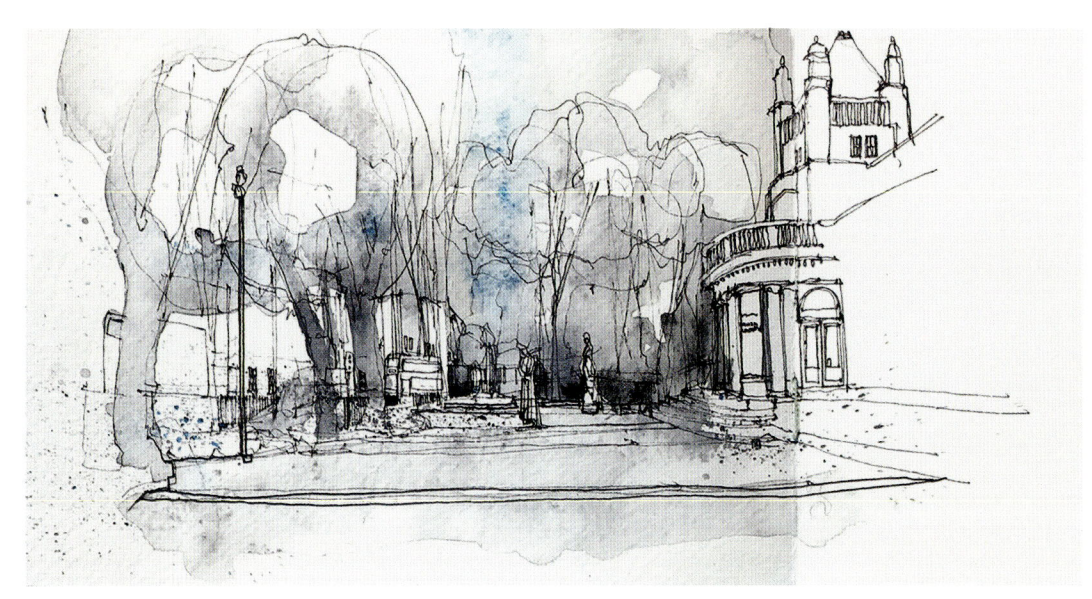

SIMONE RIDYARD, THE WHITWORTH

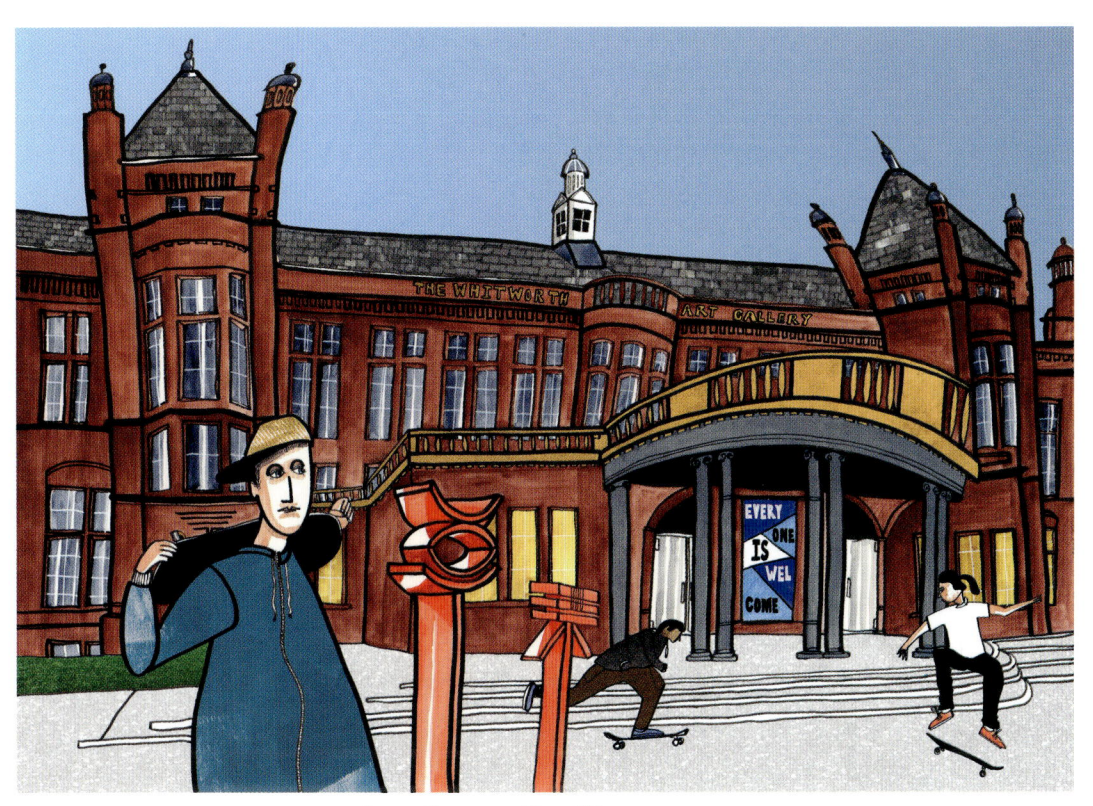

LEN GRANT, THE WHITWORTH

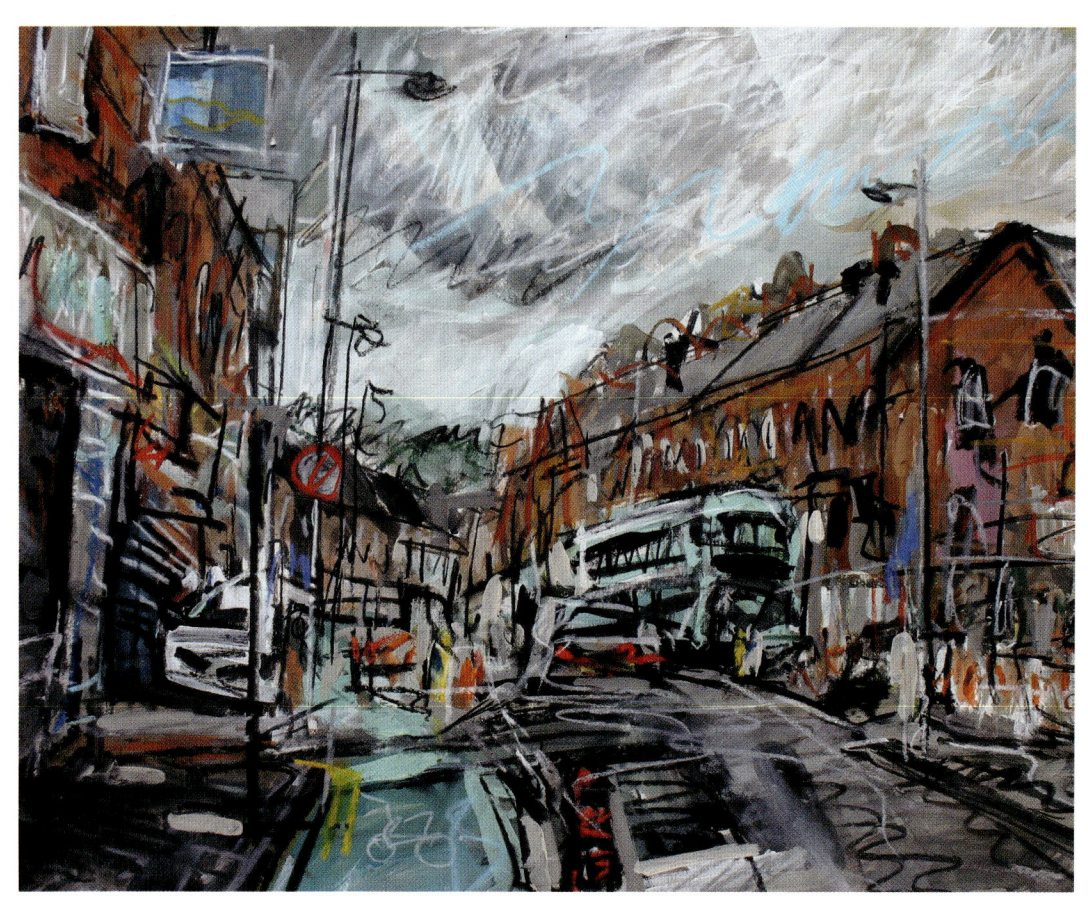

MATTHEW THOMPSON, BUS ON CURRY MILE

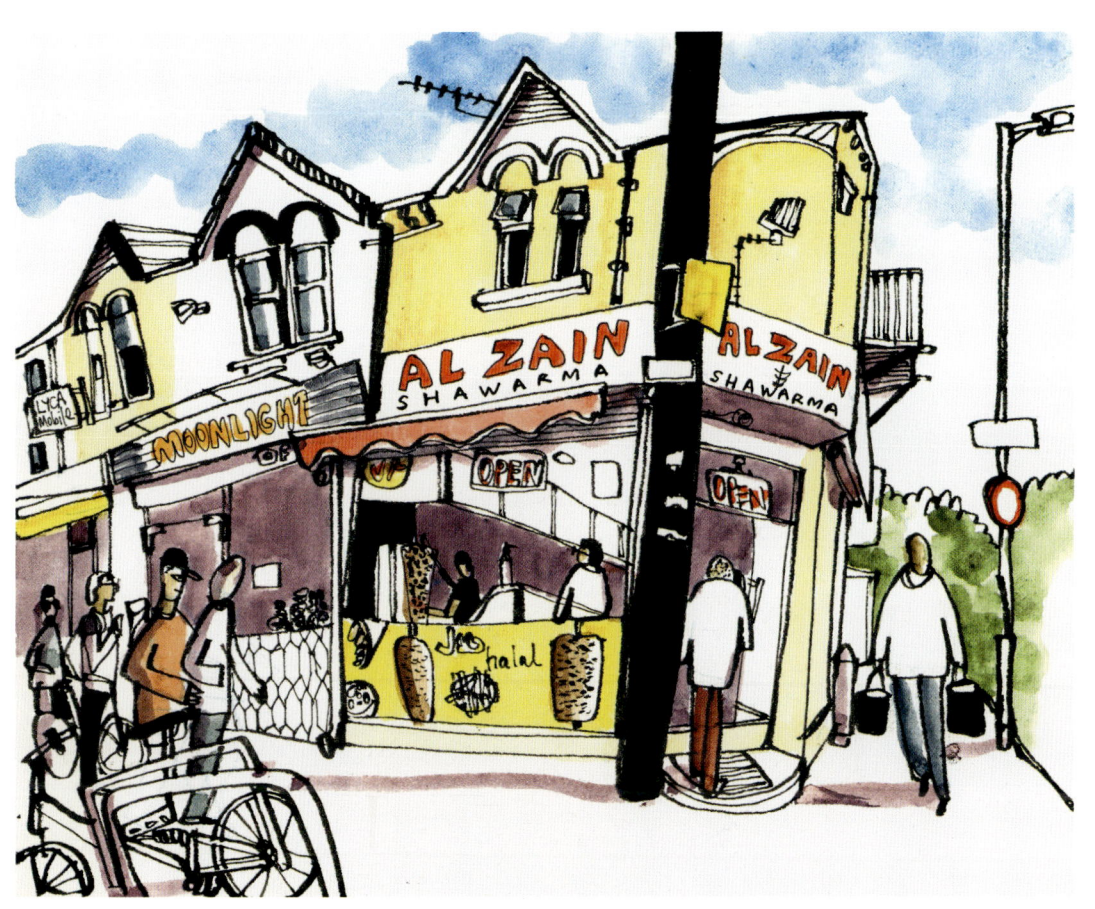

LEN GRANT, AL ZAIN SHAWARMA, RUSHOLME

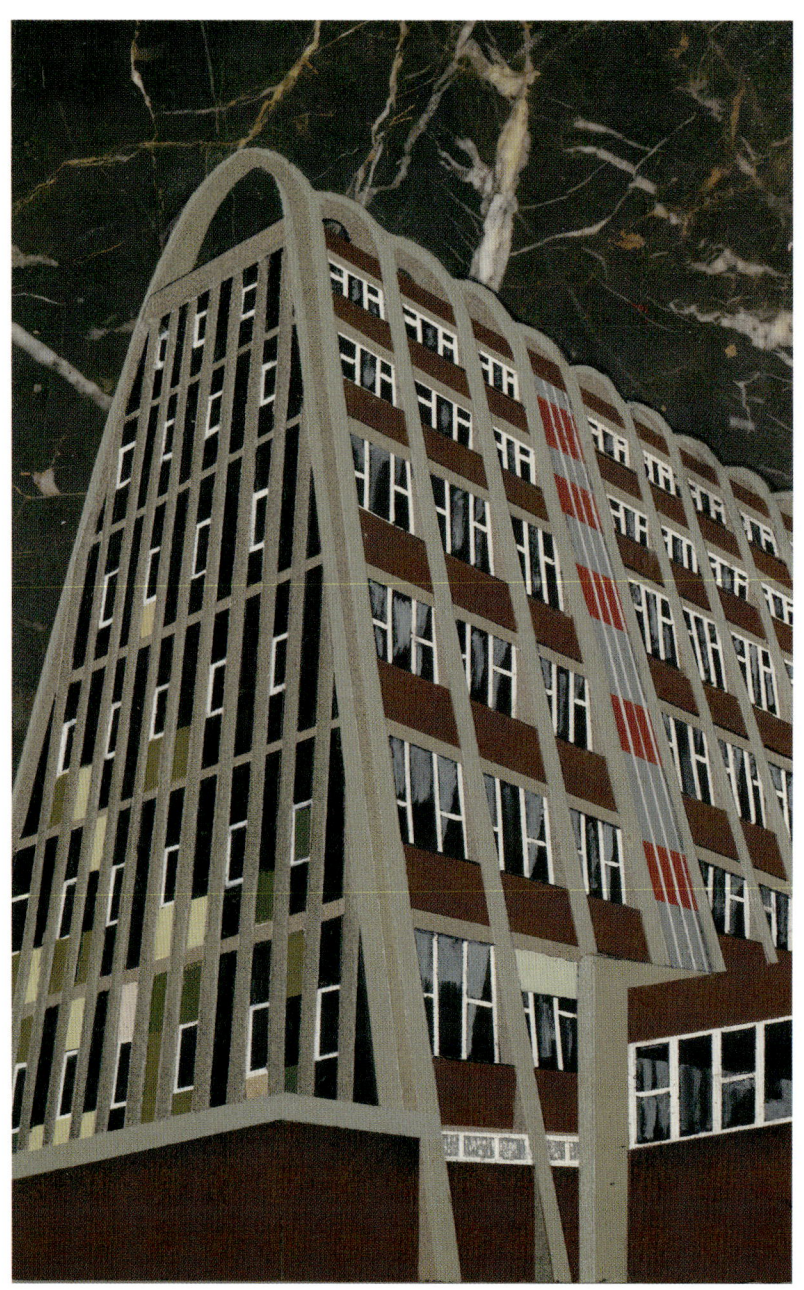

M A N D Y   P A Y N E ,   T H E   T O A S T   R A C K

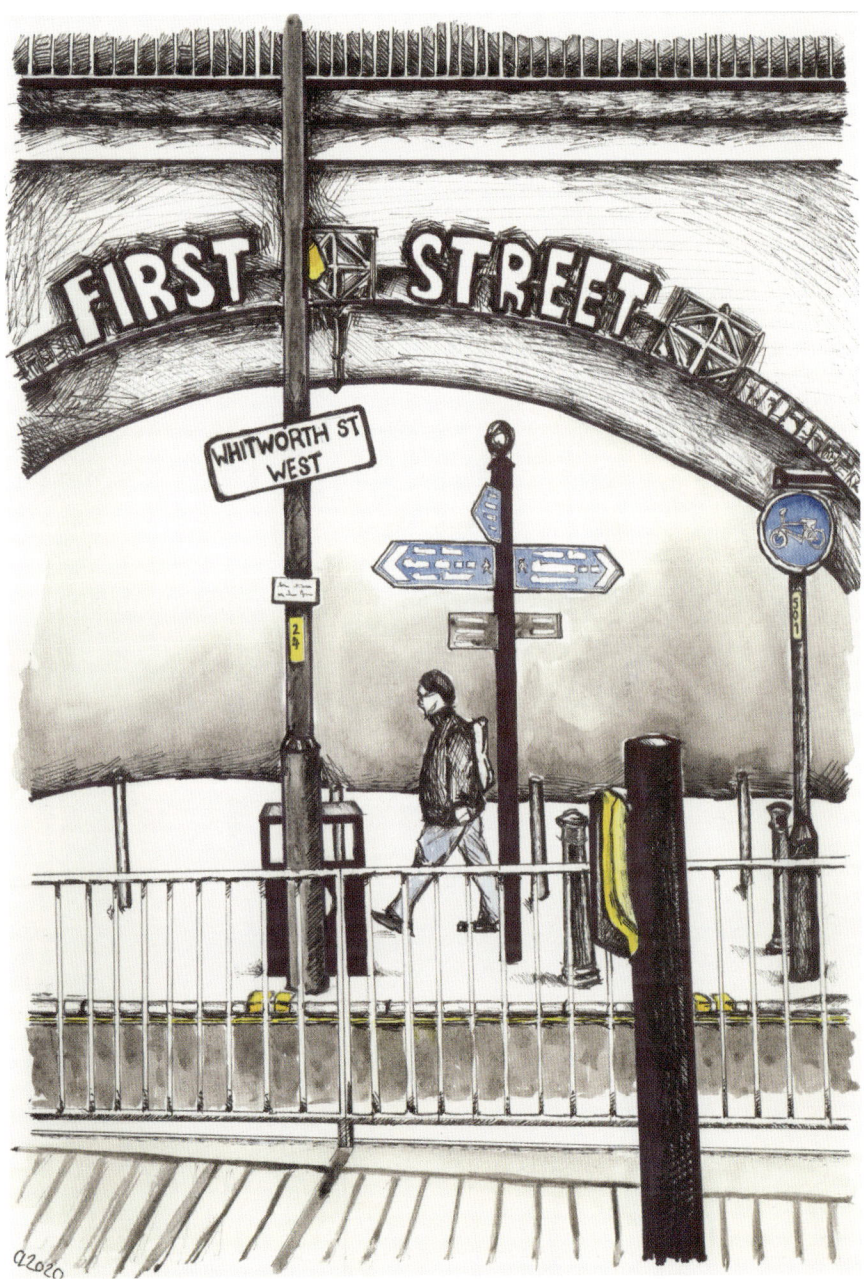

Caz Latham, First Street and Whitworth St West

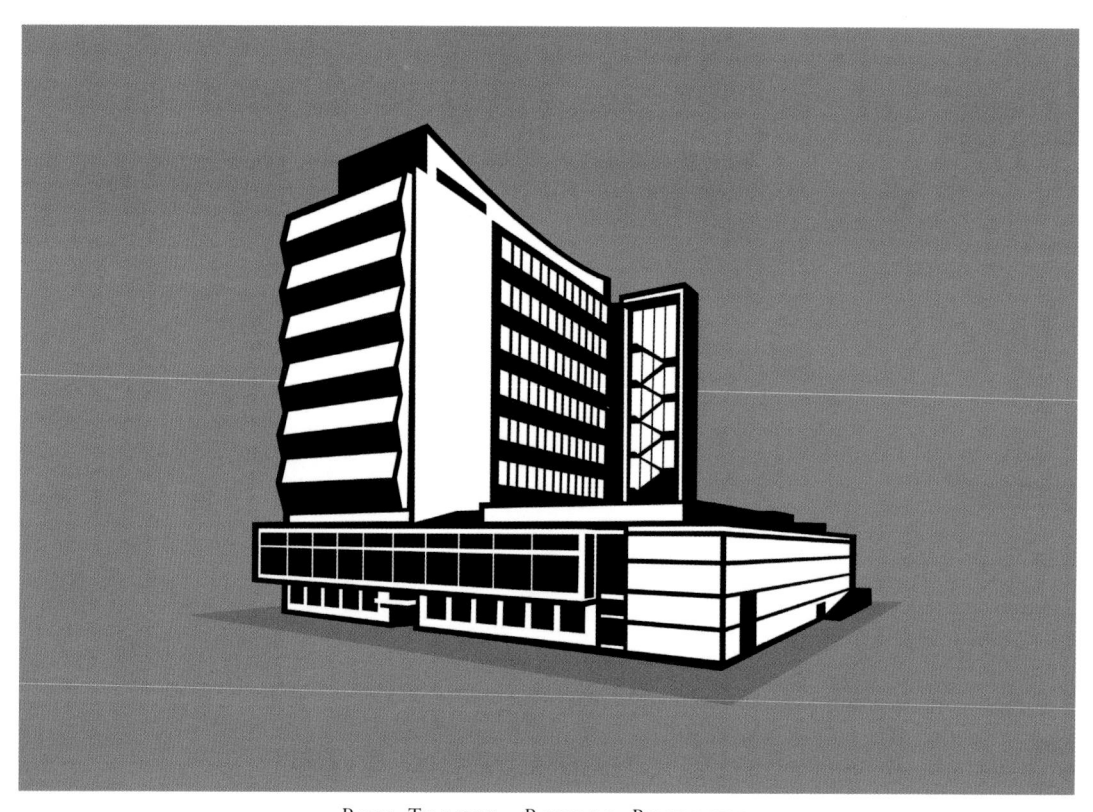

PHIL TURNER, RENOLD BUILDING

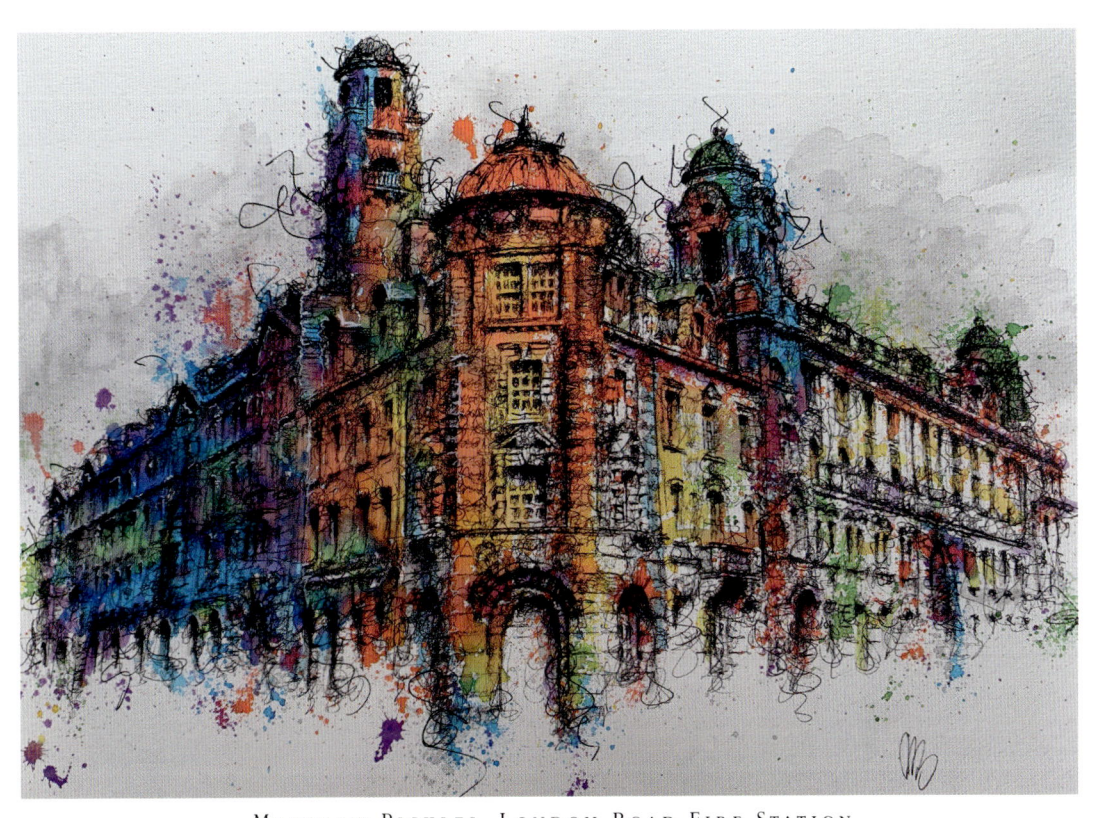

MATTHEW PICKLES, LONDON ROAD FIRE STATION

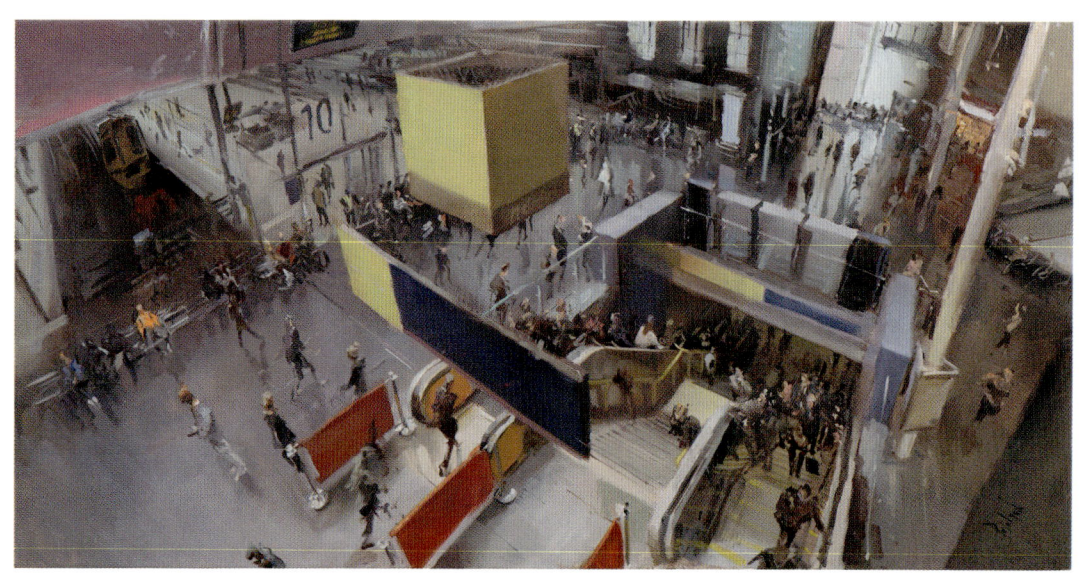

ROB POINTON, ENGINE ROOM

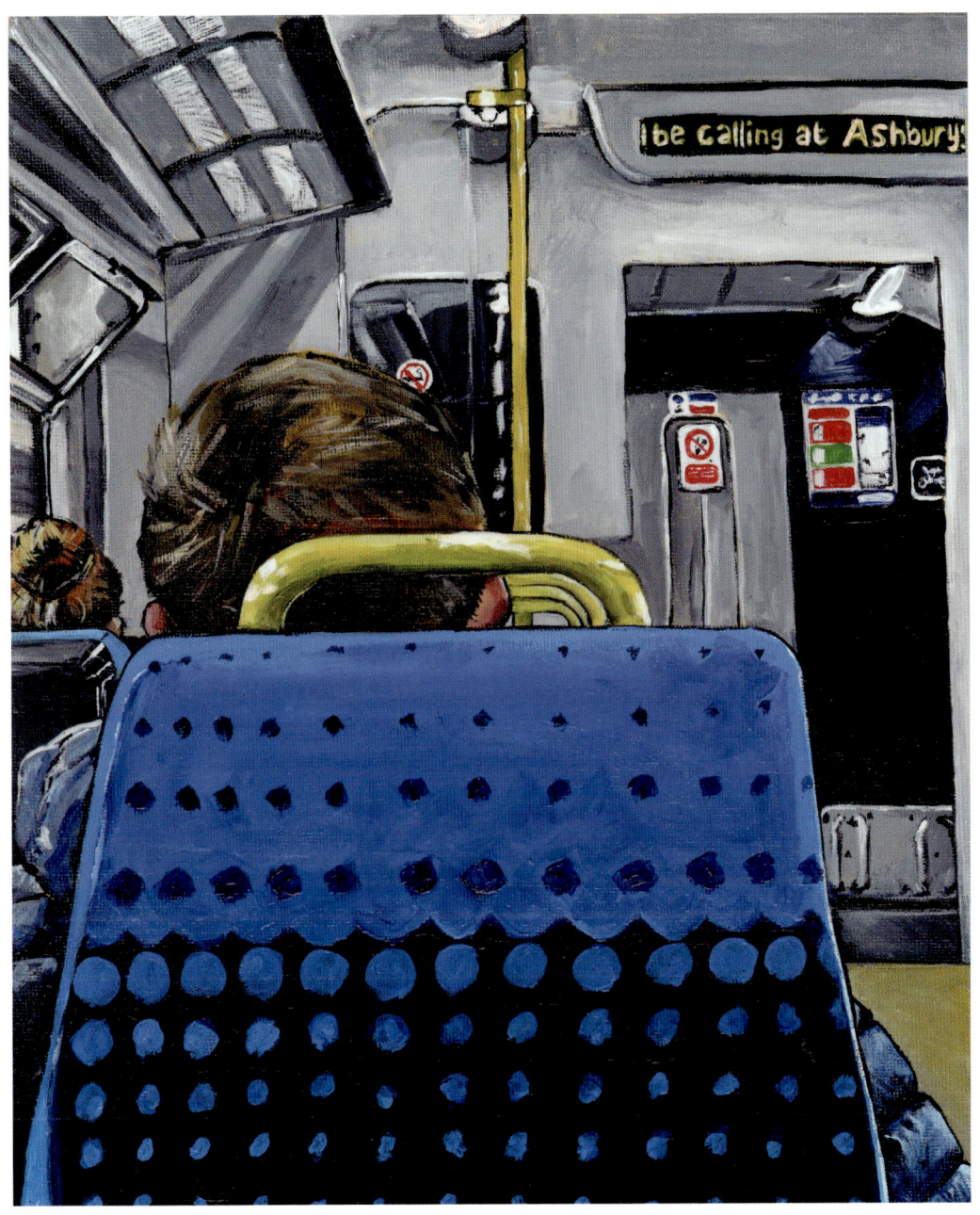

Caz Latham, Manchester Piccadilly Station towards Ashburys

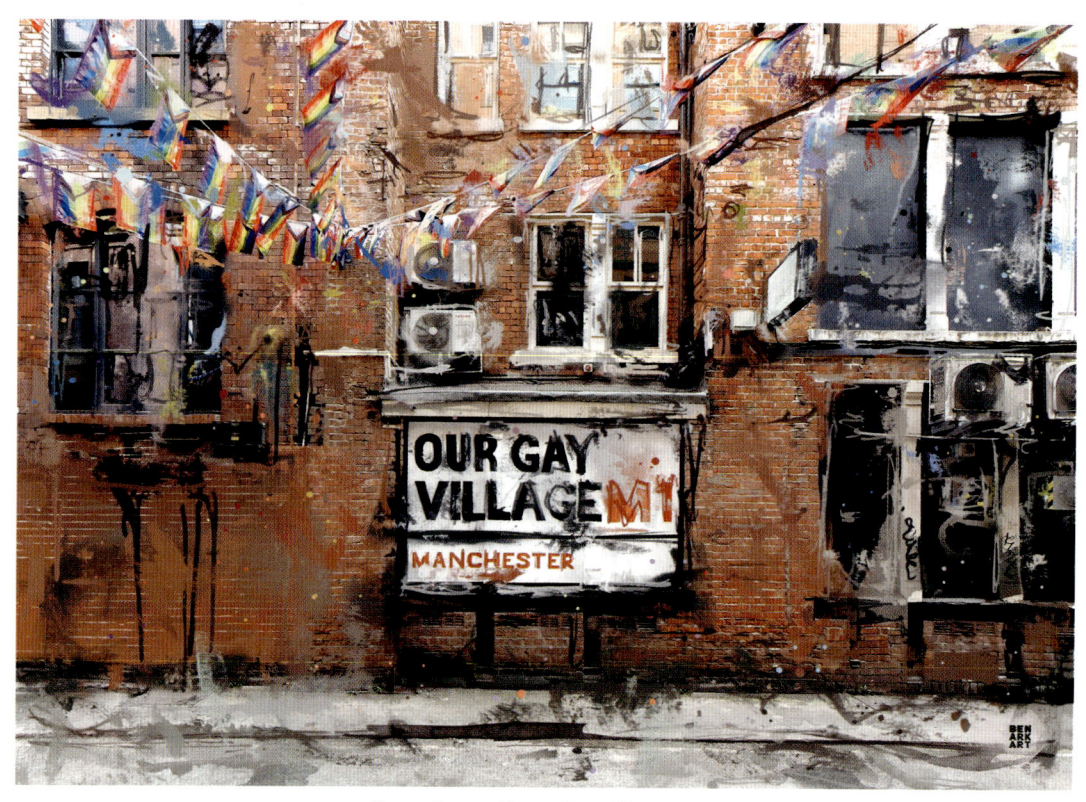

BEN ARK, THE GAY VILLAGE

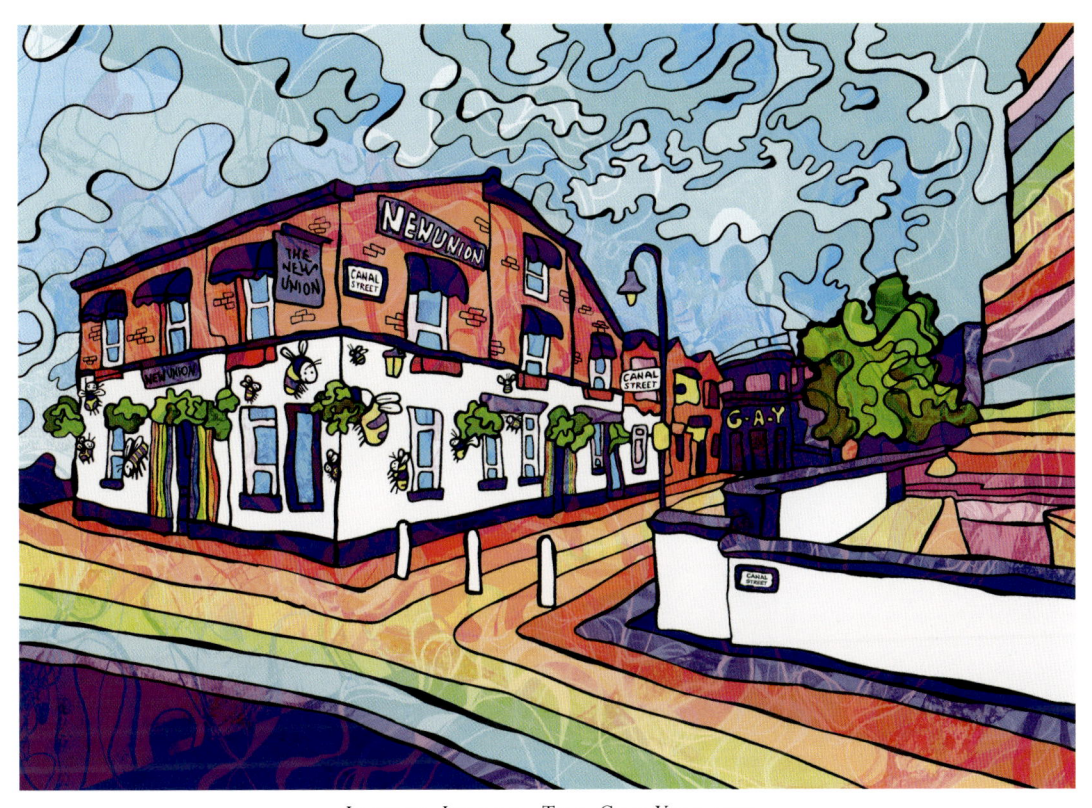

JASMIN ISSAKA, THE GAY VILLAGE

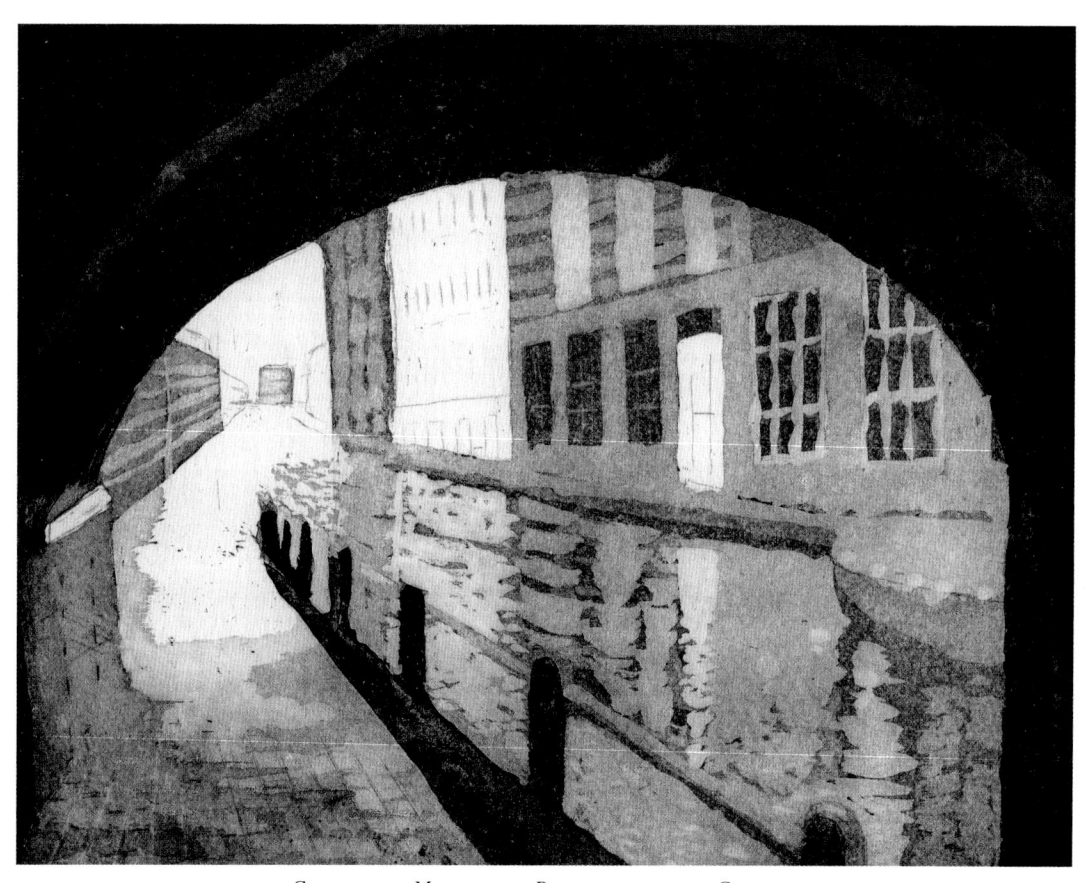

CAROLYN MURPHY, BRIDGEWATER CANAL

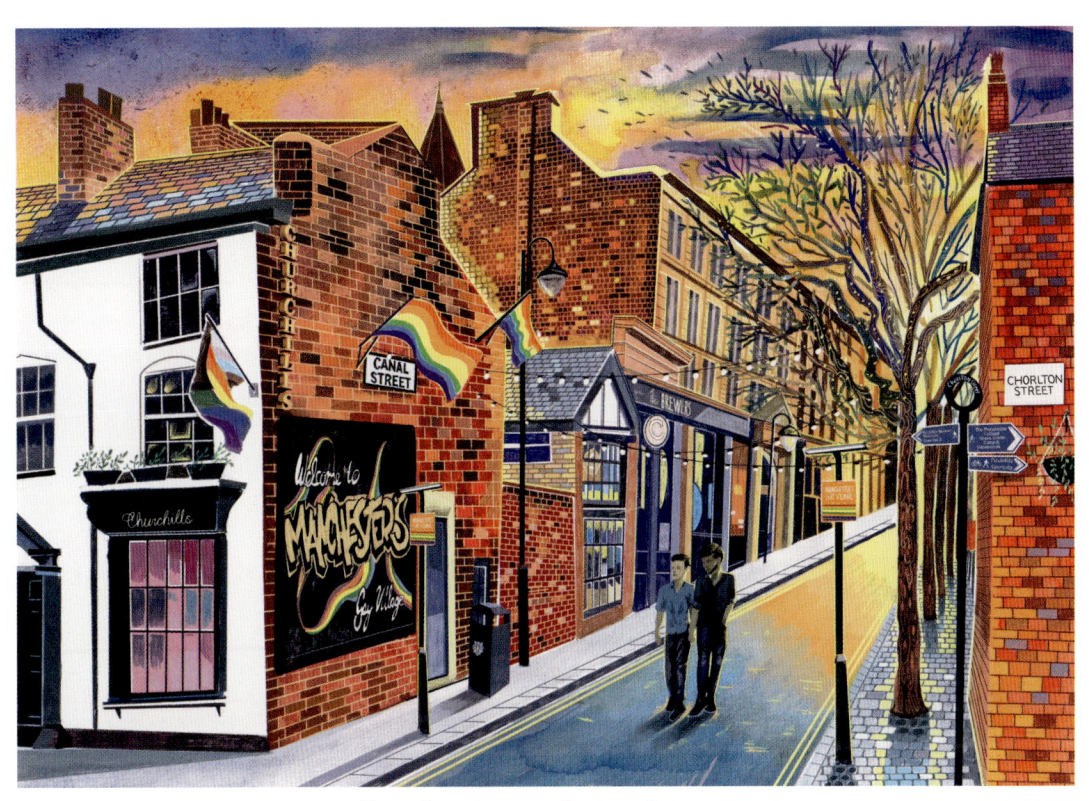

Zac Rossiter, Canal Street

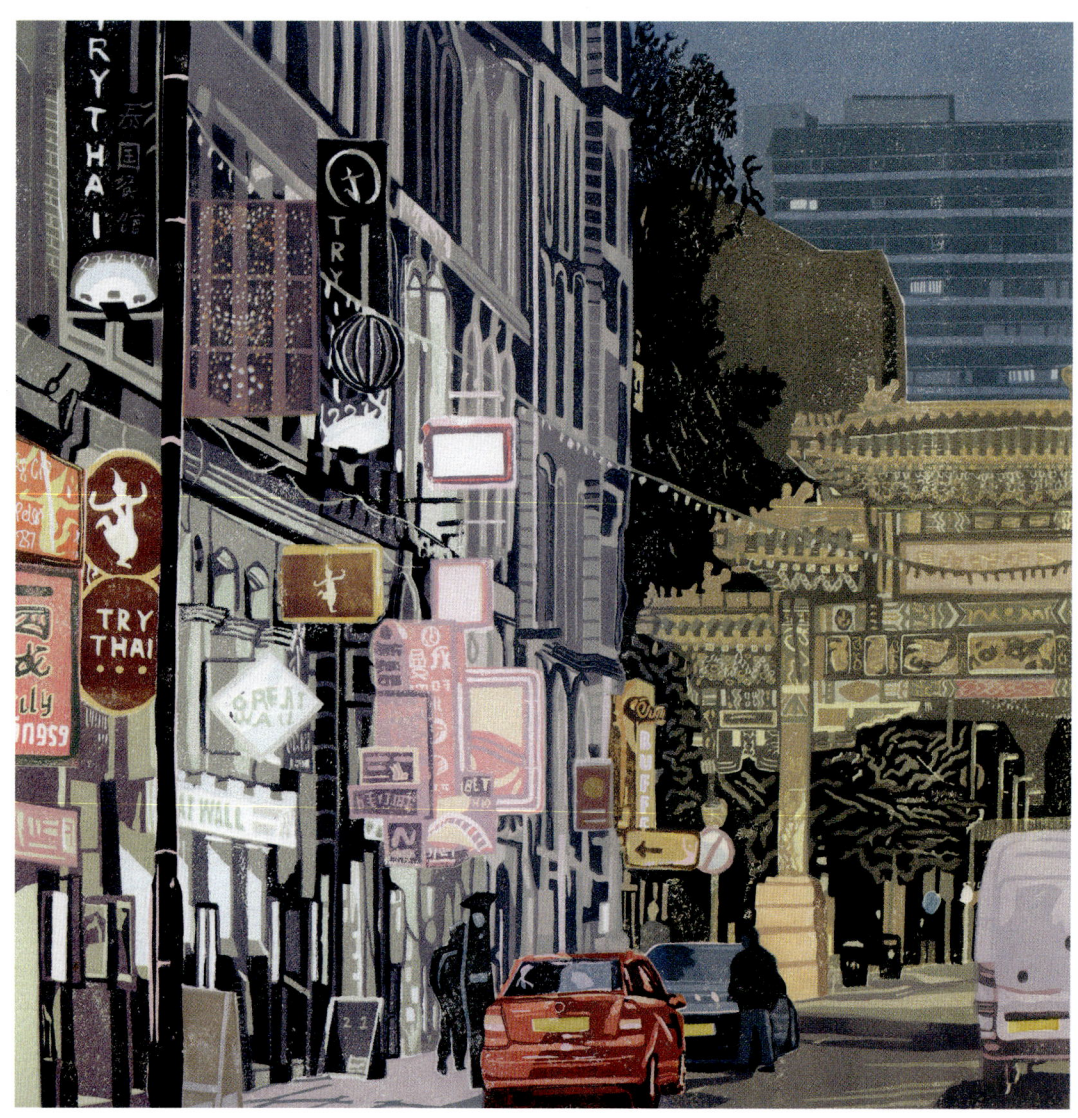

DANIEL HOWDEN, CHINATOWN

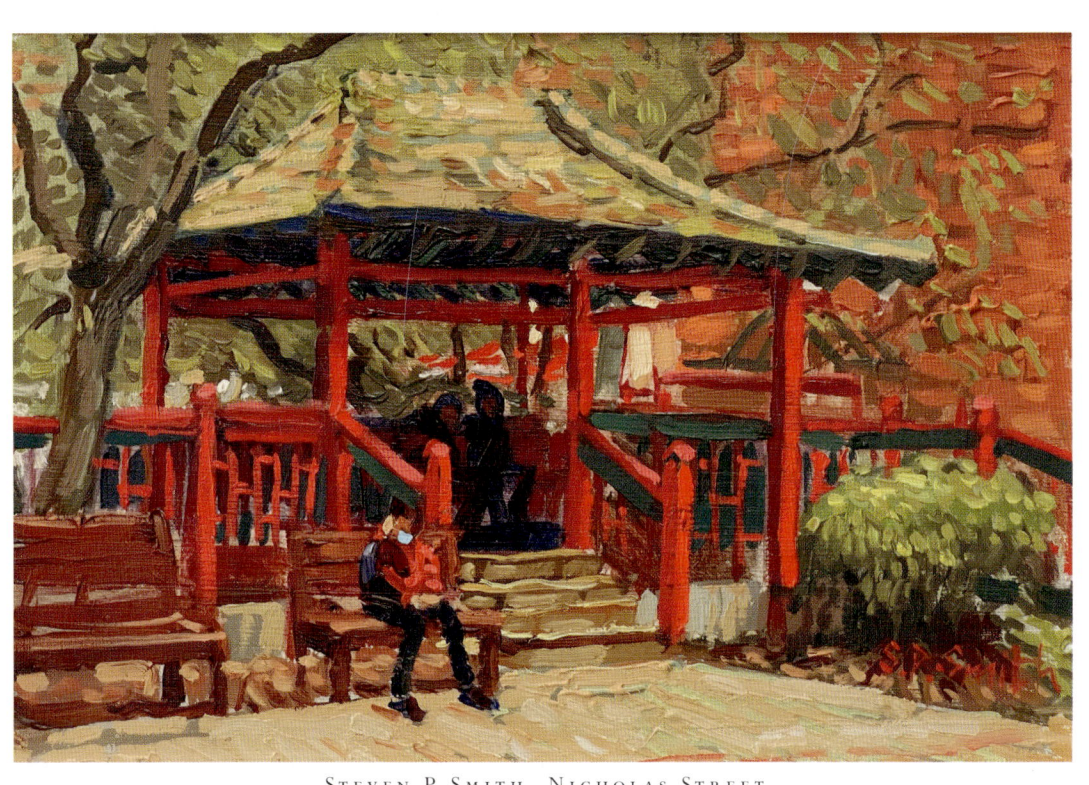

STEVEN P SMITH, NICHOLAS STREET

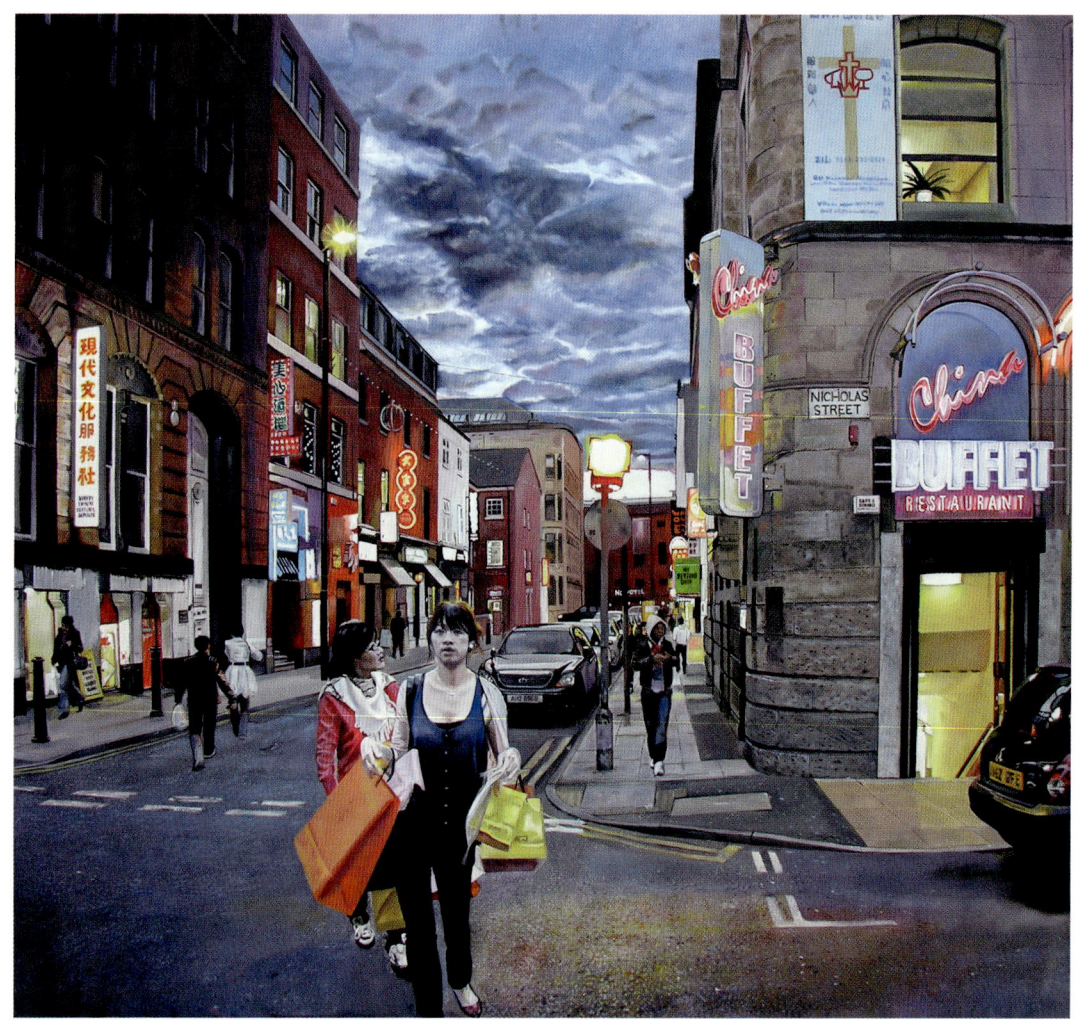

CHRIS ACHESON, CHINATOWN

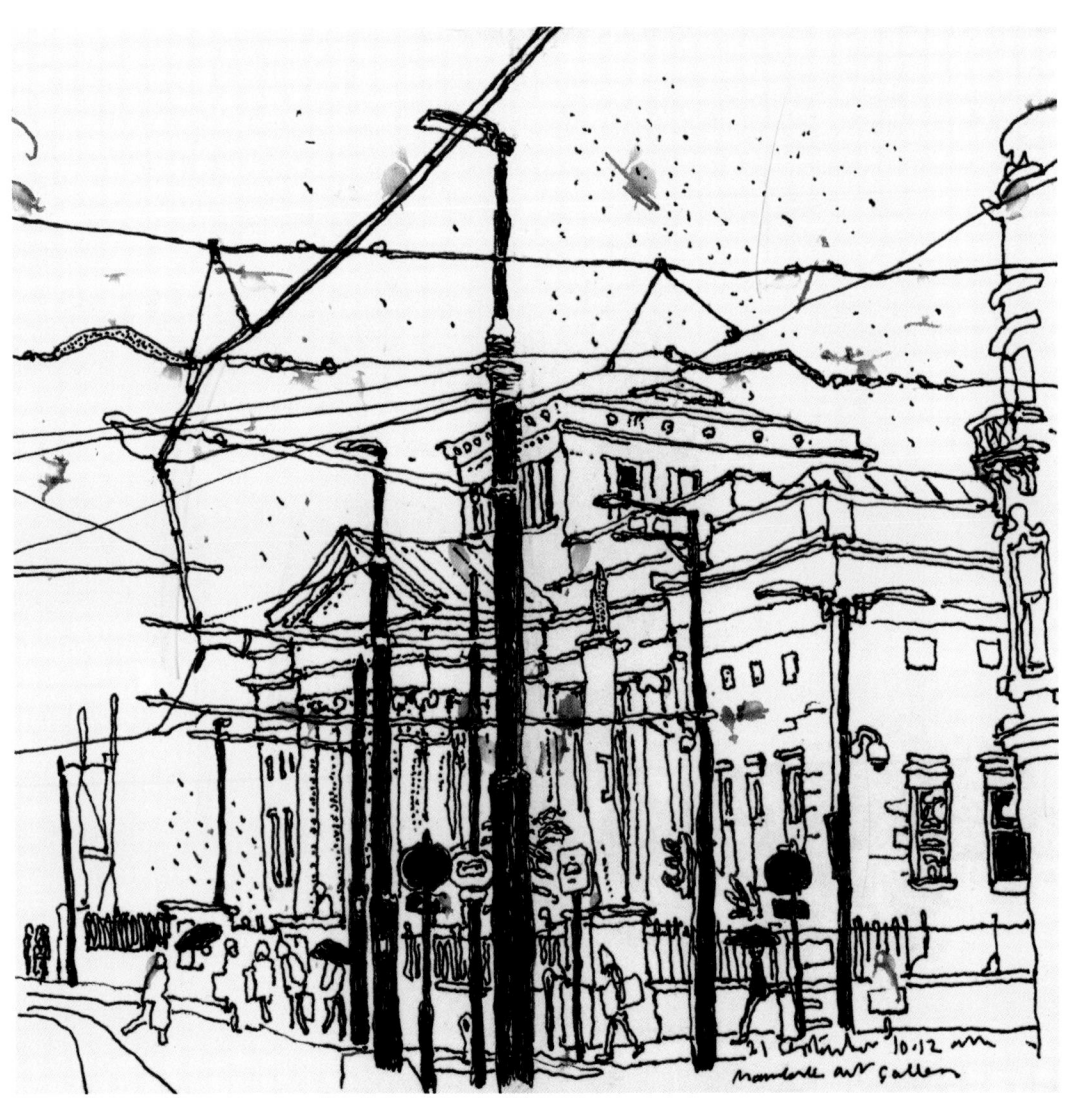

JOHN HEWITT, MANCHESTER ART GALLERY

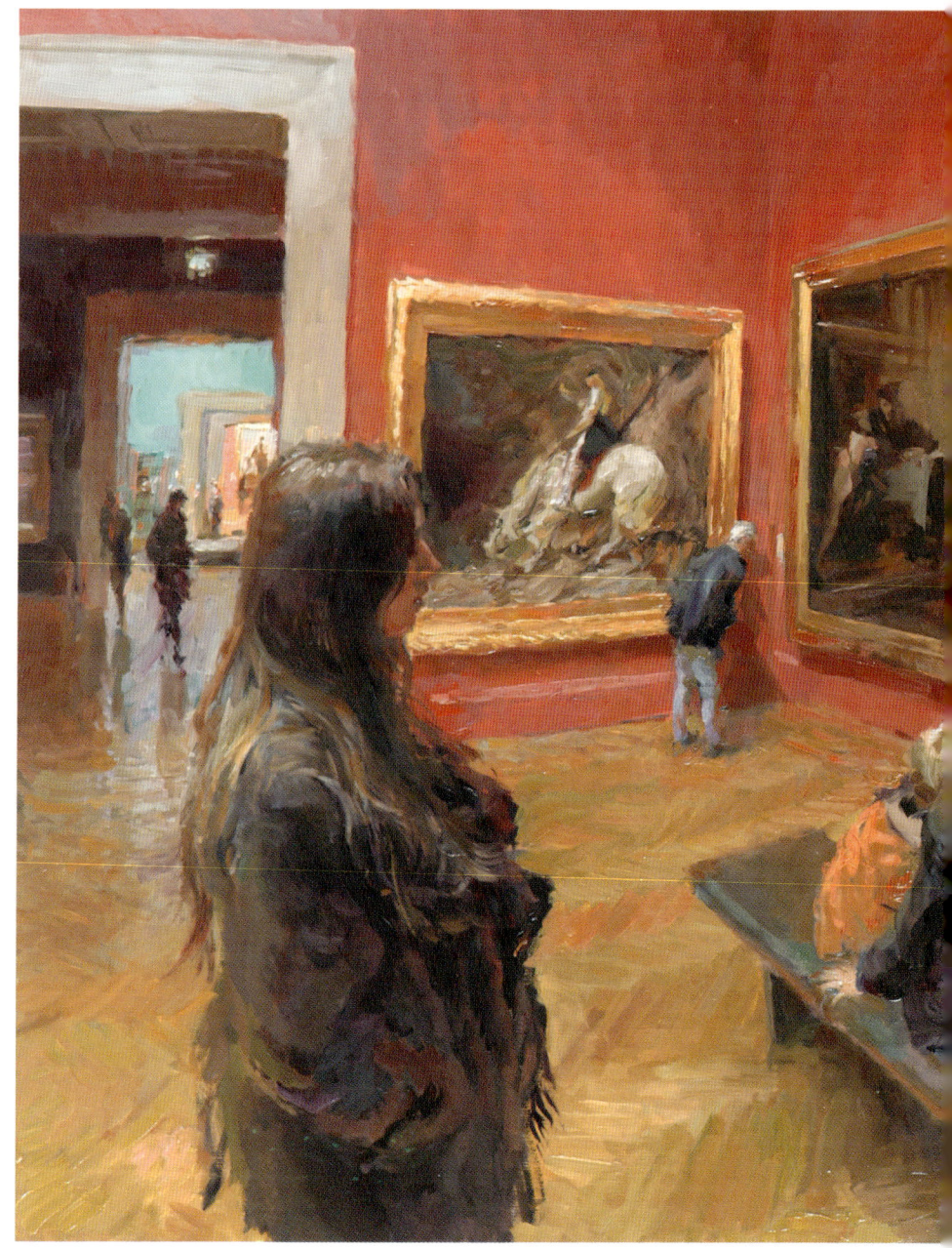

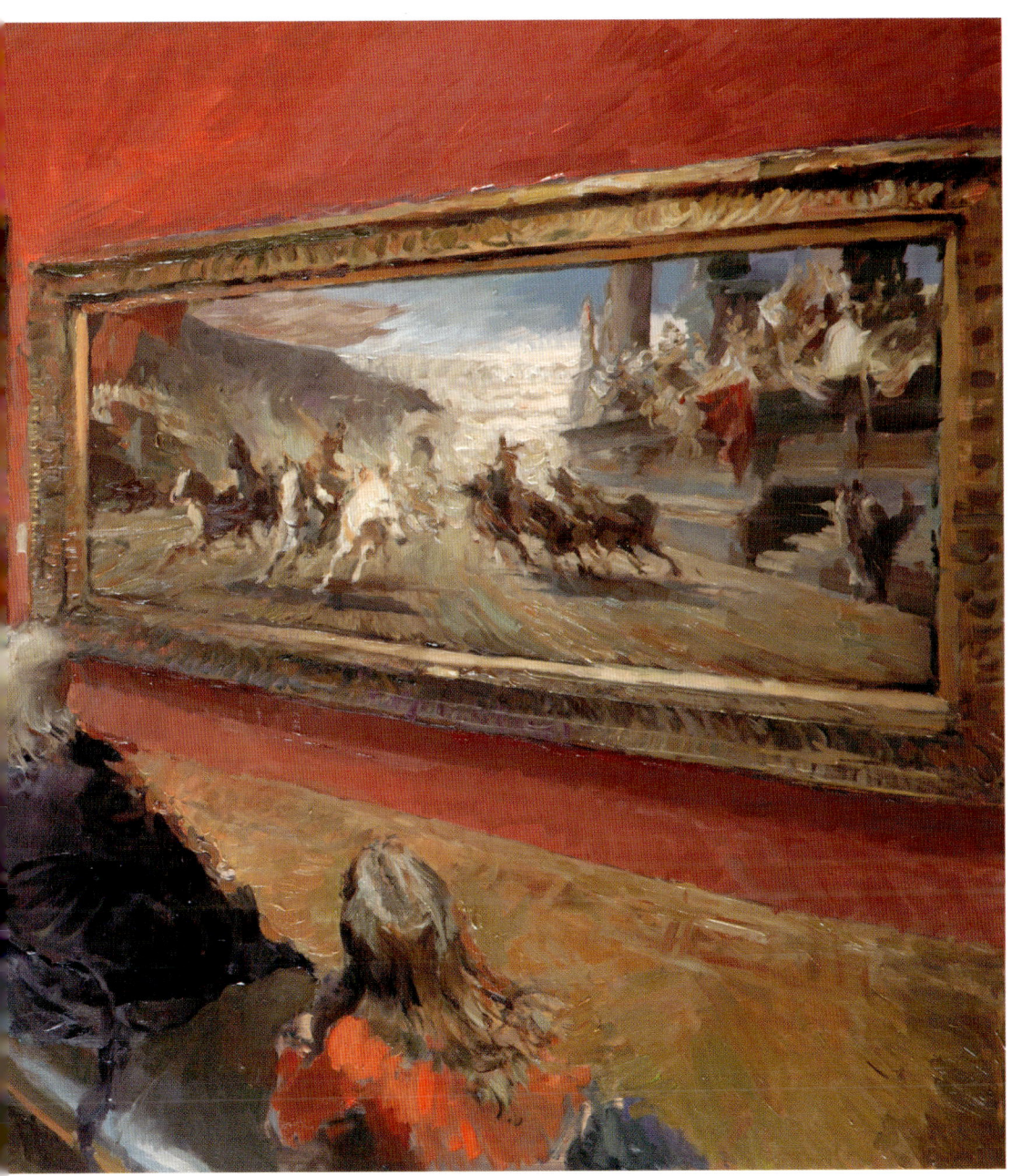

Rob Pointon, The Enchantment of Painting

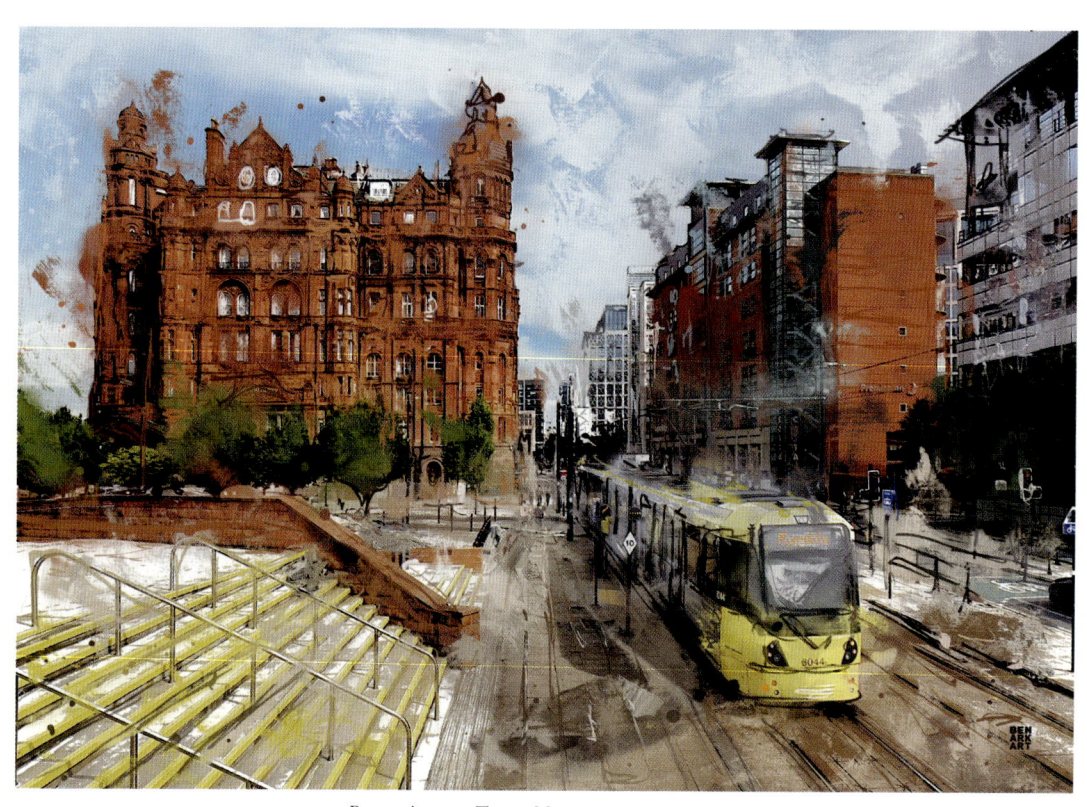

Ben Ark, The Midland Hotel

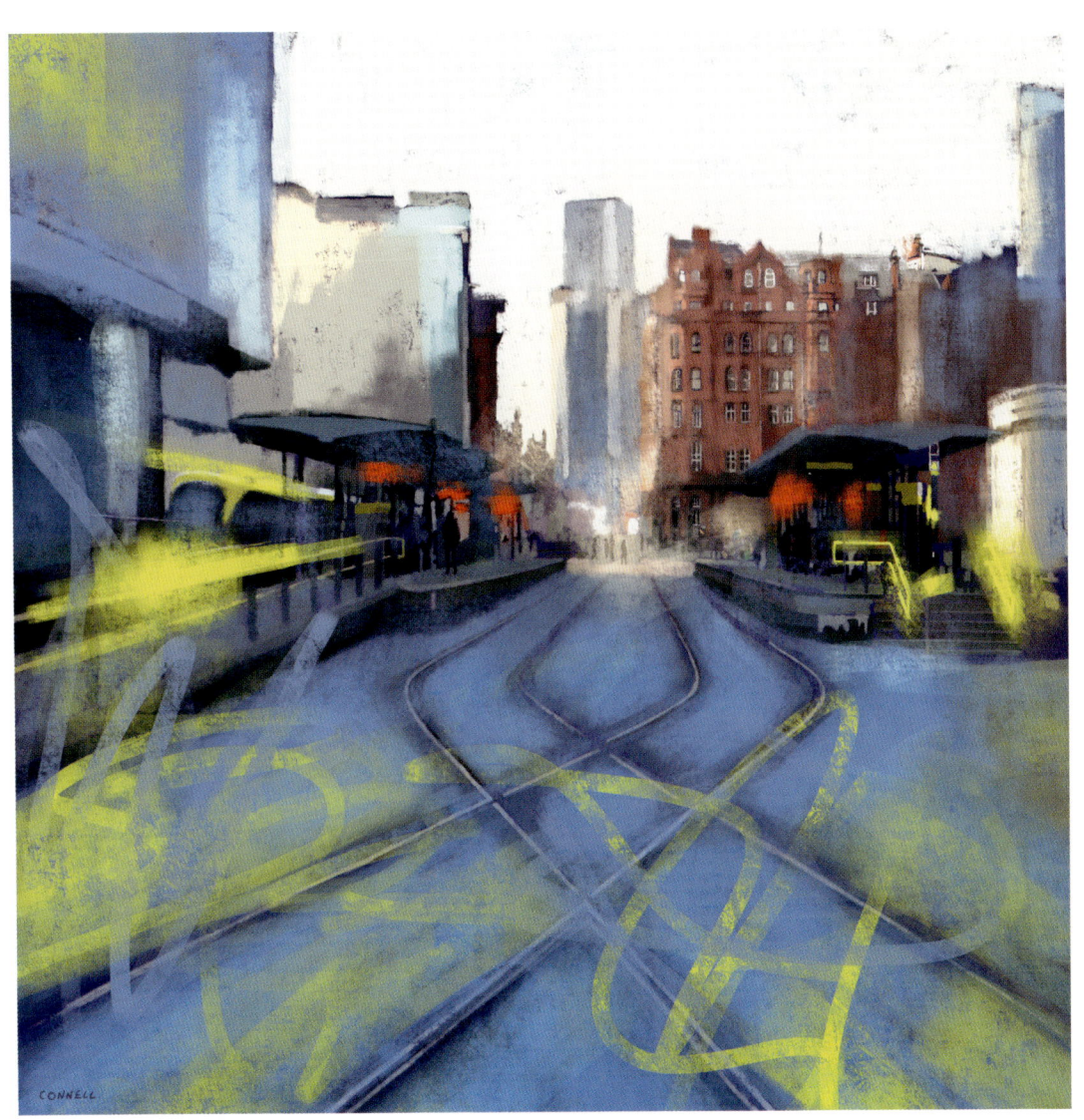

SARAH CONNELL, ST PETER'S SQUARE

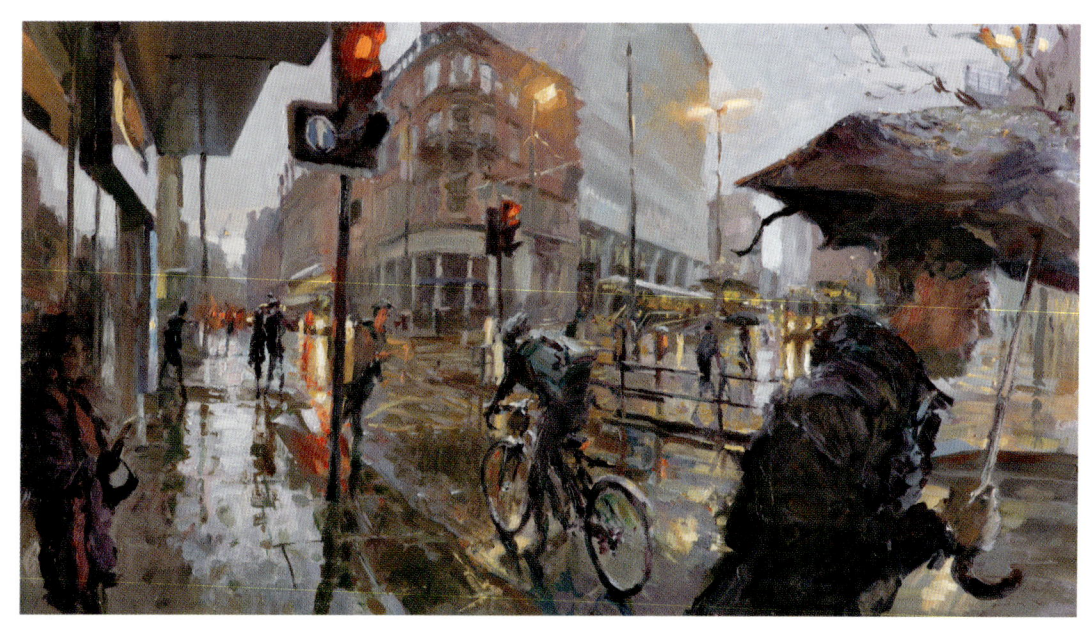

ROB POINTON, ST PETER'S SQUARE

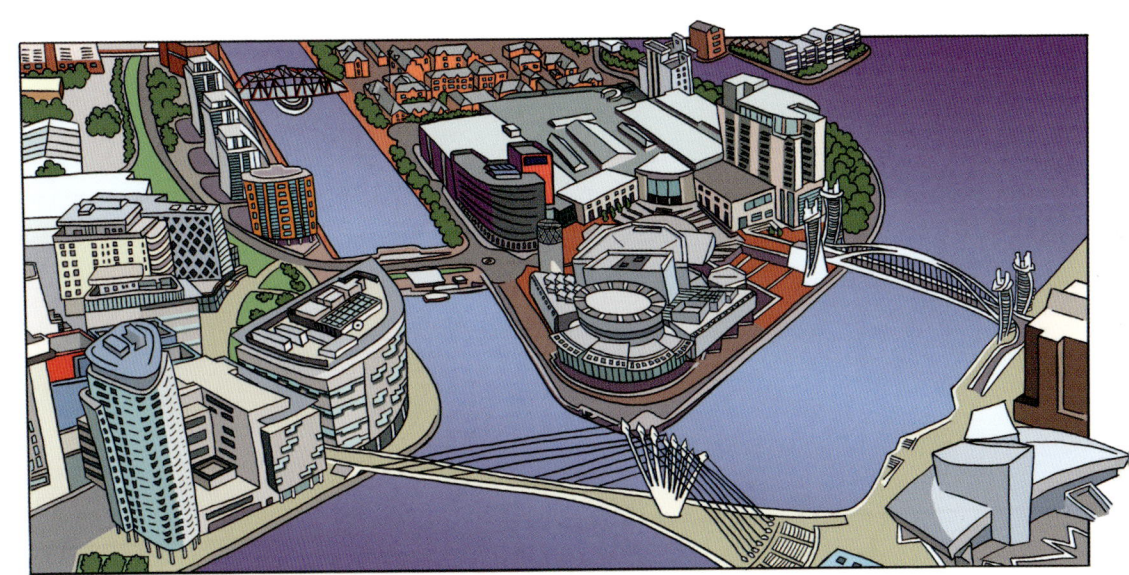

TONY PICKERING, SALFORD QUAYS

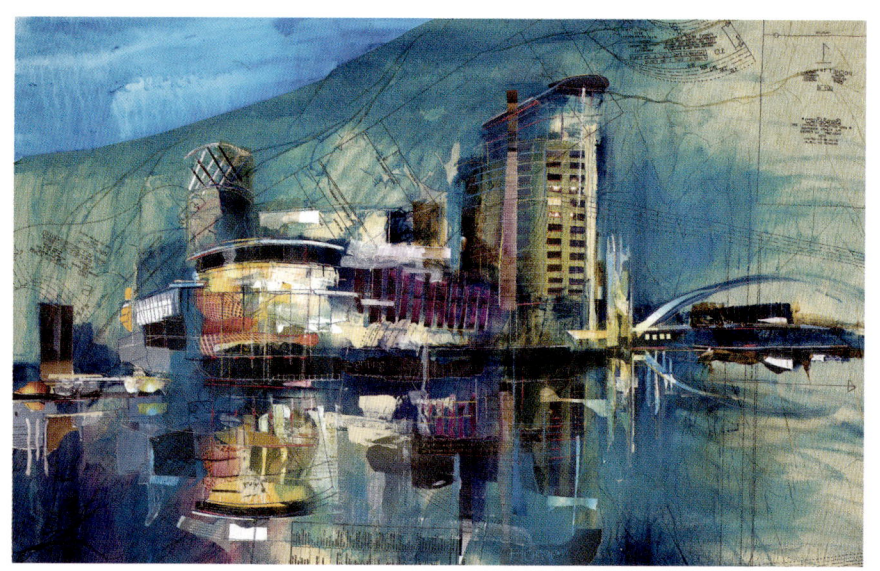

ROB WILSON, MEDIACITYUK

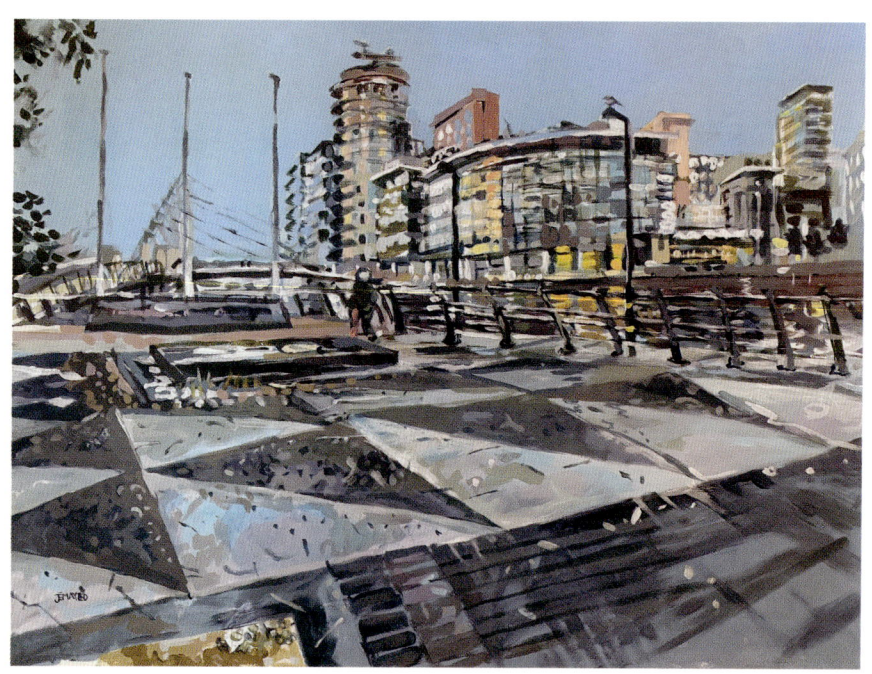

JANET MAYLED, SALFORD QUAYS

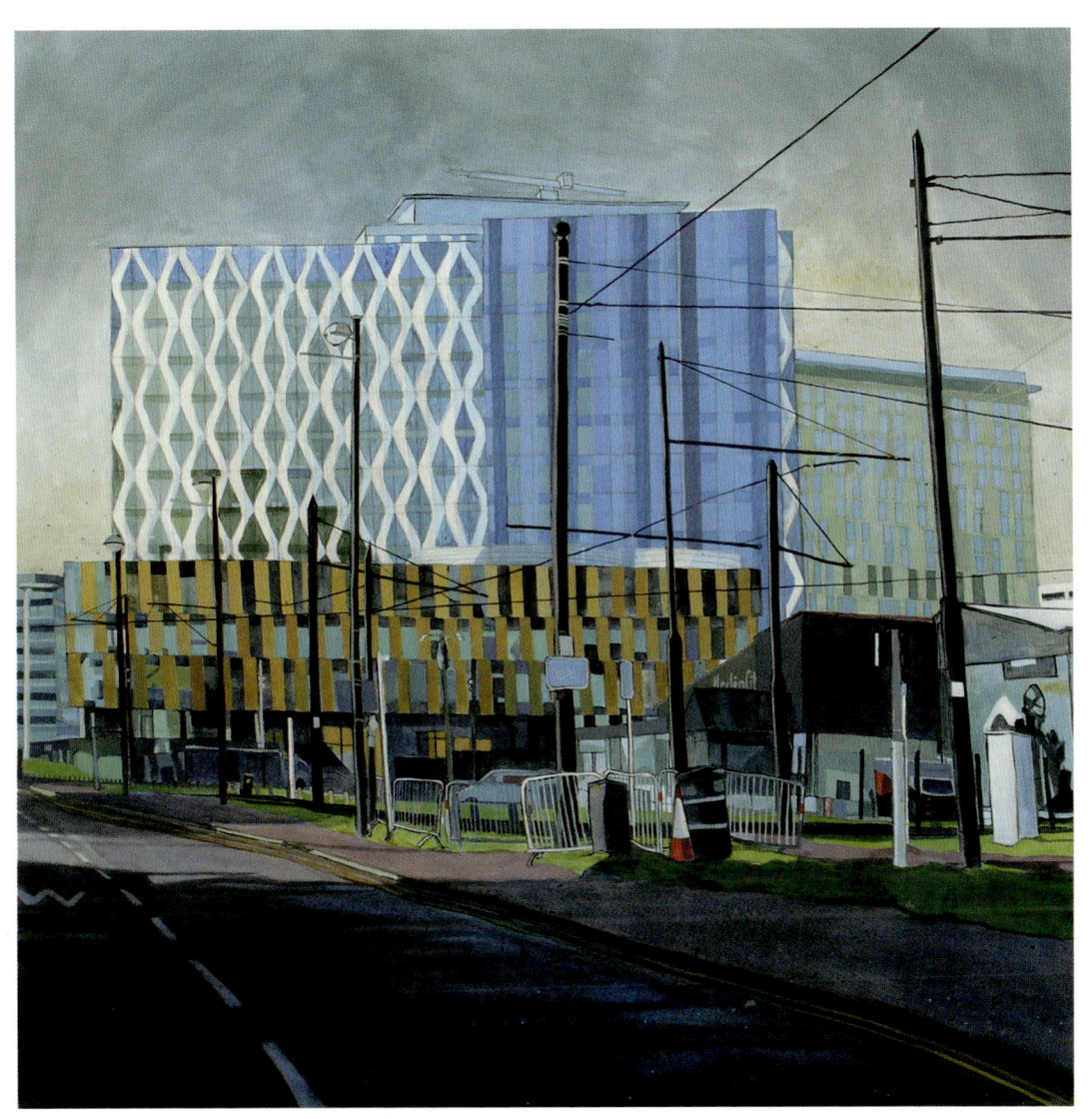

CAROLINE JOHNSON, MediaCityUK

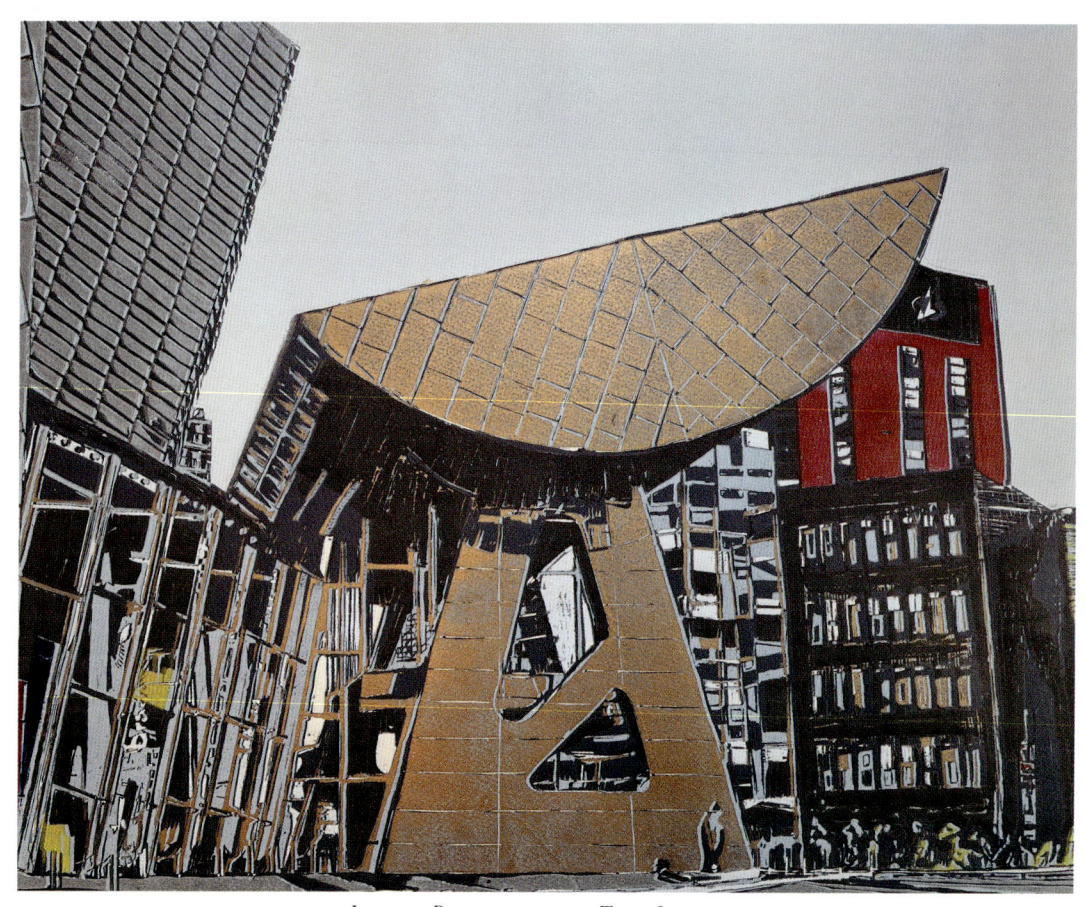

JAYNE PELLINGTON, THE LOWRY

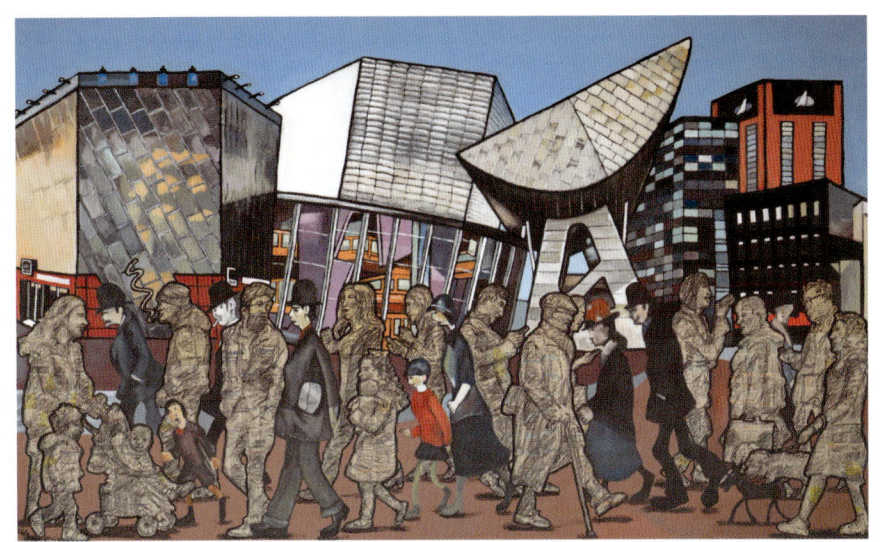

MATT WILDE, IN TWO MINDS

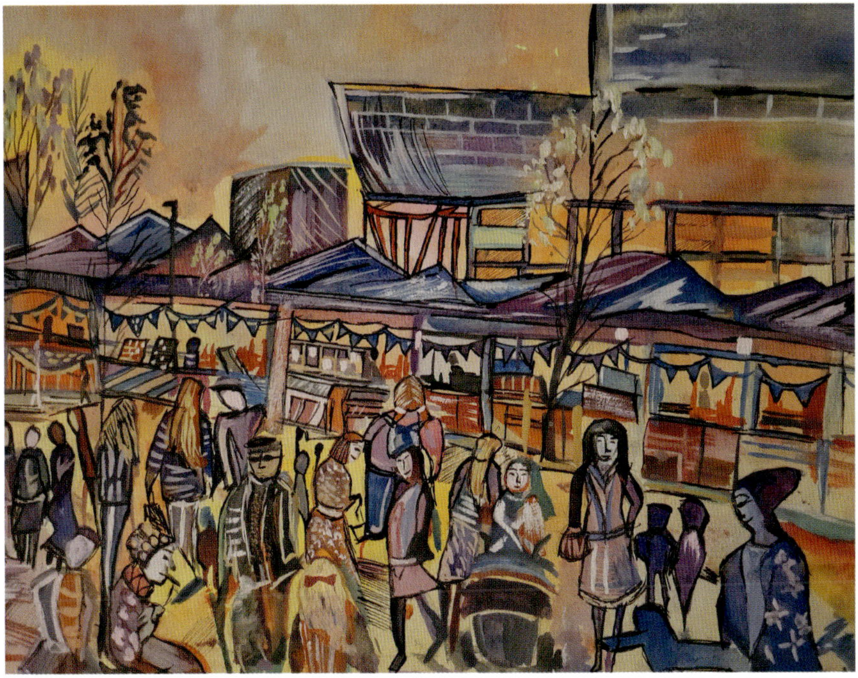

ASHLEY CUNDALL, SALFORD QUAYS

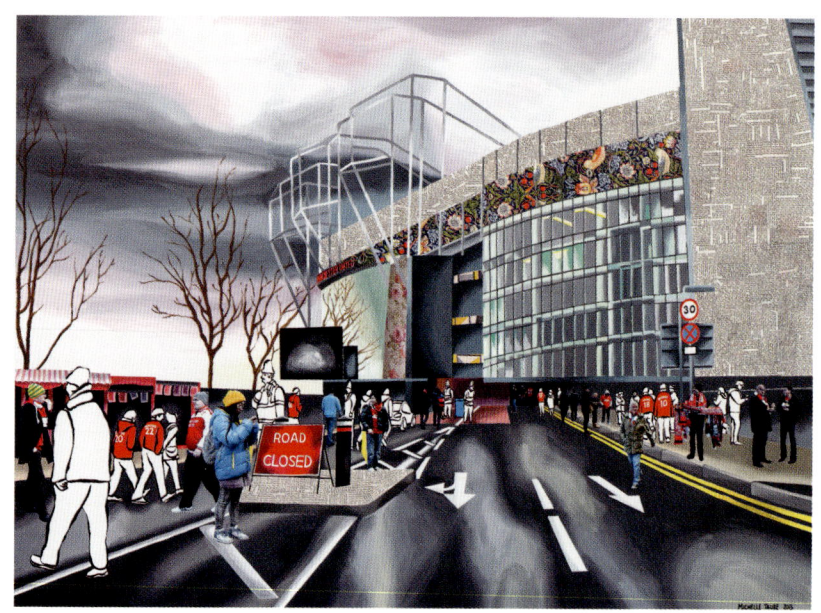

MICHELLE TAUBE, OLD TRAFFORD FOOTBALL STADIUM

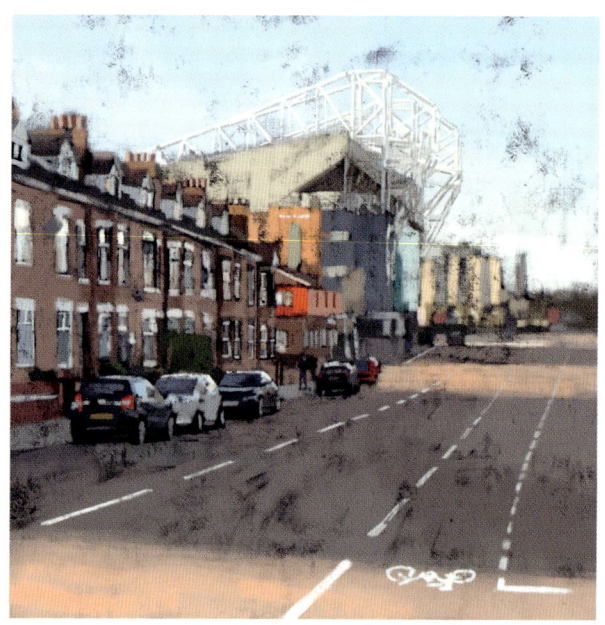

SARAH CONNELL, SIR MATT BUSBY WAY

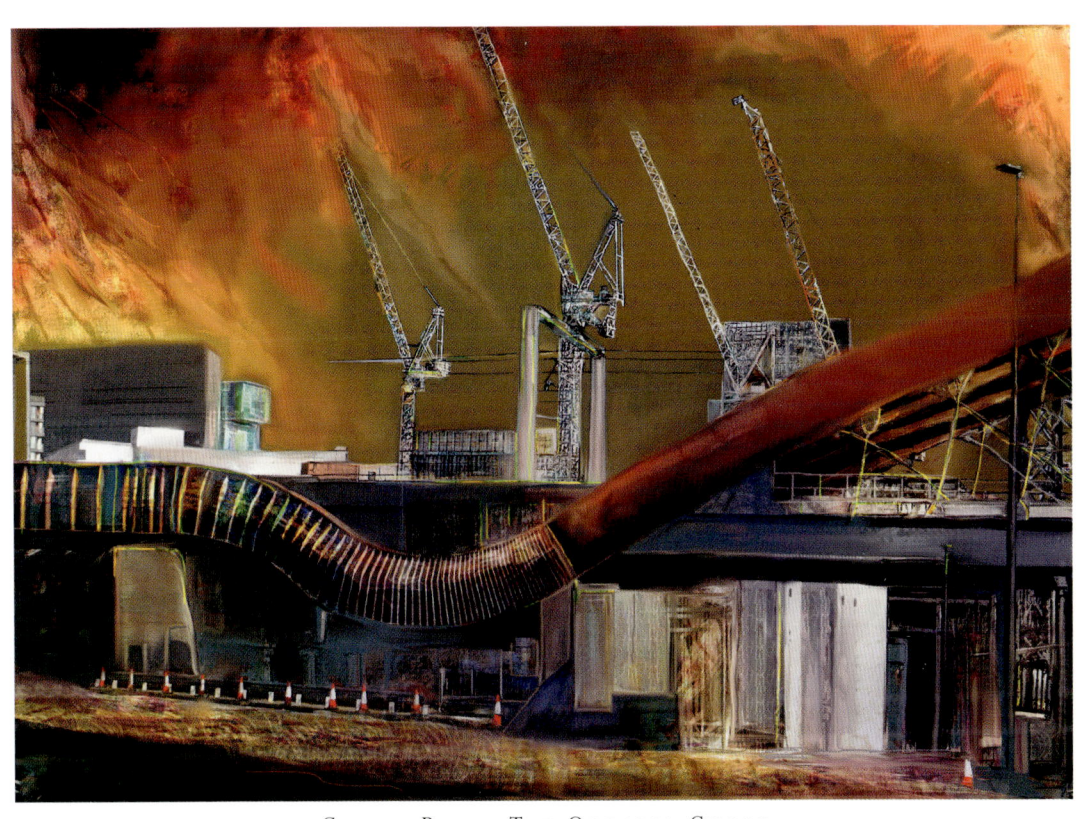

CLAIRE RILEY, THE ORDSALL CHORD

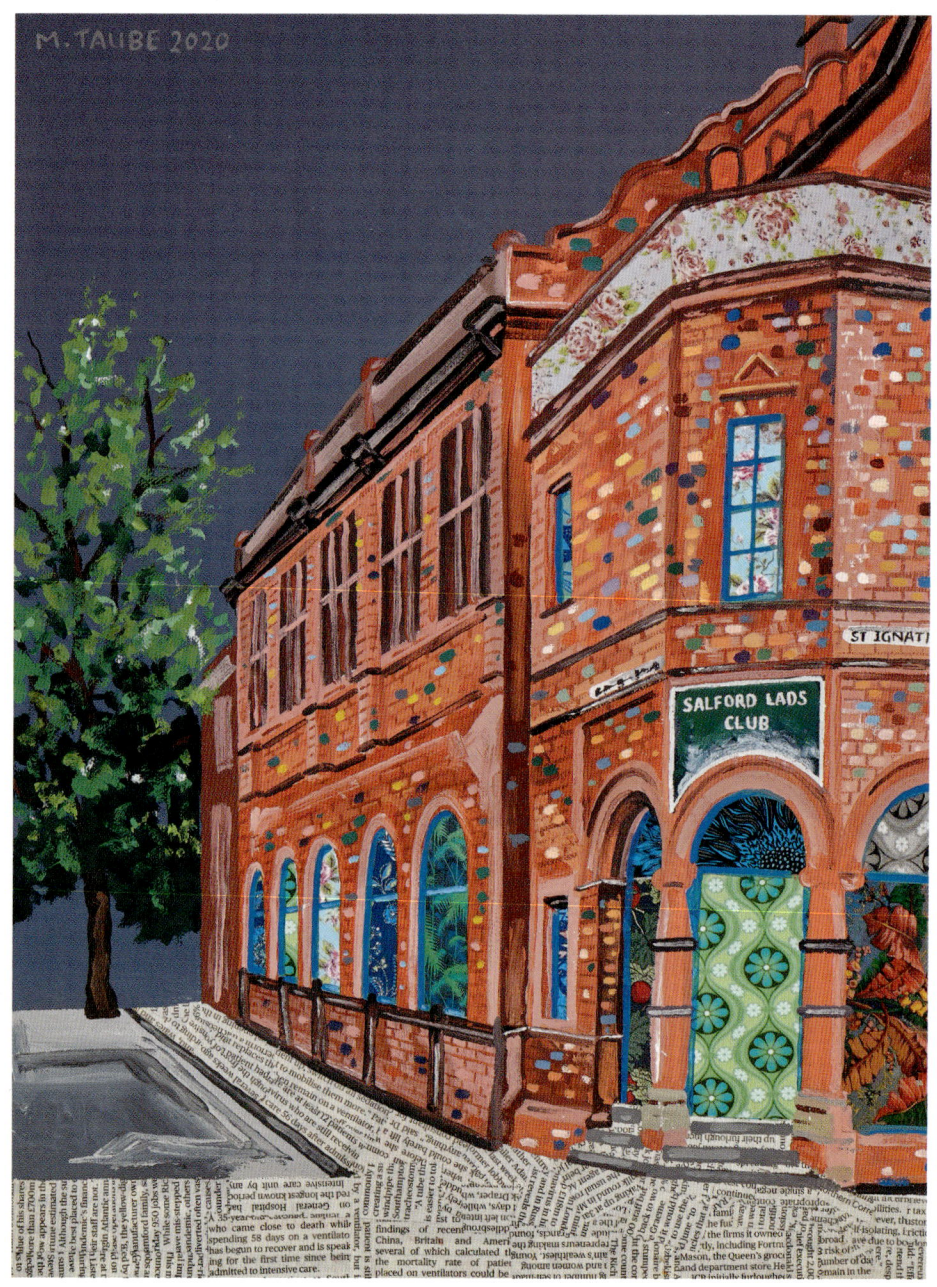

MICHELLE TAUBE, SALFORD LADS CLUB

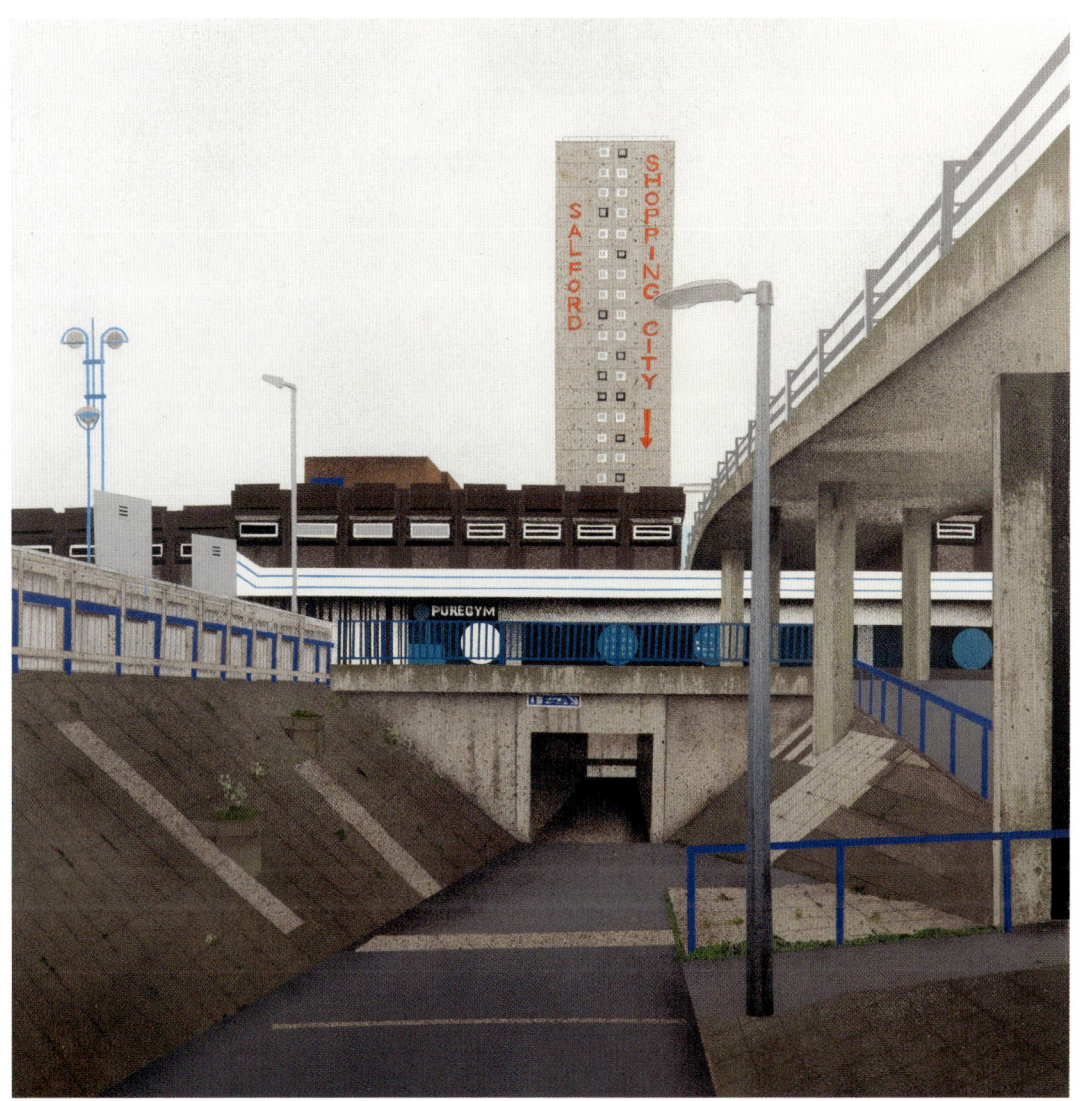

MANDY PAYNE, SALFORD SHOPPING CENTRE

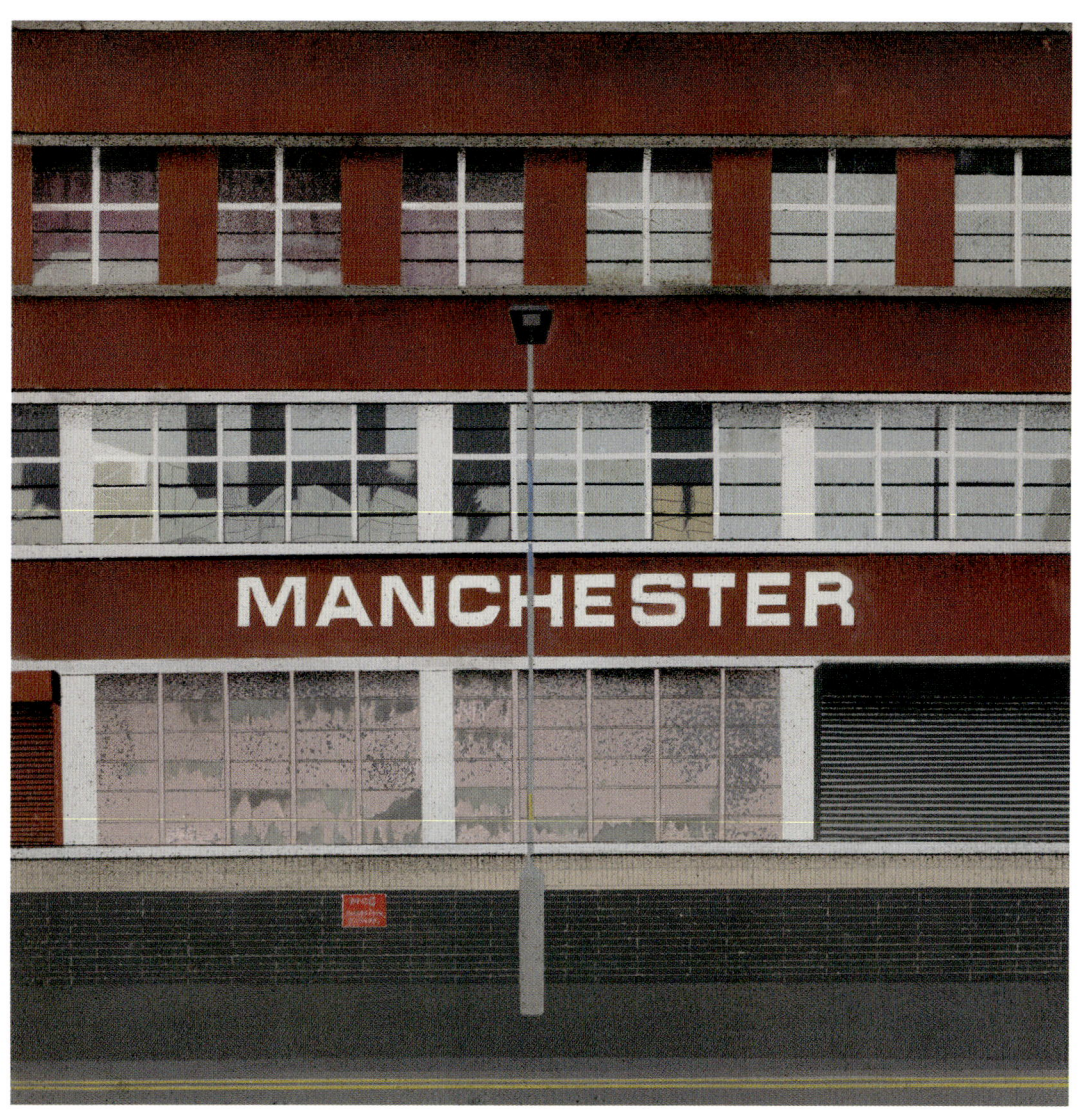

MANDY PAYNE, CHEETHAM HILL

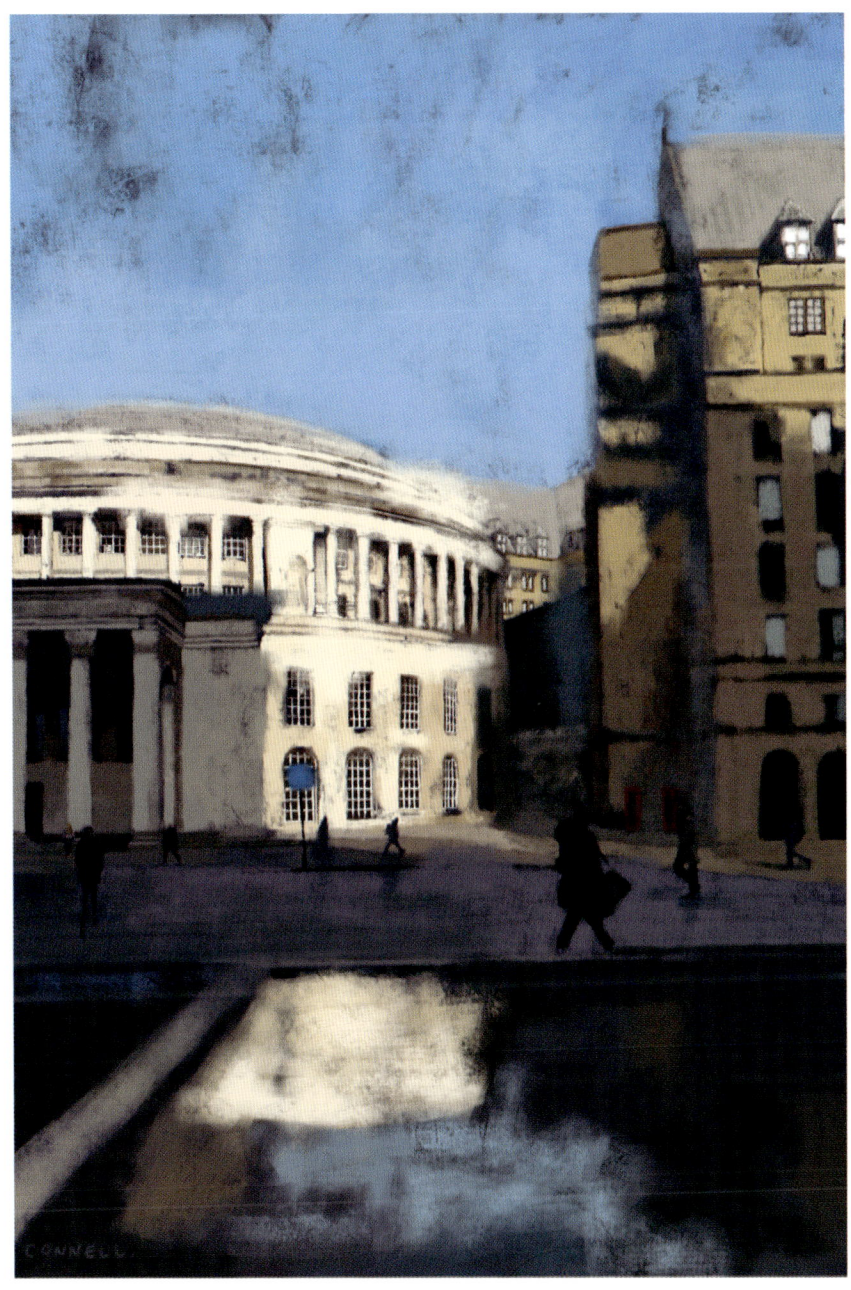

SARAH CONNELL, MANCHESTER CENTRAL LIBRARY

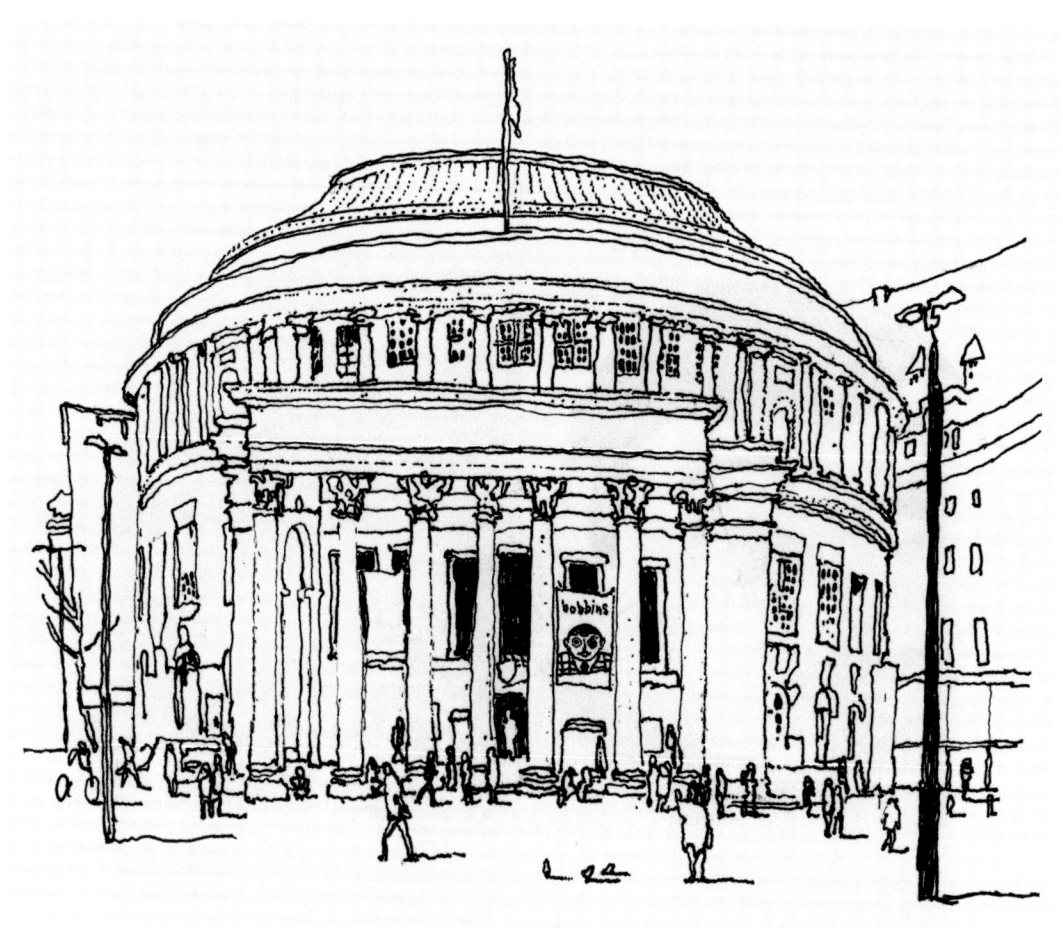

JOHN HEWITT, MANCHESTER CENTRAL LIBRARY

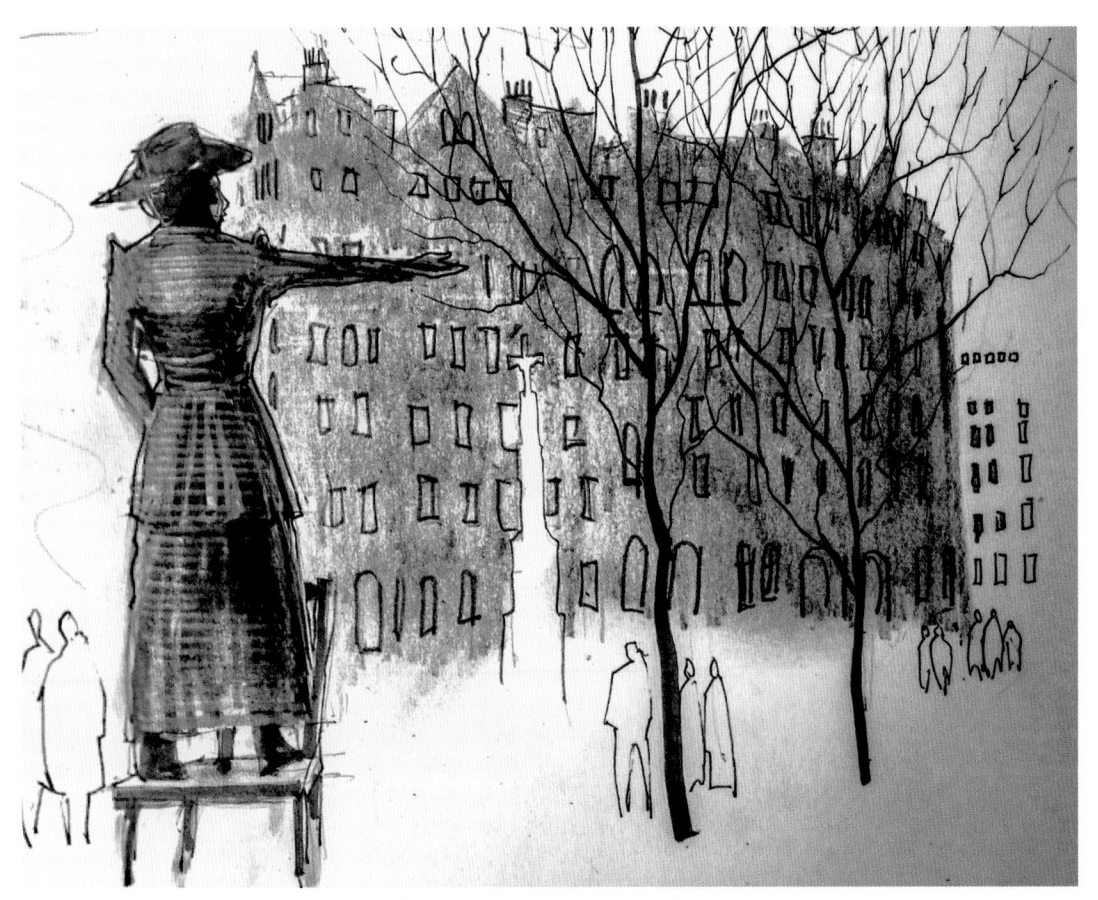

DAVID LOWTHER, EMMELINE POINTS TO THE MIDLAND HOTEL

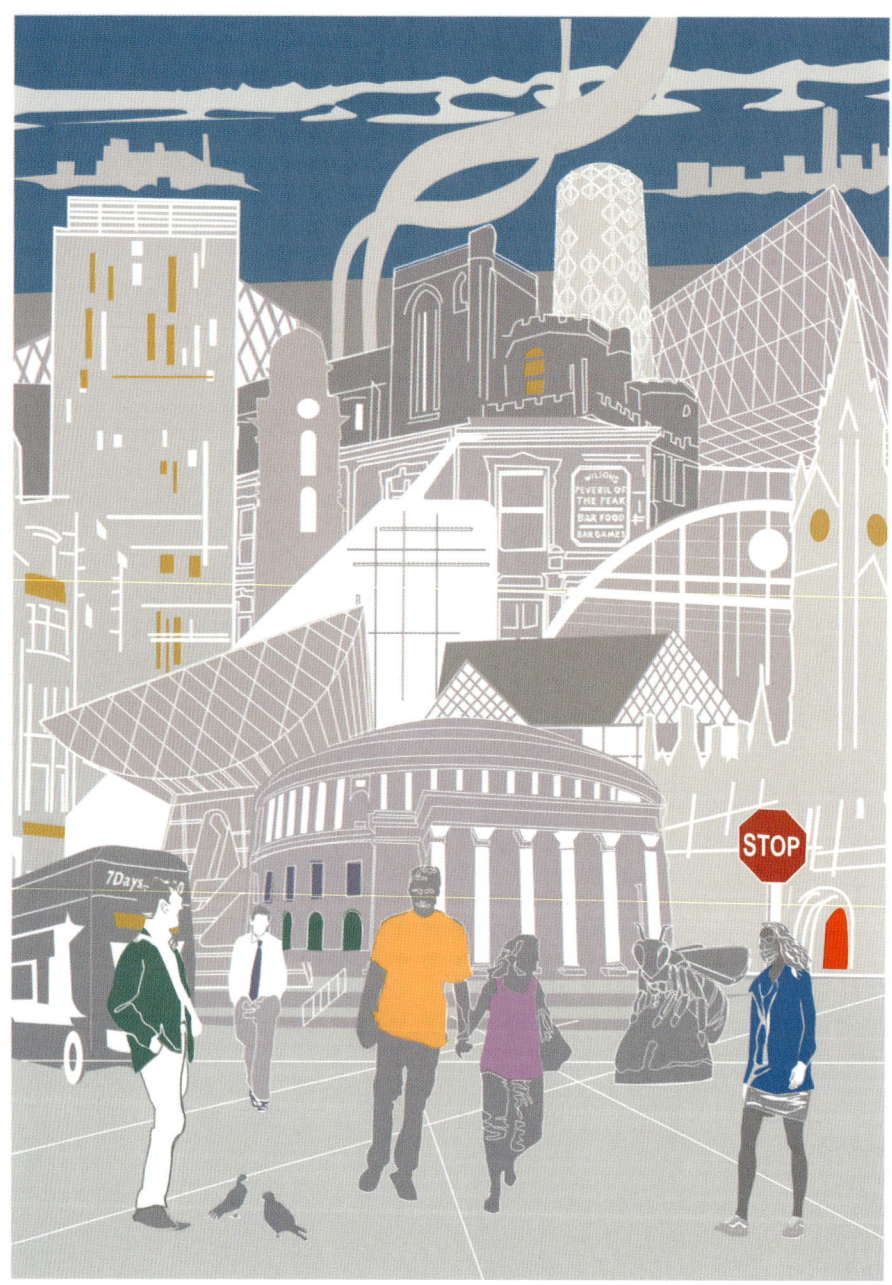

Helen Jones, Manchester buildings light

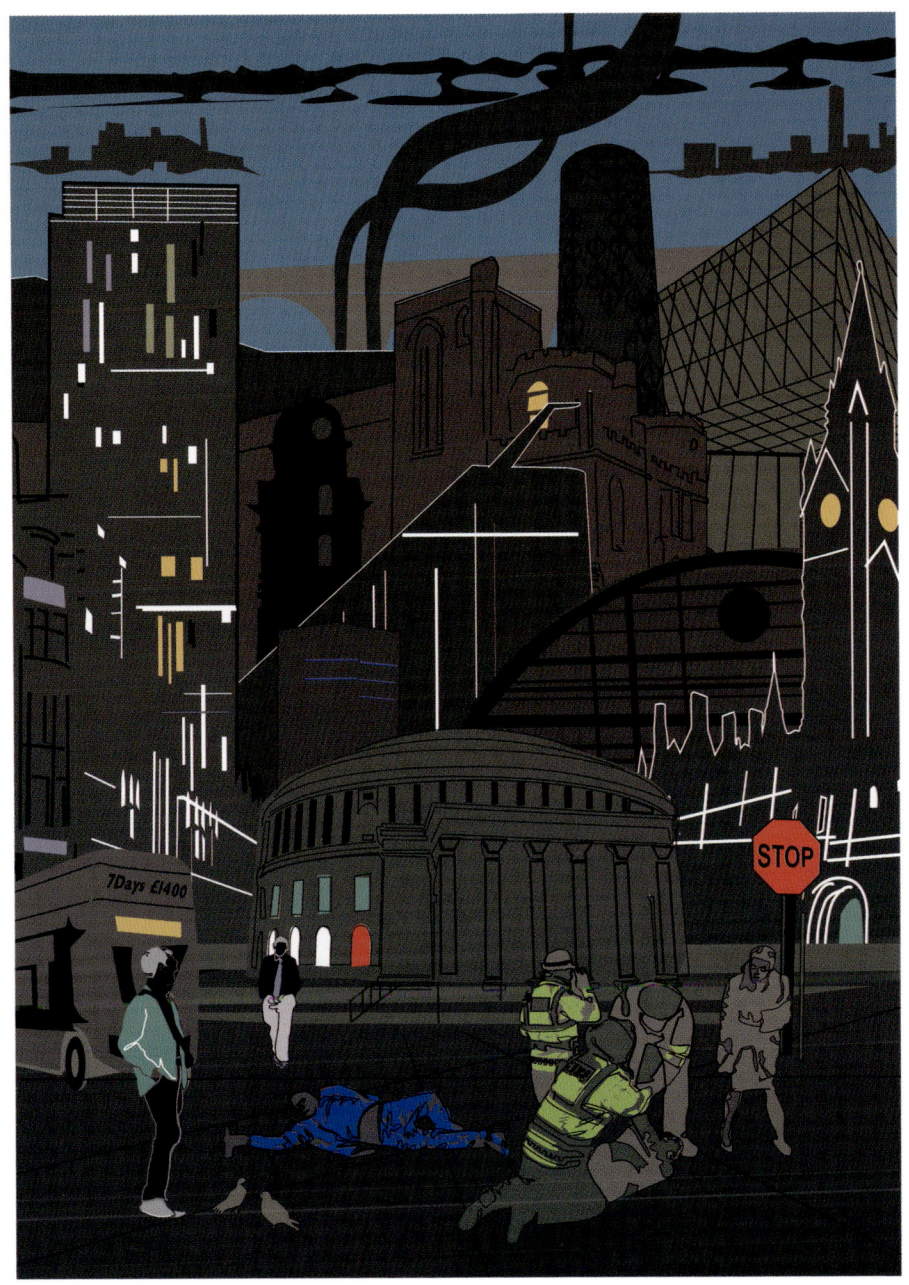

HELEN JONES, MANCHESTER BUILDINGS DARK

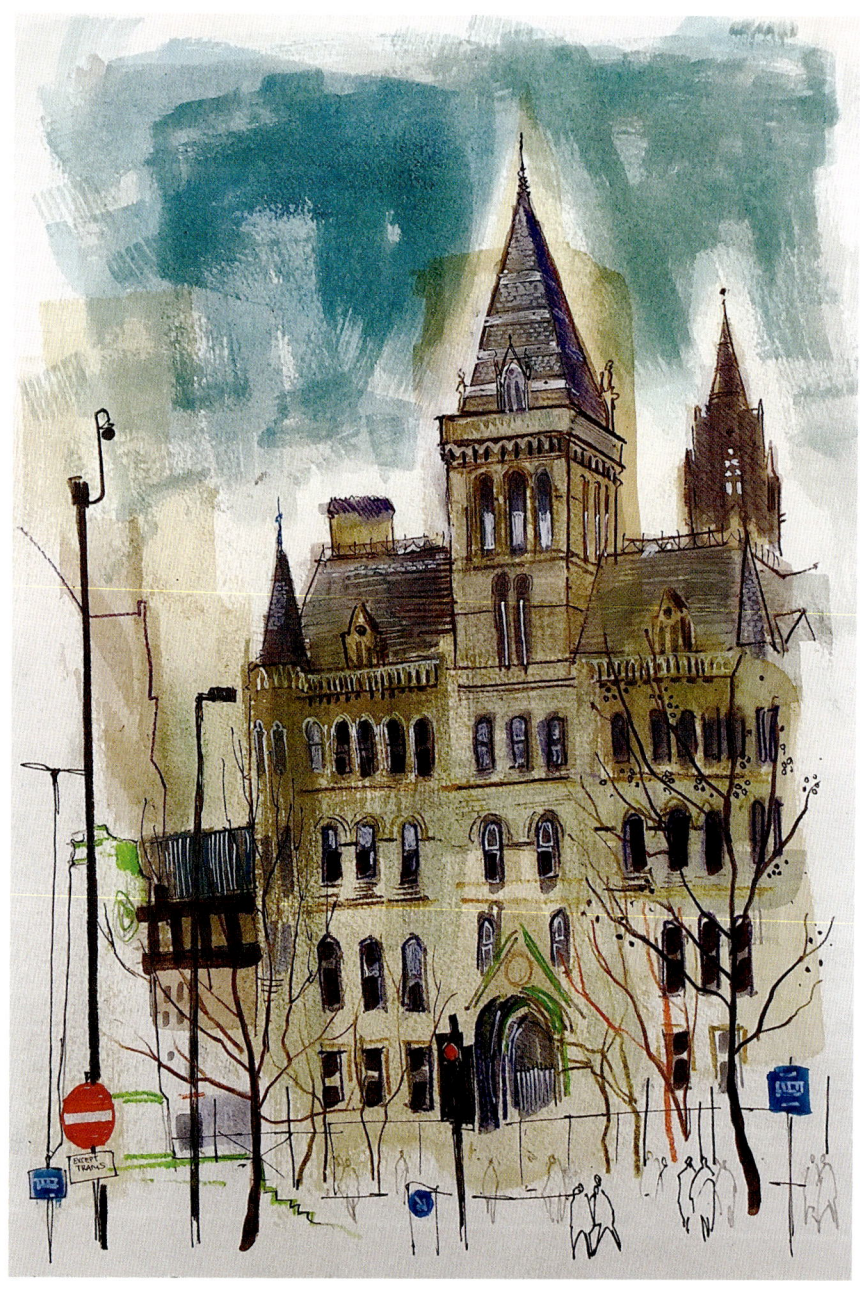

David Lowther, Manchester Town Hall

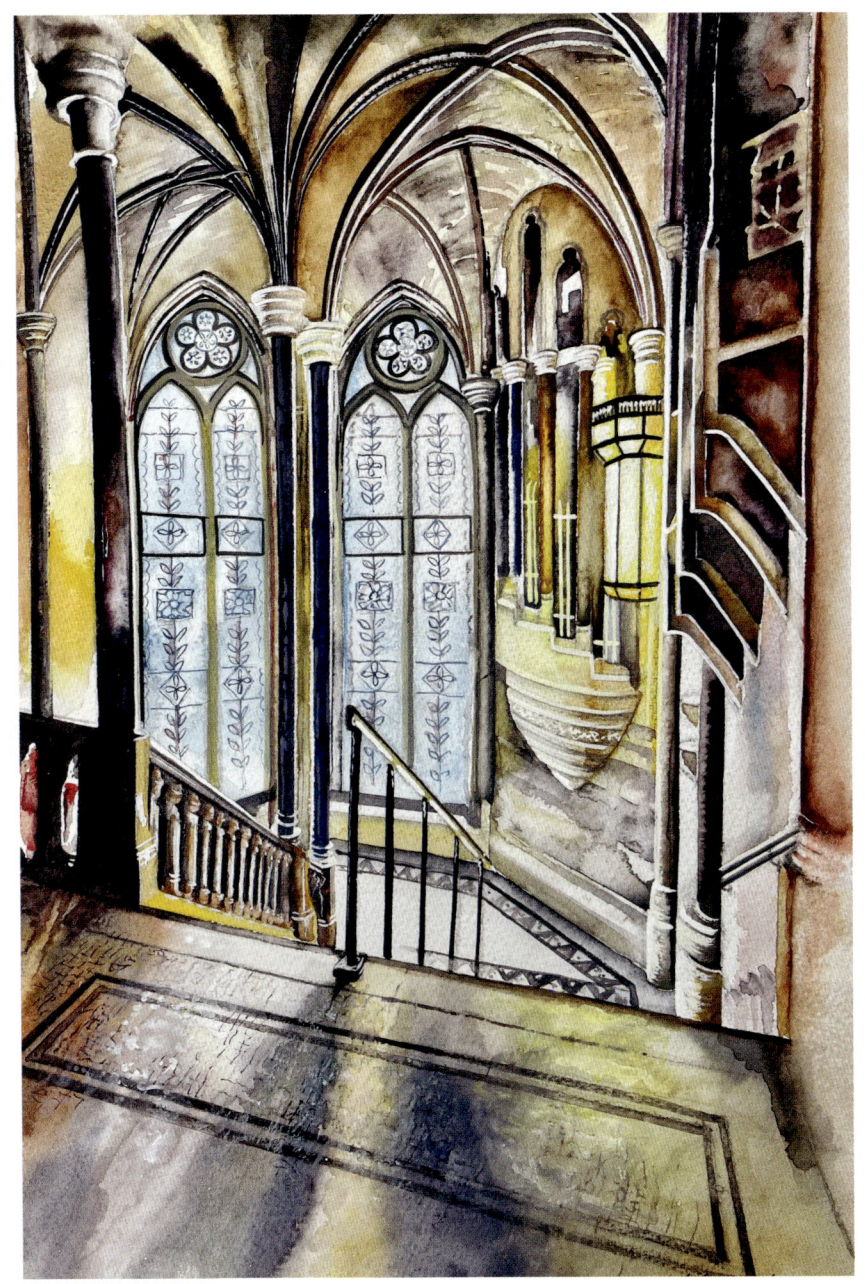

LISA HASELDEN, MANCHESTER TOWN HALL

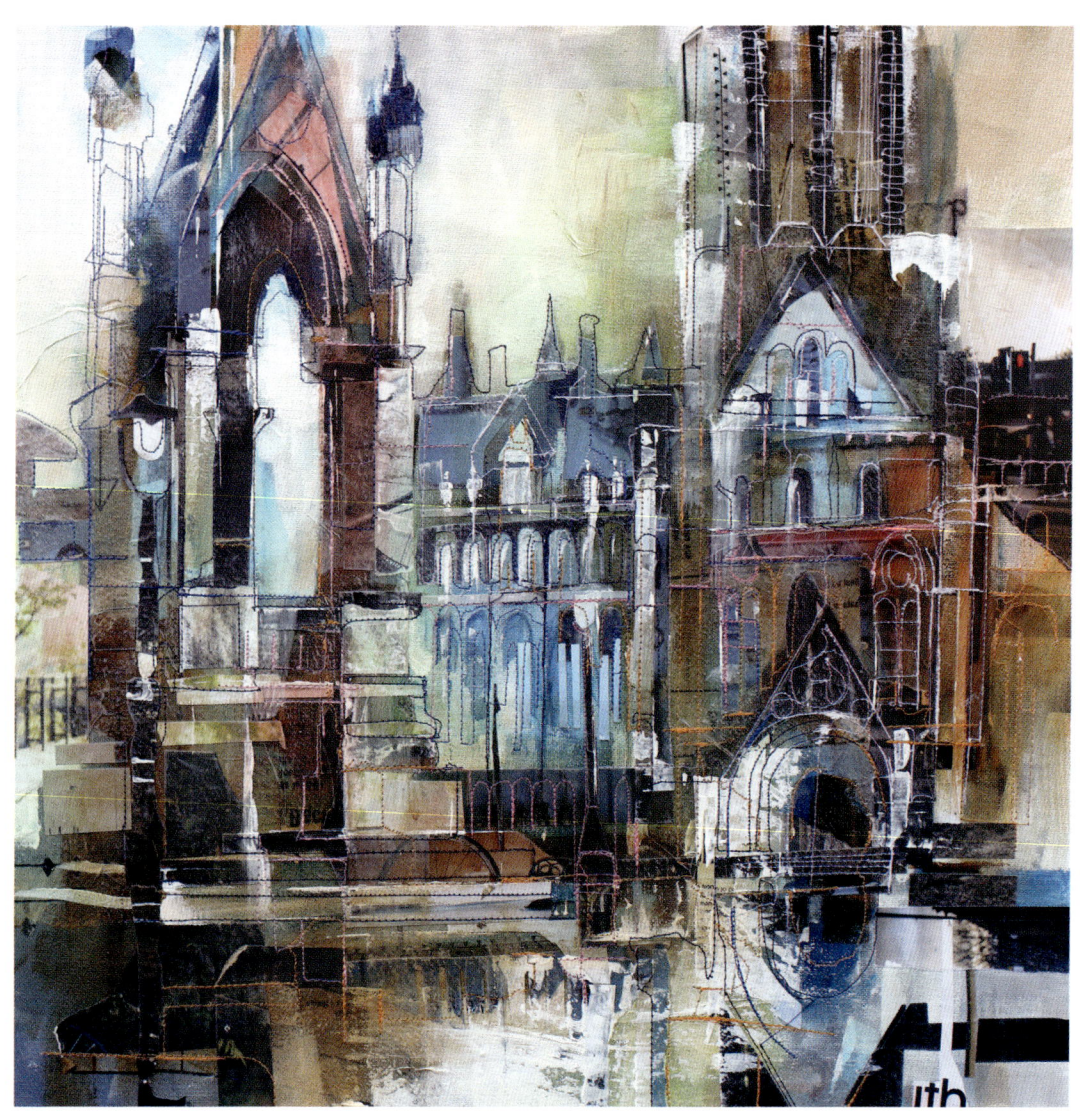

ROB WILSON, ALBERT SQUARE

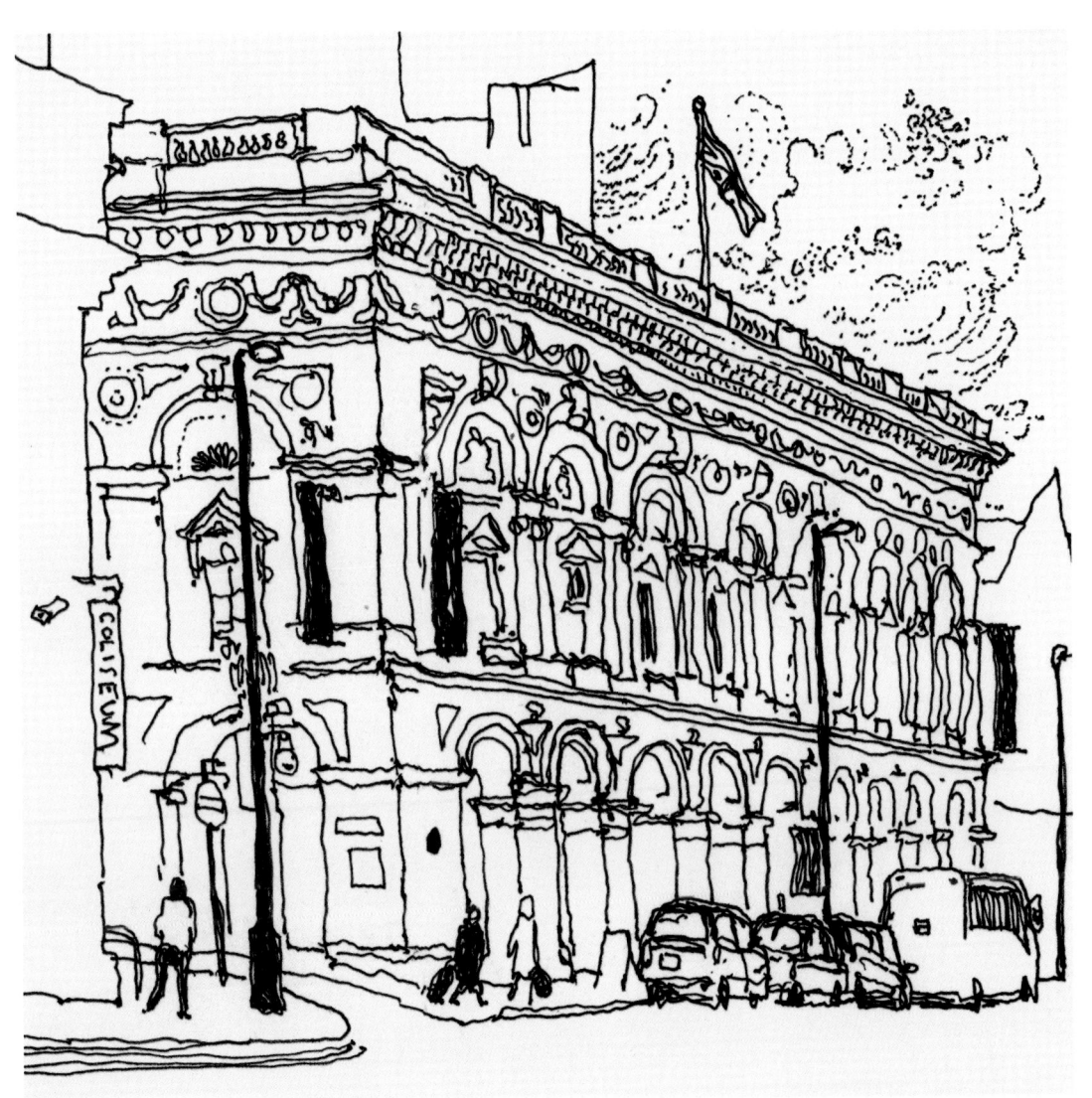

JOHN HEWITT, THE FORMER FREE TRADE HALL

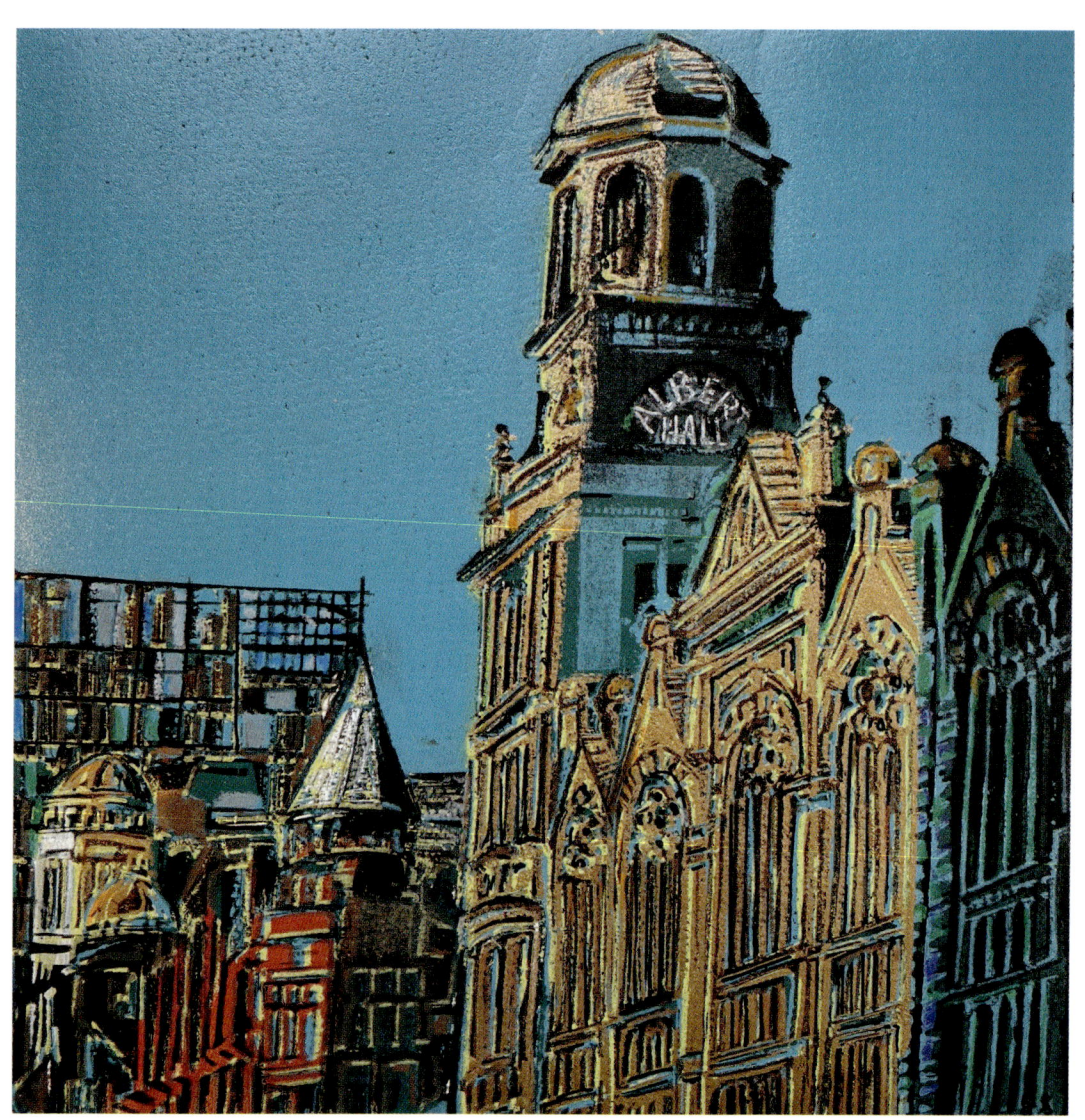

Jayne Pellington, Albert Hall

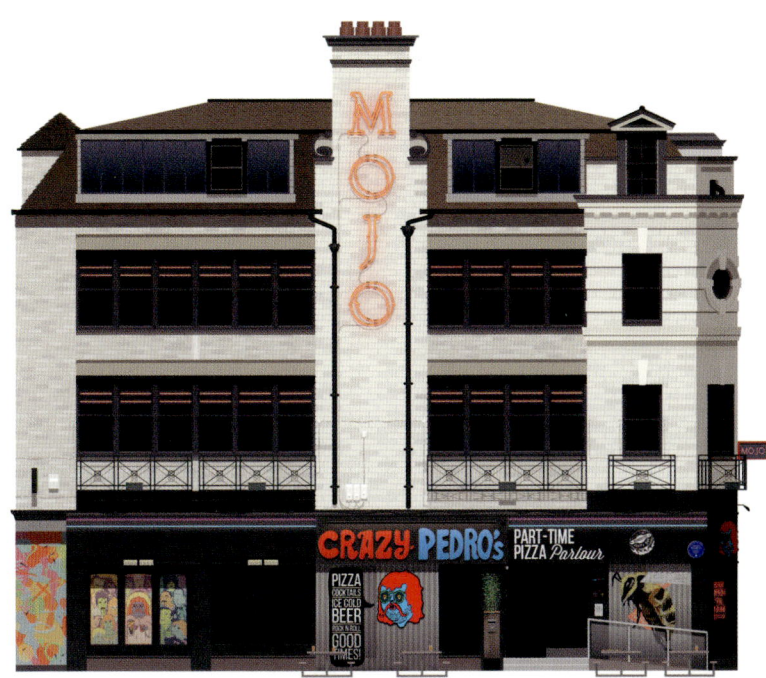

GLEN CROSS, MOJO AND CRAZY PEDRO'S

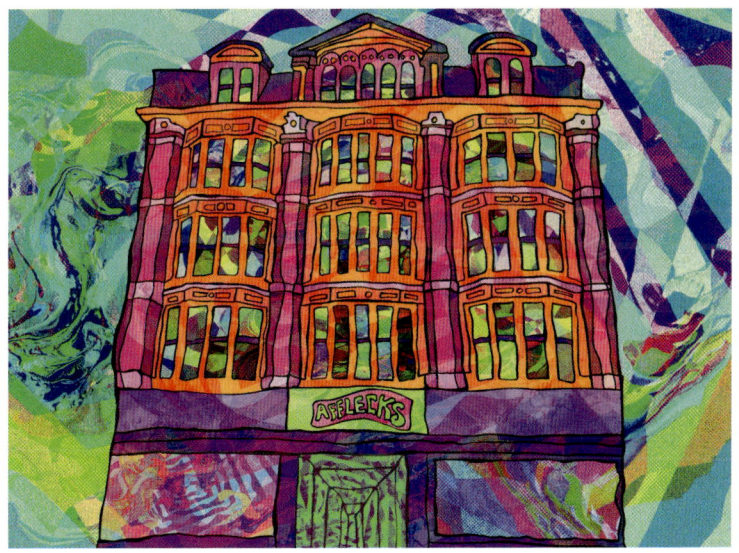

JASMIN ISSAKA, AFFLECKS

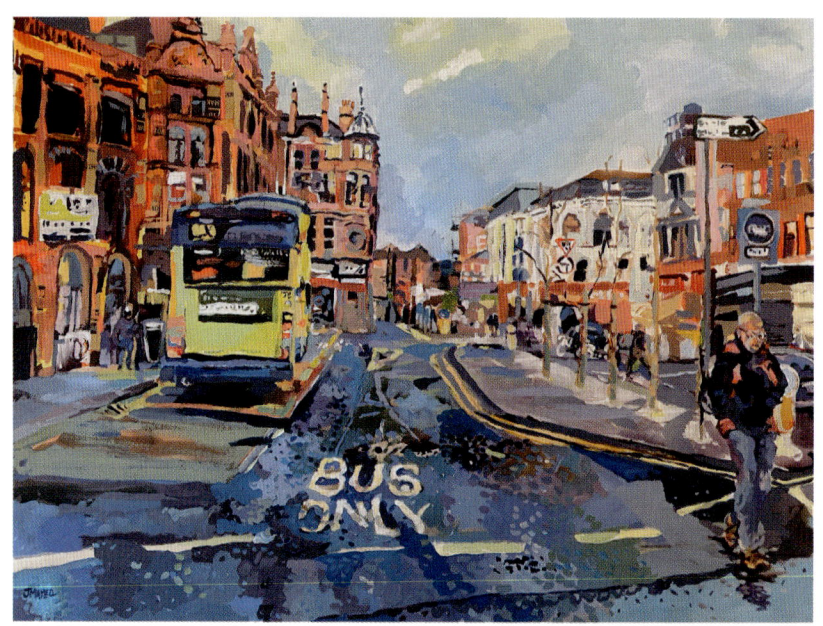

JANET MAYLED, DALE STREET

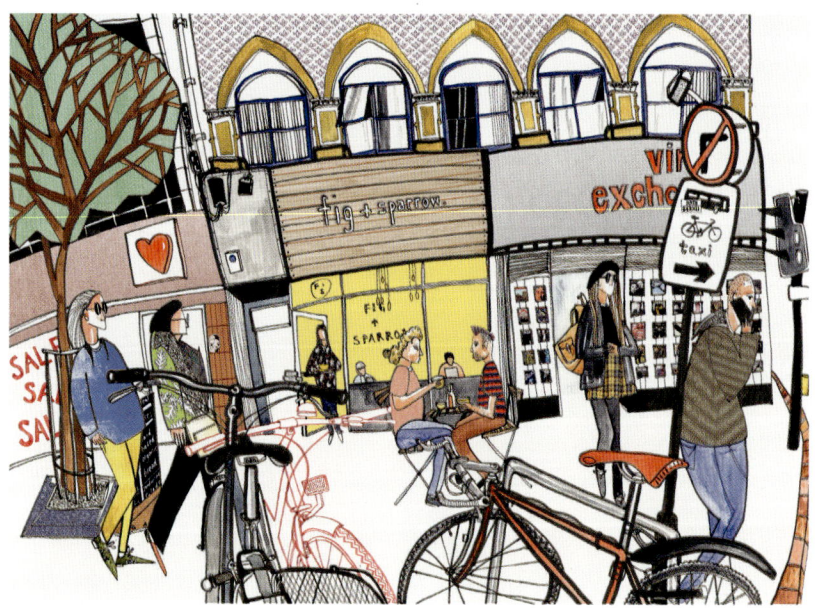

LEN GRANT, FIG AND SPARROW CAFÉ, NORTHERN QUARTER

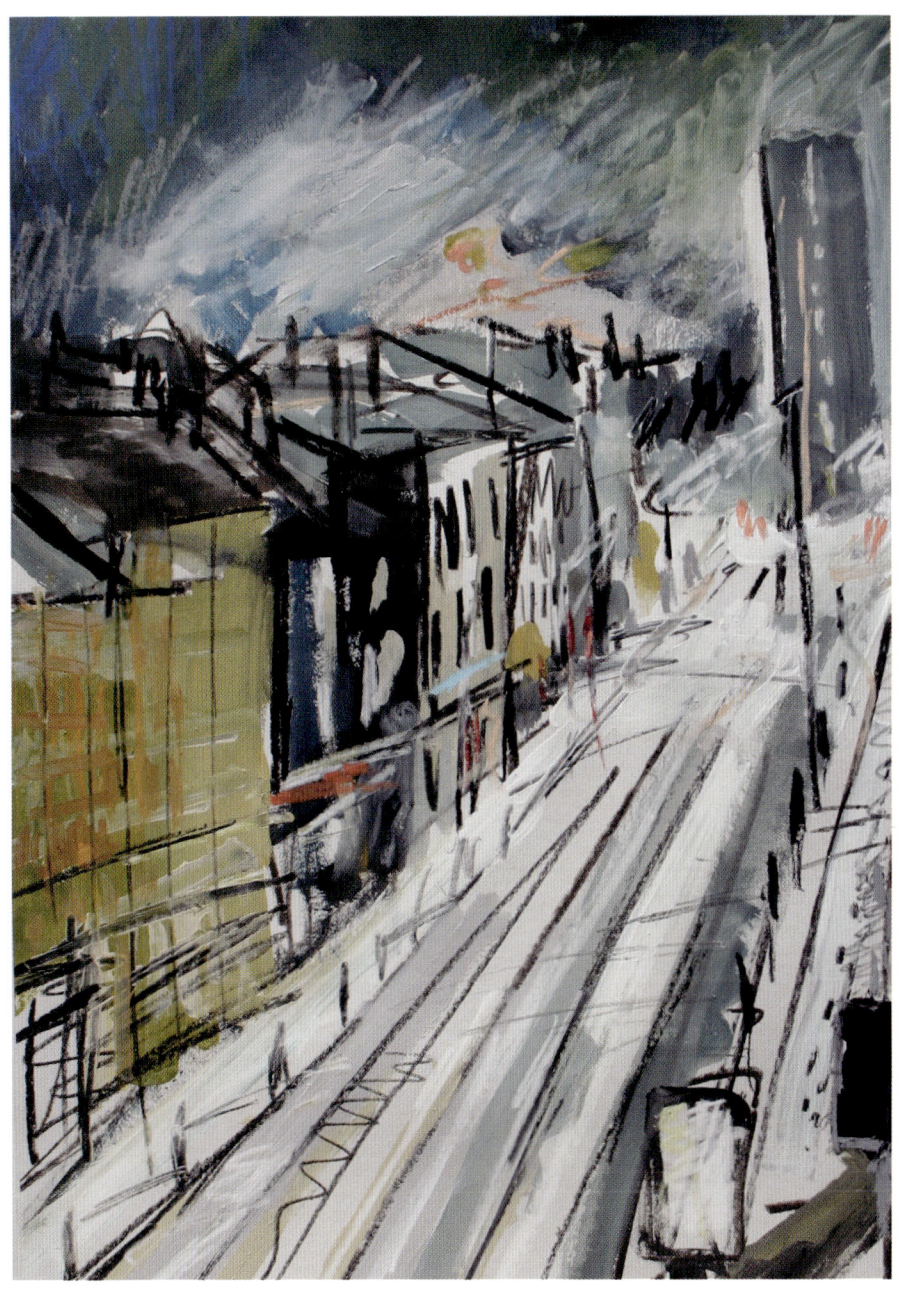

MATTHEW THOMPSON, OLDHAM STREET

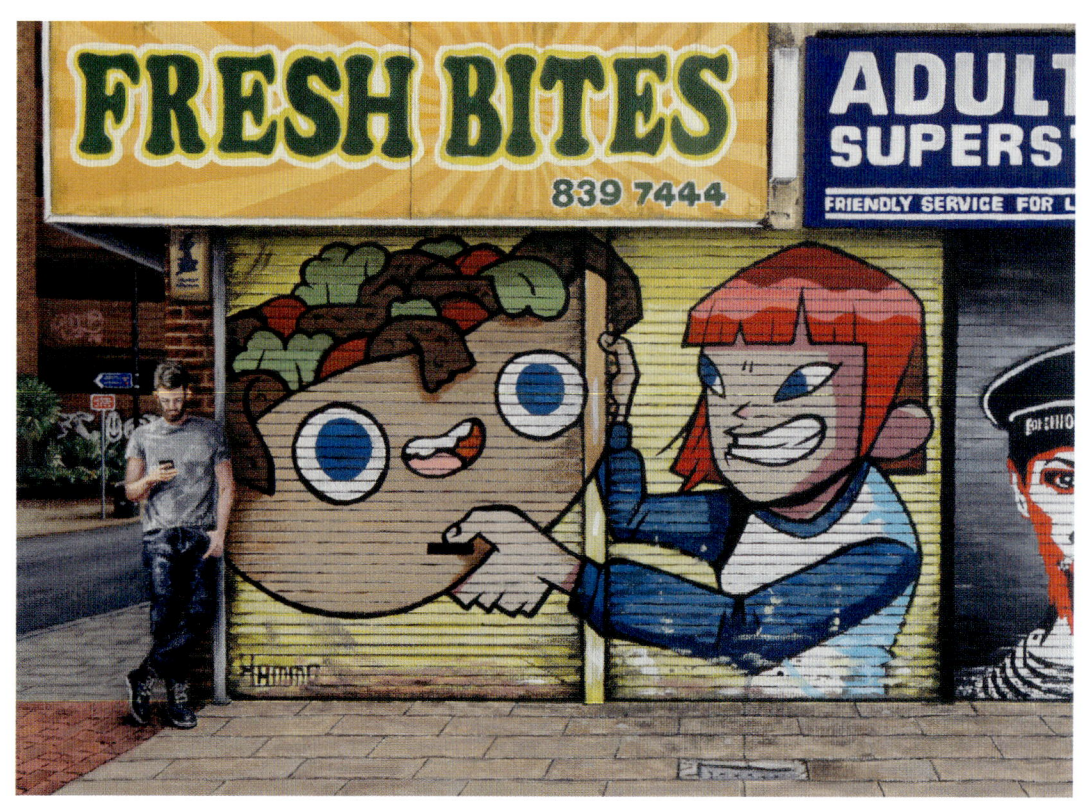

PETER DAVIS, OLDHAM STREET

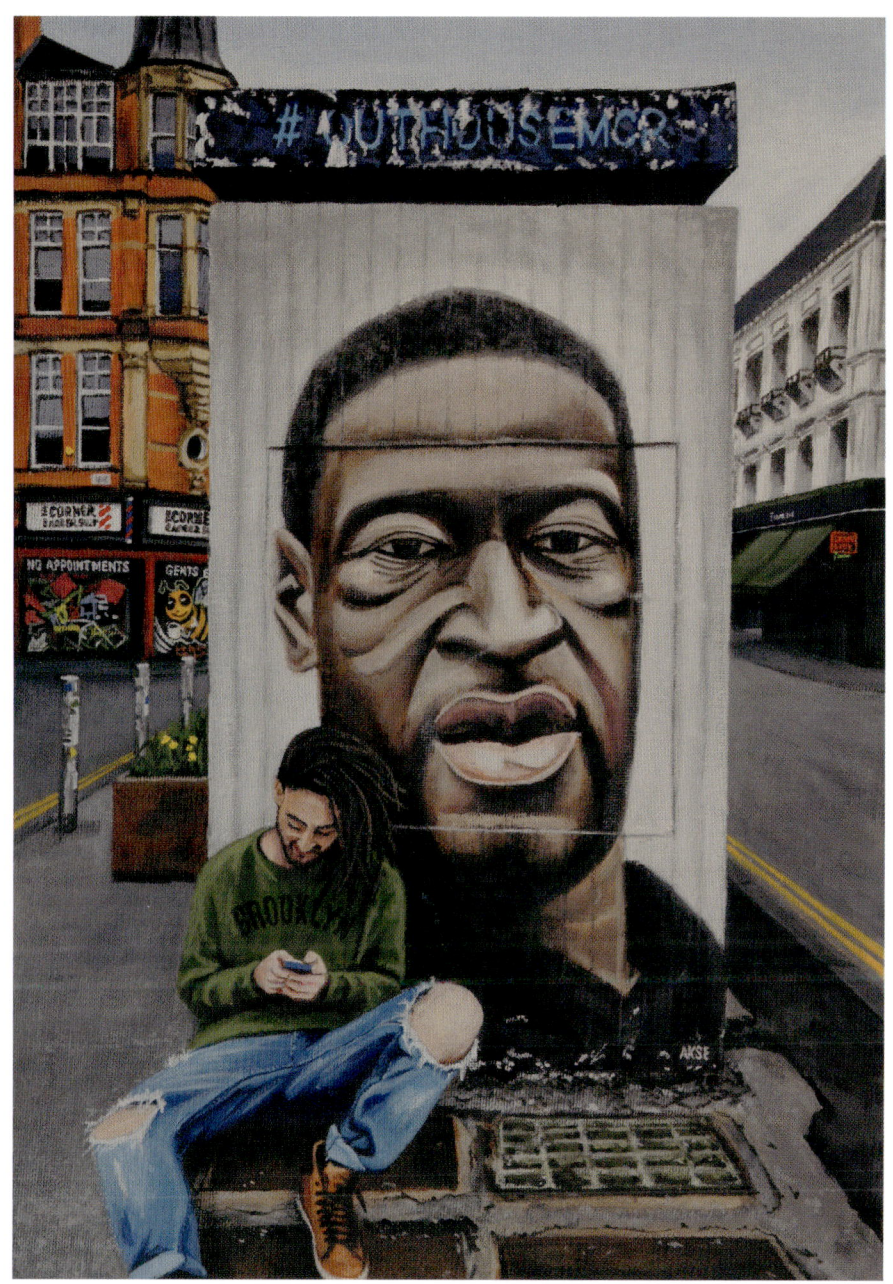

PETER DAVIS, STEVENSON SQUARE

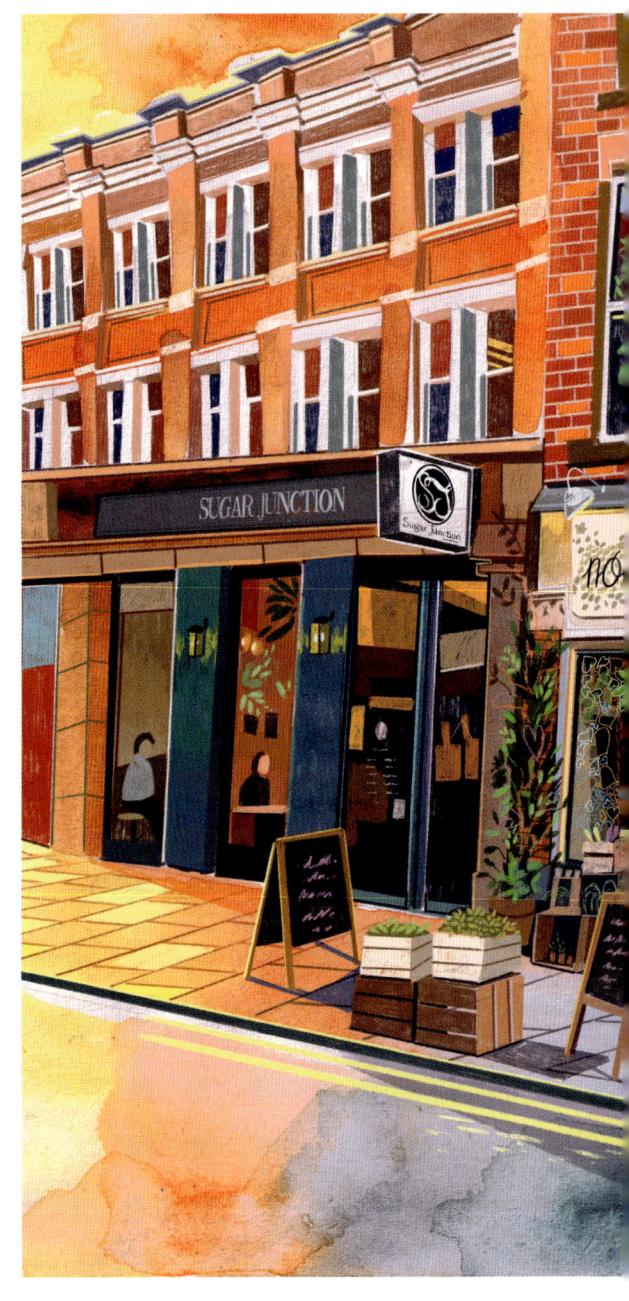

ZAC ROSSITER,
NORTHERN QUARTER

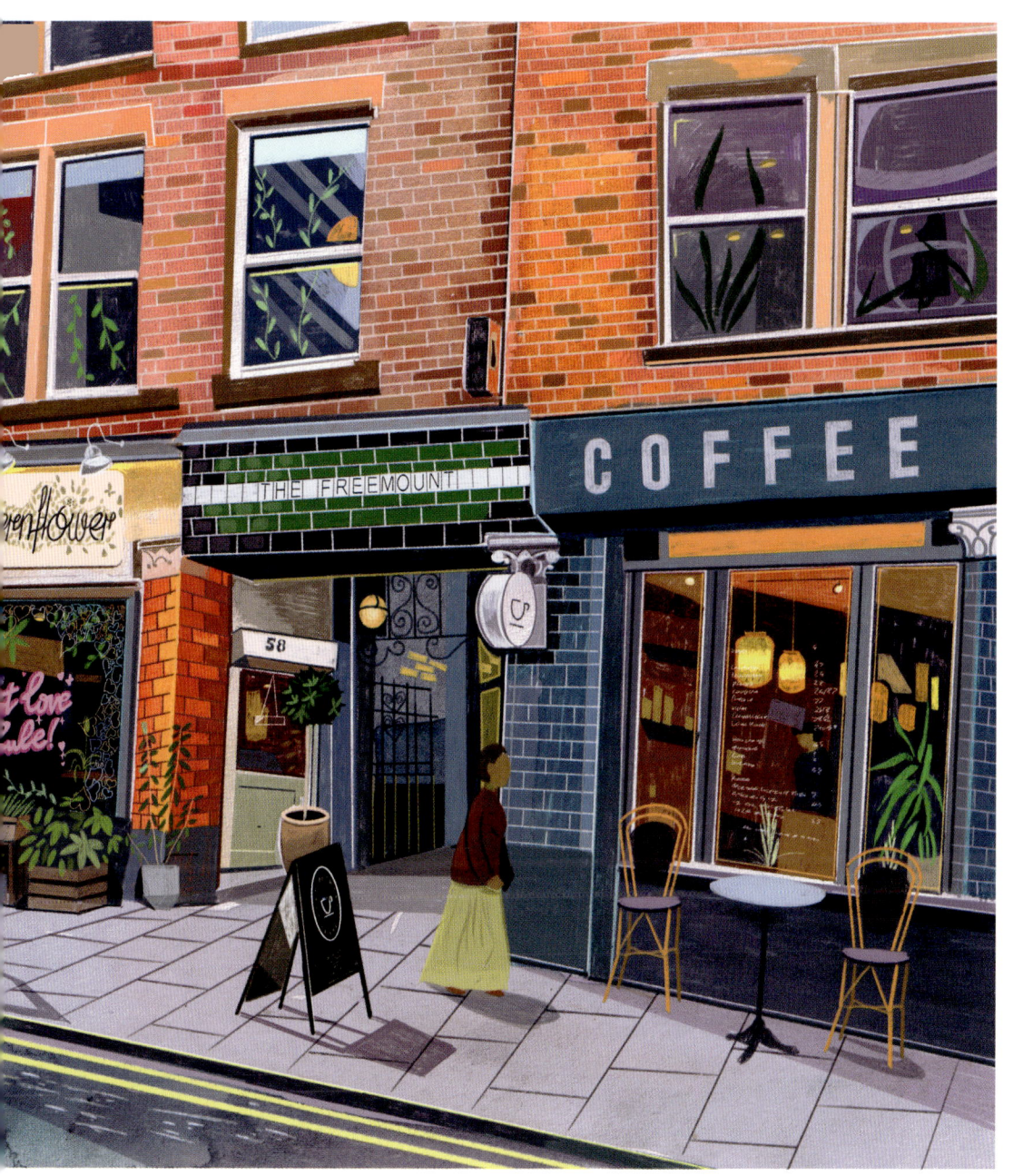

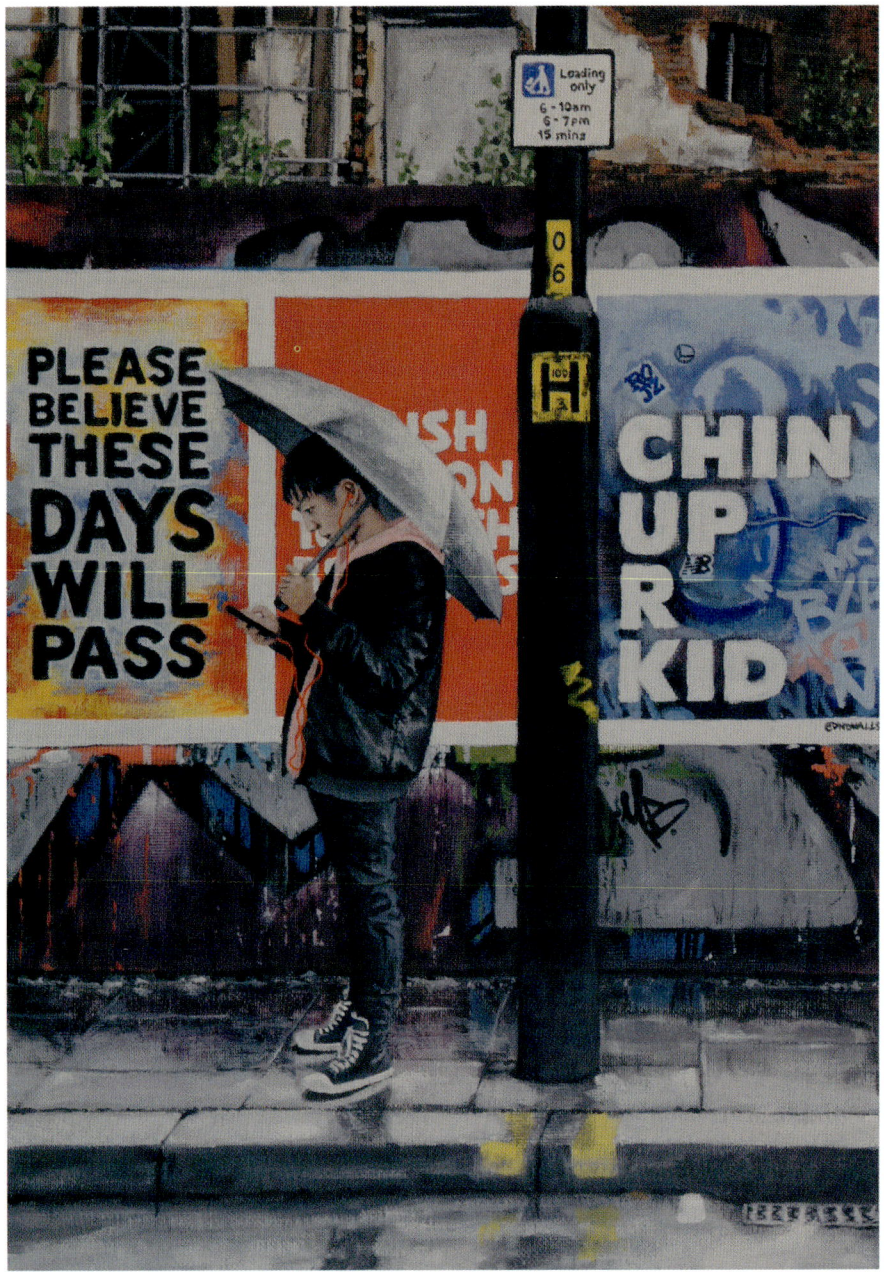

PETER DAVIS, THOMAS STREET

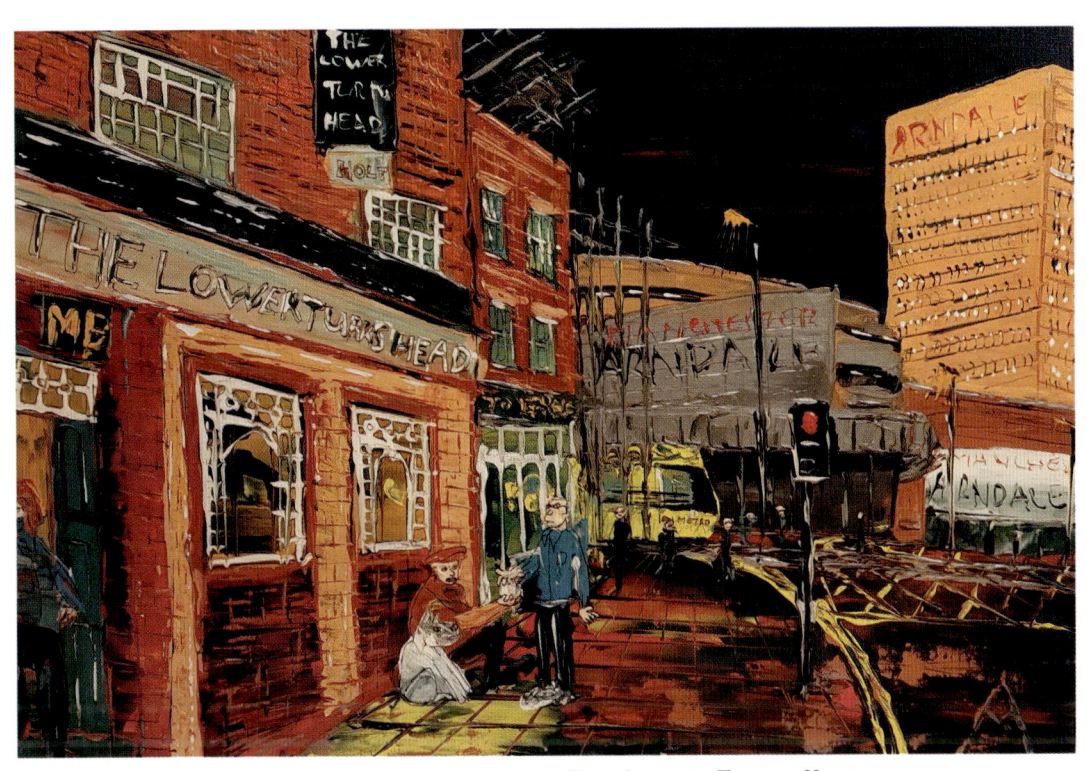

ANDREW ALAN MATTHEWS, THE LOWER TURKS HEAD

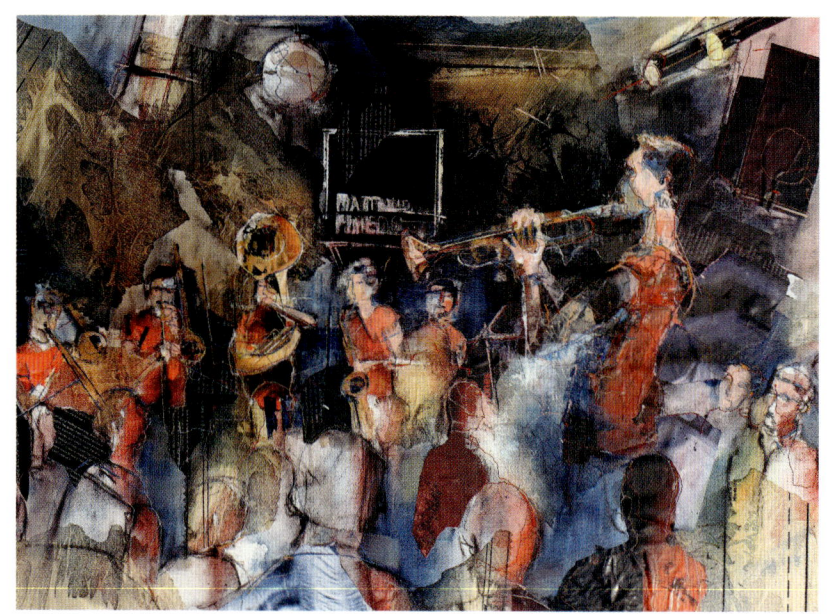

ROB WILSON, MATT AND PHRED'S

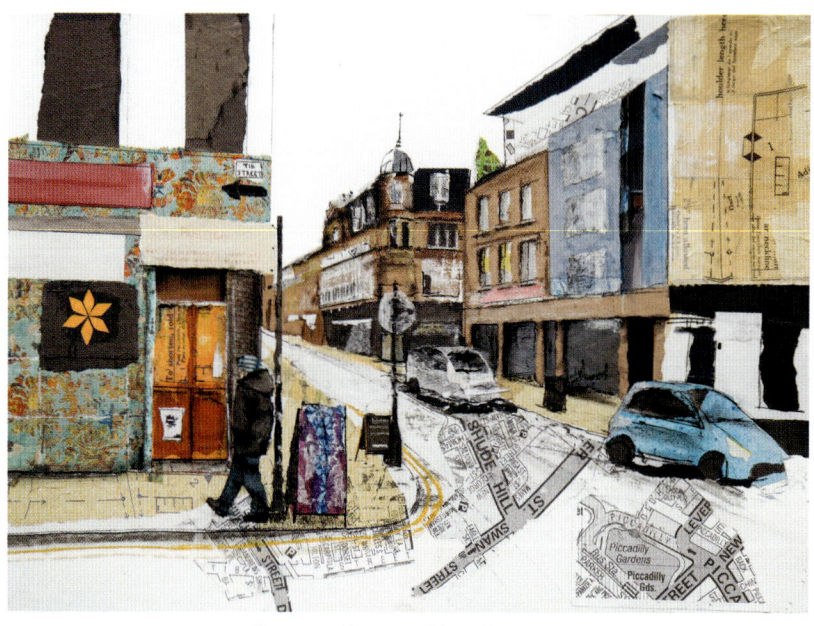

EMILY GATES, TIB STREET

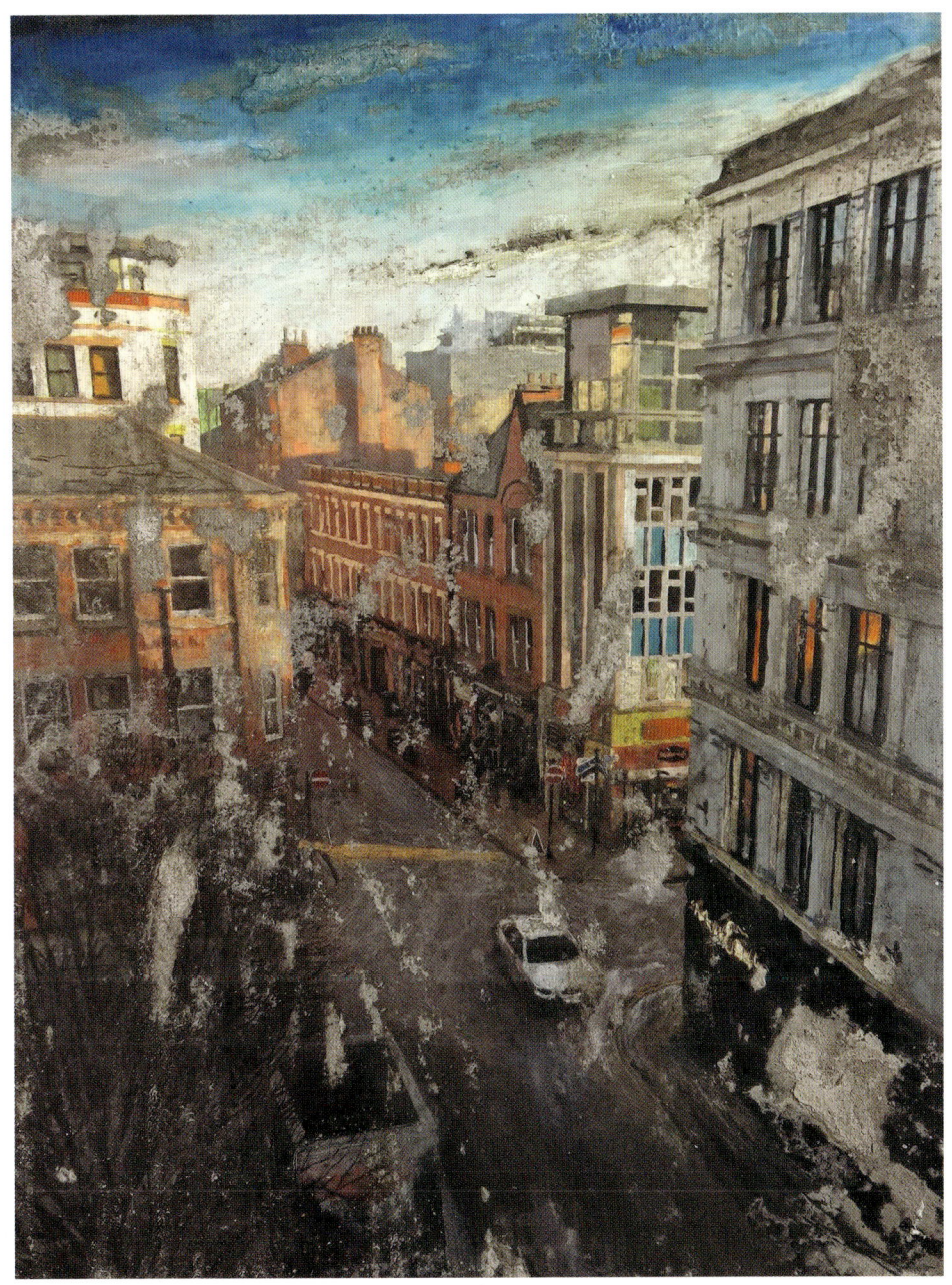

TIM GARNER, TIB STREET

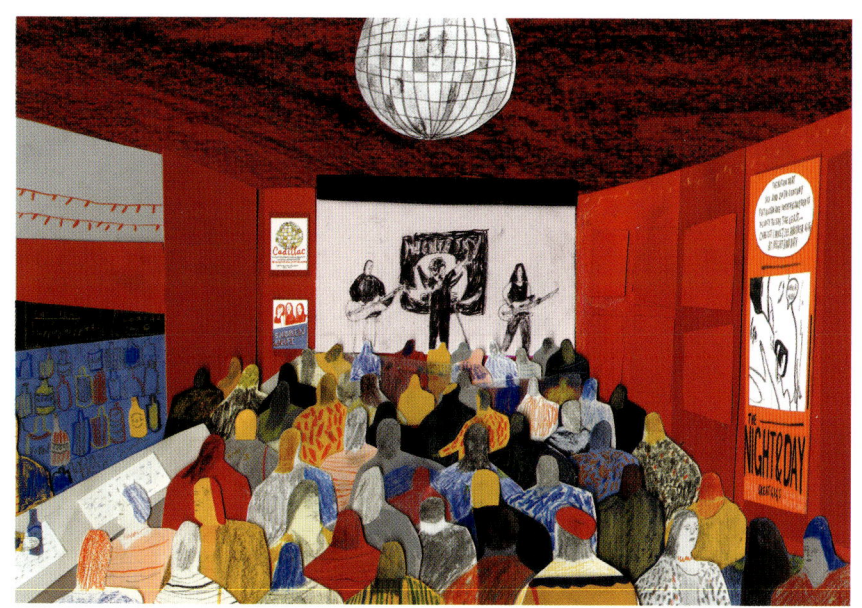

MAISY SUMMER, CROWD AT NIGHT AND DAY

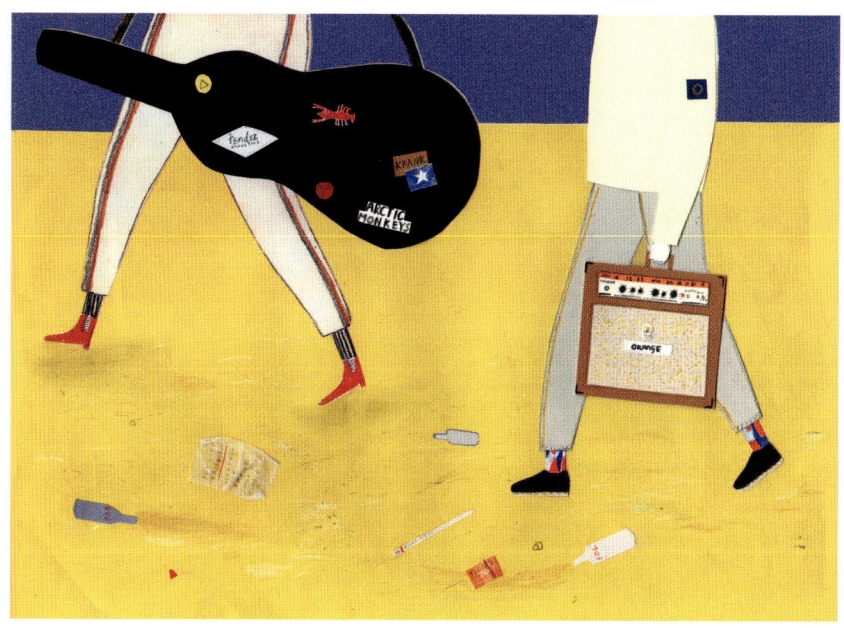

MAISY SUMMER, END OF THE NIGHT AT NIGHT AND DAY

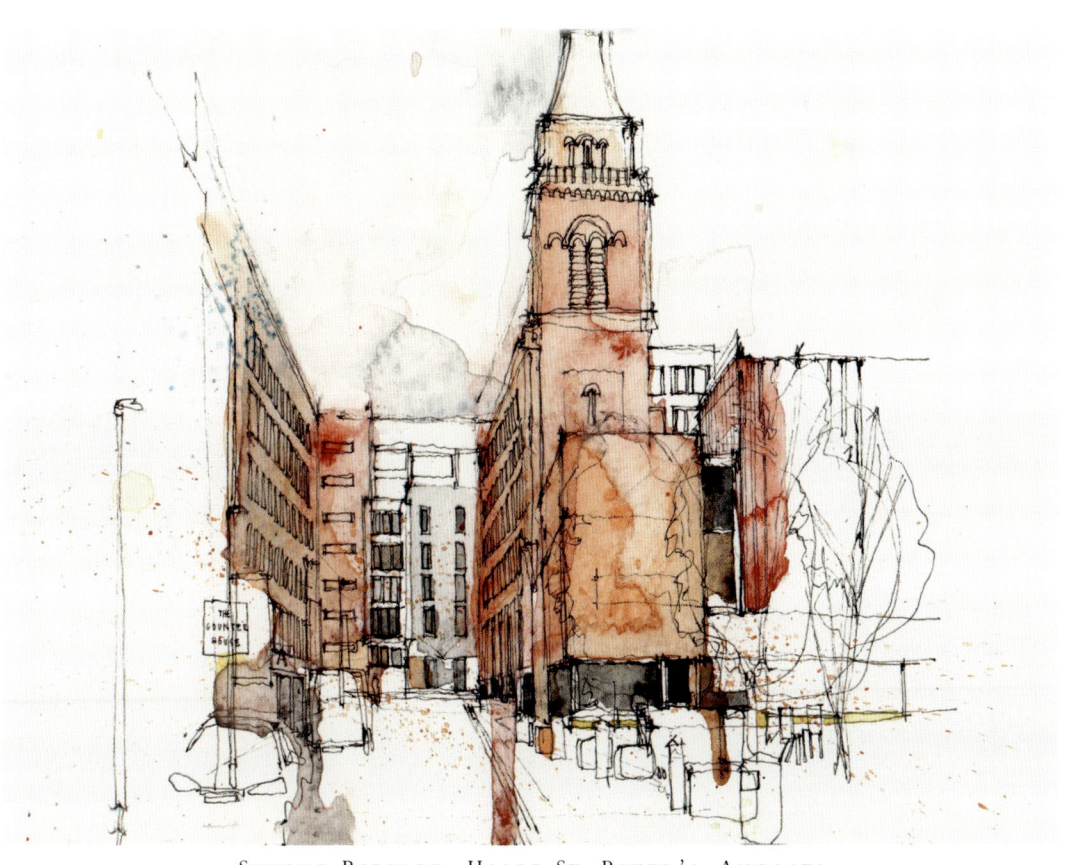

SIMONE RIDYARD, HALLE ST. PETER'S, ANCOATS

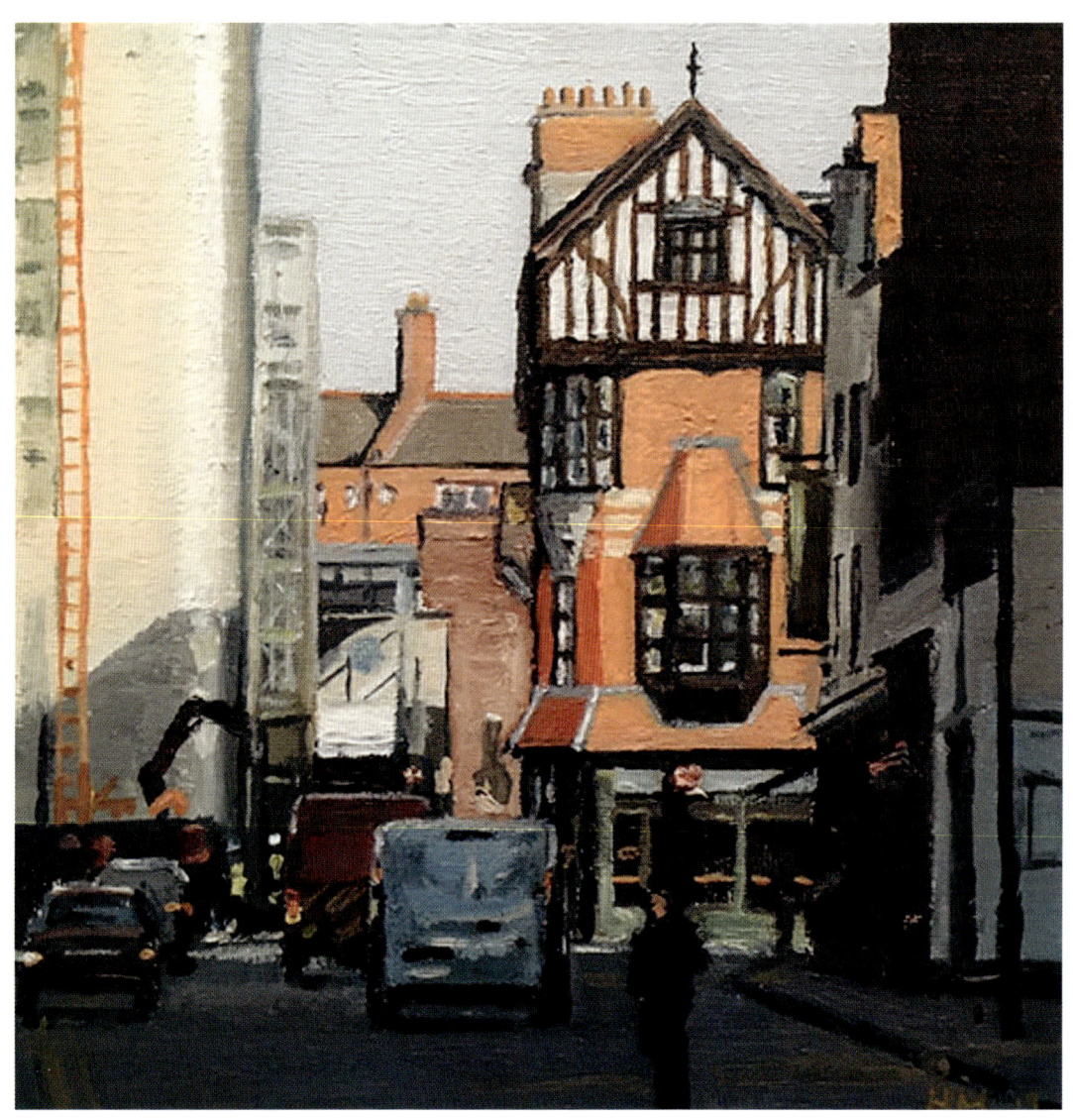

HENRY MARTIN, GREAT ANCOATS STREET

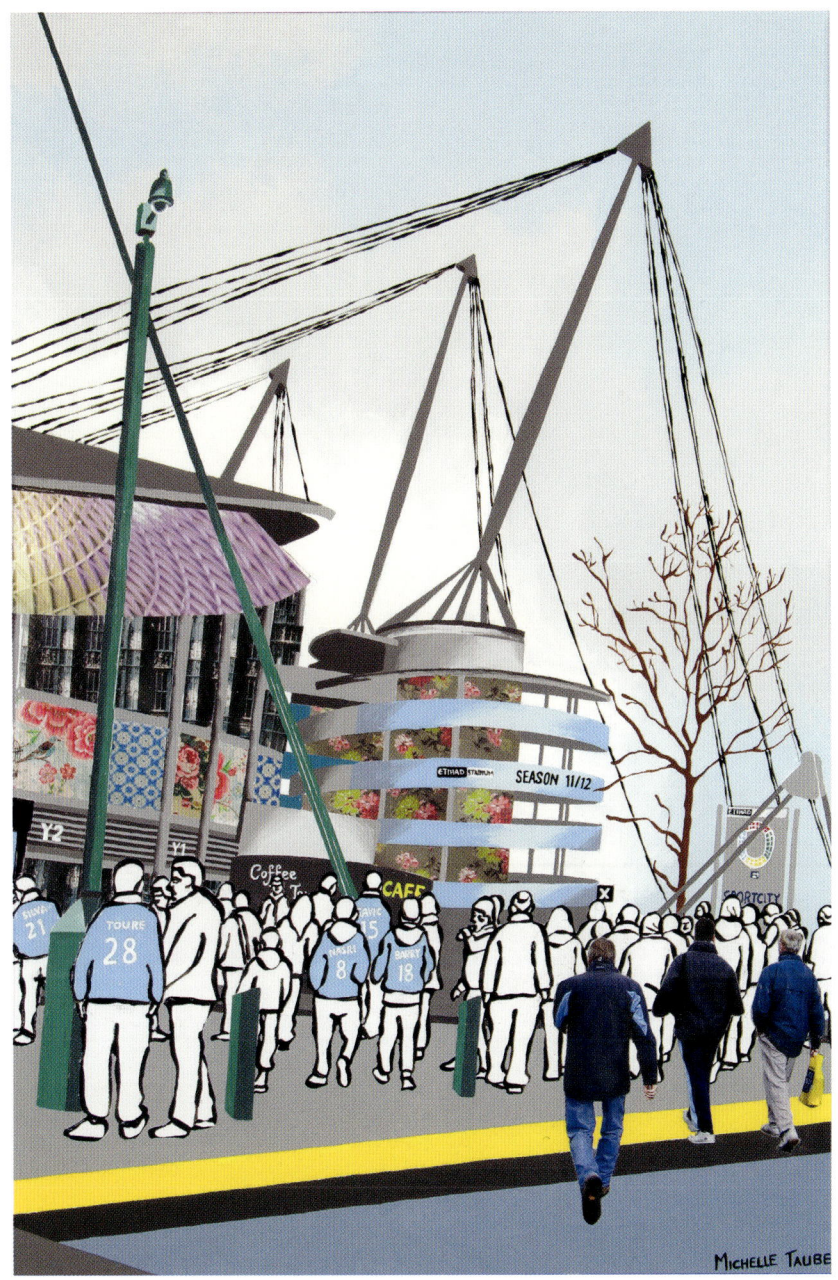

MICHELLE TAUBE, BLUE MOON RISING

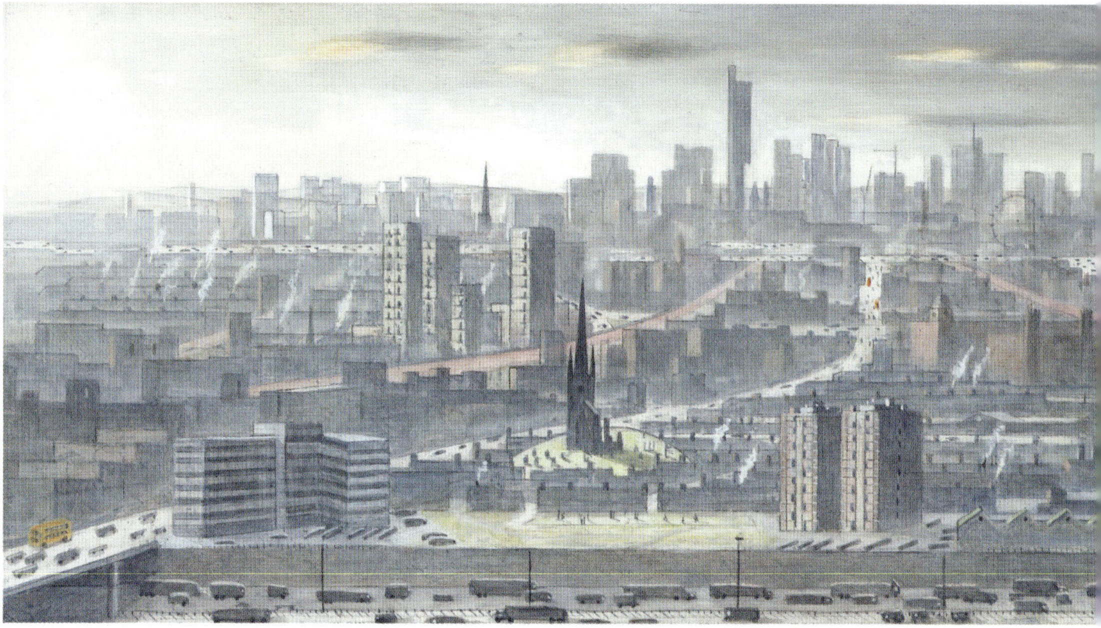

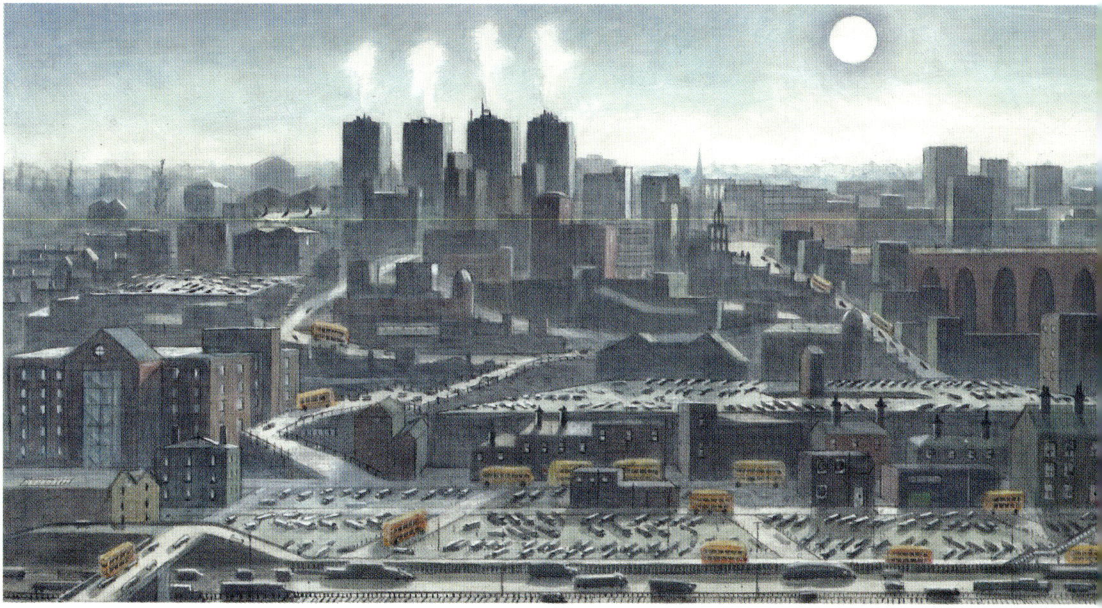

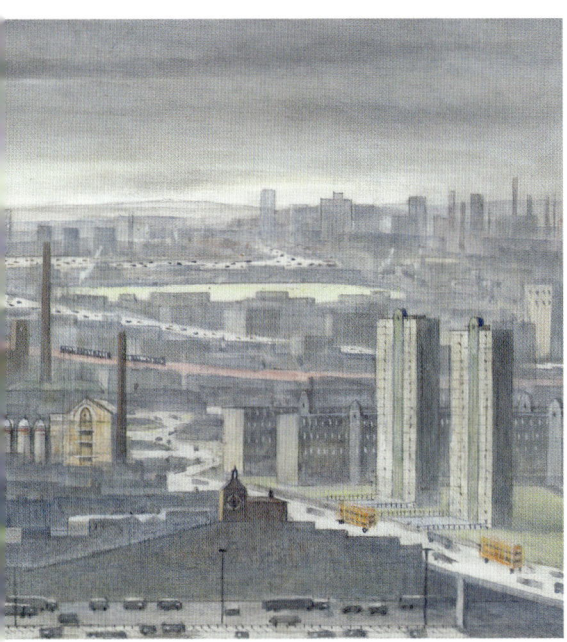

HELEN CLAPCOTT, NORTH

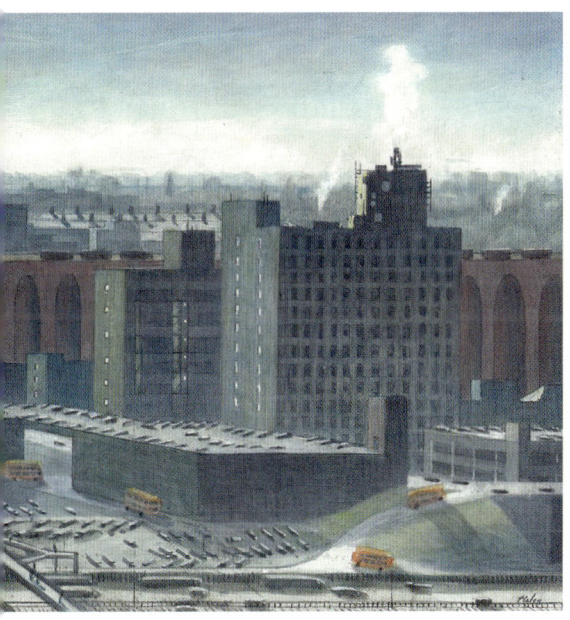

HELEN CLAPCOTT, SOUTH

ARTIST CREDITS

Adam Ralston
(49, 60)
www.adamralston.co.uk
En plein air and still life oil painter
from direct observation

Andrea Joseph
(26)
Instagram: aheavysoul
A book illustrator from South
Wales now working and drawing in
Manchester

Andrew Alan Matthews
(8, 48, 117)
andrewalanmatthews.co.uk
Mancunian artist producing cityscapes
and YouTube videos in a positive way

Ashley Cundall
(93)
artfultutorservices@gmail.com
Colourist painter inspired by the
beauty of both urban and rural
locations

Ben Ark
(42, 50, 59, 76, 86)
www.benarkart.co.uk
Mixed media collage using acrylic,
ink, resin, digital painting and
photographic elements

Ben Rock
(25)
Instagram: sketchmcr
Watercolour painting

Caroline Johnson
(15, 18, 47, 55, 91)
artistsmock@hotmail.co.uk
Fine artist, printmaker and
documentary artist

Carolyn Murphy
(78)
www.carolynmurphy.co.uk
Artist printmaker exploring
landscapes and our human impact

Caz Latham
(58, 71, 75)
Instagram: cazlathamart
Capturing the colour and character of
everyday life using paints and pens

Chris Acheson
(82)
www.chrisacheson.co.uk
Taking inspiration from popular street
culture, the themes of his work are
varied

Claire Riley
(10, 95)
Instagram: clairemancart
Digitally created artworks produced
using mixed media

Daniel Howden
(65, 80)
infohowden@gmail.com
Highly reductive linocut prints

David Lowther
(13, 20, 21, 101, 104)
Instagram: DavidLowtherArtist
Artist, Urban Sketcher, tutor and
mark maker drawing the Manchester
and beyond

Eamonn Murphy
(12, 19, 30, 50)
art.exvista.com
Expressing the inherent beauty of
architectural structures in bold,
graphic statements

Emily Gates
(23, 118)
www.emilygates.co.uk
Collage and mixed media landscape
art

Emma Bennett
(cover)
www.emmabennettillustration.com
Children's book illustrator, artist and
book creator

Eric Gaskell
(35)
www.egdesign.co.uk
Multi-block, reduction and single
colour linocuts of coast, town and
canal

Glen Cross
(109)
www.etsy.com/shop/GlenCrossDesign
Digital illustrations and prints of
familiar Manchester locations

Helen Clapcott
(124, 125)
www.paintingsofstockport.co.uk
A long walk, over a short distance,
over a long time

Helen Jones
(102, 103)
www.elluse.co.uk
Subversive, alternative edgy artist and
illustrator

Henry Martin
(122)
www.henrymartinpaintings.com
Author, painter and illustrator:
Manchester, France, Kefalonia, Faith,
Pride … and dragons!

Janet Mayled
(90, 110)
www.janetmayled.com
Acrylic and mixed media paintings
observed from a range of subject
matter

Jasmin Issaka
(63, 77, 109)
www.JasminIssaka.com
Psychedelic digital illustrator inspired
by mixed mediums, abstract patterns
and vibrant colours

Jayne Pellington
(33, 37, 92, 108)
jaynepellington.com
Variable edition reduction lino prints

Jen Orpin
(44)
www.jenorpinpaintings.co.uk
Contemporary British landscape
painter - oil paintings of urban scenes,
motorways and bridges

Jenny Seddon
(map)
www.jennyseddon.com
Illustration and screen prints

Jim Kite
(28, 36)
www.jimkiteart.com
Freehand architectural line drawings
capturing the city of Manchester and
beyond

John Hewitt
(62, 83, 100, 107)
Instagram: w_john_hewitt
Making daily observational
sketchbook drawings since 2013

Justin Twigg
(31, 53)
www.justintwigg.com
Landscape and portraits, Leek and
Staffordshire Moorlands, the Roaches
and the Peak District

Katie Patel
(37)
www.katiepatelart.com
Vibrant acrylic paintings, digital
drawings and portraiture

Len Grant
(64, 67, 69, 110)
www.lengrant.co.uk
Telling stories of the urban
environment with a sketchbook and
pen

Lisa Haselden
(14, 105)
Instagram: lisa_haselden_art
Artist working in a variety of
mediums and genres - cityscapes,
landscapes and portraits

Maisy Summer
(120)
www.maisysummer.com
Paper-cut mixed media illustration
from a publication exploring electric
and eclectic music venue Night and
Day

Mandy Payne
(70, 97, 98)
www.mandypayneart.co.uk
Paintings on concrete and marble,
inspired by urban landscape and
Brutalist architecture

Matt Wilde
(93)
www.mattwilde.co.uk
Work in various mediums such as
acrylic, oil, charcoal and mixed media

Matthew Pickles
(73)
mat.pickles72@gmail.com
Using pen, ink and watercolour to
juxtapose the psychedelic with the
Victorian

Matthew Thompson
(46, 68, 111)
www.matthewthompsonart.com
Original mixed media paintings

Michael Hitchens
(41, 45, 51)
www.michaelhitchens.co.uk
Printmaker, creating multi-layered
screen prints

Michael John Ashcroft
(40, 48)
www.michaeljohnashcroft.com
Original urban oil paintings using
the vibrant city of Manchester as
inspiration

Michelle Taube
(52, 94, 96, 123)
www.michelletaube.com
Painting with hand-cut collage and
photography

Norman Long
(19)
www.normanlongartist.com
On-site oil paintings with rich
surfaces and glowing light

Peter Davis
(112, 113, 116)
www.peterdavisartist.com
Prize-winning fine artist
specialising in urban landscape
painting and portrait
commissions

Phil Turner
(34, 57, 72)
www.subtractionism.com
Subtractionism: By reducing
back, we are left with pure form

Rob Pointon
(54, 74, 84, 88)
www.robpointon.co.uk
Painting on location to produce
movement filled, dynamic
compositions

Rob Wilson
(16, 24, 90, 106, 118)
www.robwilsonart.co.uk
Mixed media paintings
incorporating paint, collage,
texture and stitching

Ronald Haber
(17)
ronald-haber.pixels.com
Primarily a plein air painter
working in a variety of mediums

Sarah Connell
(22, 42, 87, 94, 99)
www.connell-art.co.uk
Contemporary acrylic and iPad
paintings

Sarah Franklin
(32)
www.sarahfranklin.art
Mixed media, concertina
sketchbook, on location urban
sketching, fuelled by tea

Simone Ridyard
(66, 121)
Instagram: simoneridyard
Architectural illustration and
urban sketching, founder of
Urban Sketchers Manchester

Sophie Nixon
(11, 61)
www.sophienixon.com
Oil painter and Urban Sketcher
drawn to the light in a scene

Stanley Chow
(56)
www.stanleychow.co.uk
Digital illustration

Steven P Smith
(18, 81)
steven@artsps.com
Alla prima oil paintings painted
outdoors en plein air from direct
observation

Sue Scott
(38, 39, 43)
www.slscott.co.uk
Acrylic paintings of urban and
rural landscapes from around
the UK

Tim Garner
(119)
garner_tim@yahoo.fr
Hand-ground acrylic, metal
and iridescent pigment, chalk,
cement and debris

Tony Pickering
(89)
www.pick-art.co.uk
Drawing in traditional and
digital media mapping spatial
narratives and tangents

Zac Rossiter
(79, 115)
www.zacrosso.etsy.com
Watercolour and iPad Procreate
illustration

Victoria Wood
(27)
www.sketchpadontour.co.uk
Creating with ink and
watercolour

Every effort has been made to correctly credit contributors. In the case of any omissions or errors
we would be pleased to make appropriate corrections in future editions.

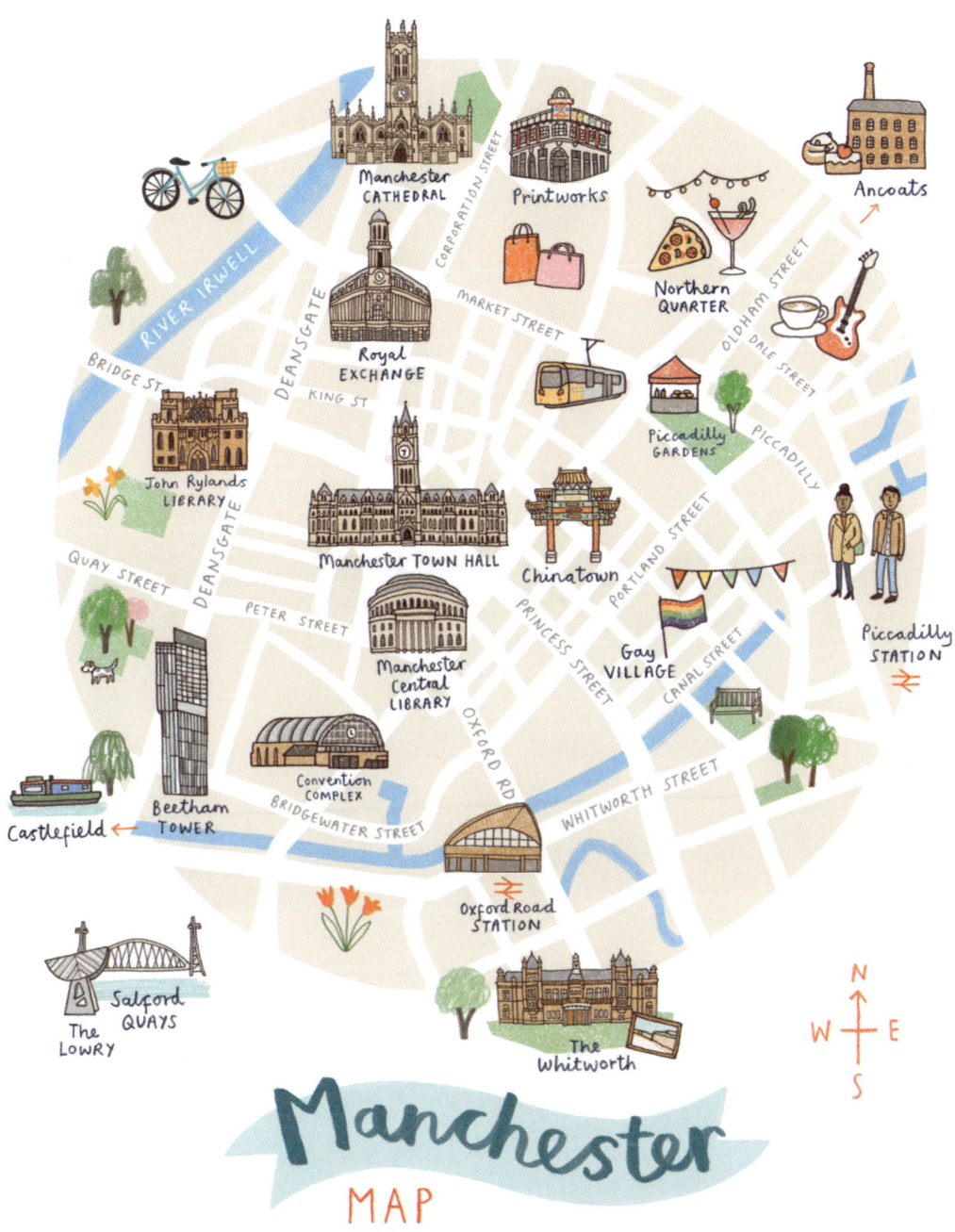

River Irwell

Manchester
CATHEDRAL

Printworks

Northern
QUARTER

Ancoats

CORPORATION STREET

MARKET STREET

OLDHAM STREET

DALE STREET

PICCADILLY

BRIDGE ST

DEANSGATE

KING ST

Royal
EXCHANGE

John Rylands
LIBRARY

DEANSGATE

QUAY STREET

PETER STREET

Manchester TOWN HALL

Chinatown

Piccadilly
GARDENS

PORTLAND STREET

Piccadilly
STATION

Manchester
Central
LIBRARY

PRINCESS STREET

OXFORD RD

Gay
VILLAGE

CANAL STREET

Castlefield

Beetham
TOWER

Convention
COMPLEX

BRIDGEWATER STREET

WHITWORTH STREET

Oxford Road
STATION

The
LOWRY

Salford
QUAYS

The
Whitworth

N
W   E
S

Manchester

MAP